Planning and control of manufacturing operations

Other titles of interest include:

Demand forecasting and inventory control
Colin D Lewis
ISBN 1 85573 241 6

Best practice in inventory management
Tony Wild
ISBN 1 85573 310 2

Planning and control of manufacturing operations

John Kenworthy

THE INSTITUTE OF
OPERATIONS
MANAGEMENT

WOODHEAD PUBLISHING LIMITED
Cambridge England

Published by Woodhead Publishing Ltd in association with the Institute of Operations Management

Woodhead Publishing Ltd
Abington Hall, Abington
Cambridge CB1 6AH, England

First published 1998, Woodhead Publishing Ltd

© 1998, Woodhead Publishing Ltd

The author has asserted his moral rights.

Conditions of sale
All rights reserved. No part of this publication may be reproduced or transmitted in any form or by any means, electronic or mechanical, including photocopy, recording, or any information storage and retrieval system, without permission in writing from the publisher.

While a great deal of care has been taken to provide accurate and current information, neither the author, nor the publisher, nor anyone else associated with this publication, shall be liable for any loss, damage or liability directly or indirectly caused, or alleged to be caused, by this book.

British Library Cataloguing in Publication Data
A catalogue record for this book is available from the British Library.

ISBN 1 85573 307 2

Typeset by BookEns Ltd, Royston, Herts.
Printed by TJ International Ltd, Cornwall, England.

Contents

Preface		*ix*
1	The manufacturing control problem	1
	1.1 Background	1
	1.2 Types of manufacturing business	5
	Exercises	14
2	Achieving control of the business	16
	2.1 A model of a manufacturing business	16
	2.2 Materials control	18
	2.3 Material Requirements Planning	26
	2.4 Inadequacies of MRP	34
	2.5 Improvements to MRP: the development of MRPII	35
	Exercises	37
3	Master Production Scheduling	42
	3.1 Introduction	42
	3.2 Exception messages	44
	3.3 The firm planned fence	44
	3.4 Master Production Scheduling policies	46
	3.5 Sales orders, sales forecasts and Available to Promise	52
	3.6 Formats for the Master Production Schedule	57
	3.7 Summary	58
	Exercises	59
4	Manufacturing orders	65
	4.1 The order life cycle	65
	4.2 Requirements	67
	4.3 Receipts	68
	4.4 Nomenclature	68

CONTENTS

	4.5	Summary	72
		Exercises	73
5		Order policies	74
	5.1	Order quantities	74
	5.2	Setting order quantities	77
		Exercises	81
6		Lead times and safety stocks	83
	6.1	Setting purchasing lead times	83
	6.2	Setting manufacturing lead times	83
	6.3	Consequences of incorrectly set lead times	86
	6.4	Safety stocks	89
	6.5	Setting safety stock levels	90
		Exercises	94
7		Bills of materials	96
	7.1	Yields and shrinkages	96
	7.2	Phantom bills of materials	99
	7.3	Planning bills of materials	99
	7.4	Option Planning	101
	7.5	Nomenclature	104
		Exercises	106
8		Sales forecasting and Distribution Requirements Planning	109
	8.1	How are forecasts made?	109
	8.2	How far ahead should forecasts go?	111
	8.3	Accuracy of forecasts	114
	8.4	Making forecasting easier	117
	8.5	Distribution Requirements Planning	120
	8.6	Summary	123
		Exercises	124
9		Capacity planning and short term scheduling	127
	9.1	Capacity Requirements Planning	128
	9.2	Rough Cut Capacity Planning	134
	9.3	Short term scheduling	137
	9.4	Finite planning and scheduling systems	141
	9.5	Automated finite planning and scheduling	141
	9.6	Categorisation of finite capacity planning and scheduling systems	143

	9.7	Queues and scheduling	150
		Exercises	154
10		Optimised Production Technology	160
	10.1	Bottlenecks	160
	10.2	Effect of random variations in output	161
	10.3	Gateing the input stage	162
	10.4	OPT software	163
		Exercises	165
11		Just in Time and Continuous Improvement	166
	11.1	What is Just in Time?	166
	11.2	Lead times, order sizes and JIT	168
	11.3	Reducing change-over times	170
	11.4	Reducing movement or transport times	173
	11.5	Reducing product complexity	178
	11.6	Reducing process complexity	179
	11.7	Purchasing and JIT	180
	11.8	Summary	183
	11.9	JIT and MRPII	184
	11.10	Total Quality Management	185
	11.11	TQM and JIT	187
		Exercises	188
12		Implementing manufacturing control systems	192
	12.1	Initiating the project	192
	12.2	Project organisation	195
	12.3	The project plan and time scale	197
	12.4	Educational activities	198
	12.5	Project publicity	201
	12.6	Technical activities	201
	12.7	Cutting over to the new system	205
	12.8	Operating MRPII	206
	12.9	Performance measures	206
	12.10	Postscript	208
		Exercises	209

Answers to exercises   *211*

Index   *259*

Preface

This book is intended to be a practical guide to planning and control in manufacturing industry, suitable for manufacturing managers, attendees and presenters of 'in-house' training courses, students studying for professional examinations in operations management such as the Diploma of the Institute of Operations Management and for undergraduates following engineering or industrial studies courses who need an introduction to manufacturing control techniques.

My intention was to write a practical book, based on over 20 years' experience as manager, academic and consultant in the field. I have tried to write an easy-to-understand and readable book rather than an intellectually rigorous tome with arguments and statements supported by literature searches and references.

Twenty-five years ago, even though I was an experienced industrial manager, I had very little understanding of the problems of operations management and even less of their solutions. Since then my understanding of the subject has developed as a result of reading other people's books, taking part in discussions and attending courses and conferences. Many friends and colleagues may detect the influence of their ideas and war stories in the book. I am grateful to all of them. It would be impossible to produce a comprehensive list of influencers, but friends and colleagues in the Institute of Operations Management (formerly BPICS), Zeneca (formerly ICI), The Manufacturing and Logistics Group, R B Management Consultants, Manufacturing Management Ltd and Cincom Systems (UK) have all played significant roles. However, I accept complete responsibility for all errors and misunderstandings.

John Kenworthy

Presenter's pack

A presenter's pack has been produced to accompany this book with the aim of saving valuable preparation time for anyone making a presentation on the material covered by the book. The pack includes masters for over 250 overhead slides with a prompt page giving the main points to be made about each slide. It is available only from: Woodhead Publishing Ltd, Abington Hall, Abington, Cambridge, England CB1 6AH. Telephone +44 (0)1223 891358. Fax +44 (0)1223 893694.

1

The manufacturing control problem

1.1 Background

1.1.1 Mass production

It is almost a century since Henry Ford started to manufacture Model Ts on a production line. As long as he made the same number of cars each day, week or month, his manufacturing control was relatively simple. If he was making 100 cars per day, he needed 100 engines per day, 400 wheels, 100 radiators, 200 headlamps, etc. It was easy to tell the supplying operations how much to make. Provided that the assembly line schedule did not change, both the internal and external suppliers made the same this week as they did last and could confidently predict that it would be the same next week.

Of course, as in any successful business, the rate of production had to increase from time to time. Increased supplies of components had to be synchronised with the change in line rate and no doubt temporary problems arose but if the new rate following a step change remained constant, problems could be quickly sorted out.

If Henry had given his customers a choice of colour, trim or engine size, the rate and model of production would have had to respond to customer preferences. Although it is claimed that Henry's famous dictum, 'They can have any colour they like as long as it's black,' was to take advantage of the fact that black paint dried faster than other colours, it is difficult to believe that he was not also aware that limiting customer choice minimised his production control problem.

1.1.2 Batch production

Control of the manufacture of one-off products, or of small batches of items does not appear to have been a major problem during the first four decades of the century. In general businesses were not as large as they are now and it was possible for one experienced man, supported by simple mechanical techniques such as Order Point (see Chapter 2) or a simple scheduling board, to plan most things in his head. In the 1930s even the building of a complex product such as an ocean liner was largely controlled by one person. Such a person would spend much of his time on site observing progress at first hand and would schedule the delivery of the large number of different items required for fitting out, using little more than his own experience and common sense. It is possible that standards of control were less demanding then than they are now. Interest rates were in general lower so holding stock or accepting early delivery cost less than now. Also, in an environment where not having a job often meant serious deprivation, workers were more flexible and would accept short time when work was scarce or unreasonable levels of overtime when needed, in a way which, fortunately, employers do not now expect.

1.1.3 Developments in Europe and the USA

Techniques for controlling mass production continued to develop and were given a boost by the Second World War when equipment and munitions were produced in vast quantities. Operations Research – the use of mathematical analysis to aid decision taking – became recognised as a discipline. Outside the mass production environment, devices such as new airborne radar, navigation aids and electronic counter measures were designed, developed and manufactured with remarkably short lead times and often in quantities much too small for mass production techniques. Production controllers used product knowledge, experience and common sense to plan their way around material shortages, bombed factories and sunken supply ships. Achieving production volumes was more important than productivity.

After the war, outside the USA, almost everything was in short supply. Customers were glad to have what was available and in general did not complain about late delivery or poor quality. A plant manager's main objective was to keep the plant working in order to achieve the maximum possible production. Again production volume was more important than productivity and the production planner's position in most factories was a lowly one. Senior management knew little about planning and control and, more seriously, often did not recognise that there was more to be known. It is not surprising that in many cases they established a 'hands-off' approach, monitoring carefully the output but often leaving to junior employees the important decisions on what to make or buy. Clerks who were not authorised to sign for pencils from stores, were allowed to initiate manufacturing and purchase orders worth tens of thousands of pounds.

1.1.4 The advent of computers

During the 1950s and 1960s the manufacturing environment changed. Competition increased as new factories were built or were switched from armaments manufacture to civil production. Management recognised that customers were looking for better service and quality but were not sure how to meet these demands. In the USA and Europe, computers were being used successfully to automate routine tasks such as payroll and accounting and, as a logical development, some companies attempted to use them to assist production planning and control. Success can most kindly be described as 'mixed'. The computers operated only in batch mode. Transaction records, such as movements in or out of stores had to be written on to punching sheets, which were accumulated and then once or twice a day passed to a keyboard operator who produced a punched card for each transaction. The cards were then verified by a second operator re-keying all the data into a machine which compared the second input with the cards. Any discrepancies had to be resolved before the cards could be used to update the computer.

Since in many cases the punching facilities were remote from the manufacturing site, completing the update within 24 hours was not always possible. Data within the computer could not be accessed directly, and planners and controllers worked from print-outs produced after the previous update. These had limited use for planning and control because they were out of date as soon as the first new transaction took place and a planner could not, for example, assume that stock shown on the report was still available. It could have been issued to another job since the previous update.

In spite of their limitations, batch input systems revolutionised management information. Stock and production figures for the end of an accounting period could be sorted, summarised, aggregated, reported by value, work content, volume and weight, etc. The value of such information can only really be appreciated by someone who has tried to manage a large business without it. Previously, an army of clerks would have been required to produce similar information, and even if completed before the next period end, the incidence of arithmetic errors remained unknown but was probably high.

Although the computer systems were vulnerable to errors in the data input, they did not in general make arithmetic errors. For the first time, managers of large or complex manufacturing businesses could base some, but not all, control decisions on real information rather than intuition.

1.1.5 Integrated on-line computer systems

The real benefits of using computers for manufacturing control came with the development of on-line systems using integrated data bases during the 1970s. A transaction such as recording the partial completion of a manufacturing order could be entered through a terminal on or close to the shop floor or the stores. Both the stock record of the item made and the quantity still expected from the order would be updated simultaneously and a subsequent enquiry from any terminal on the network would see the latest information.

In the ideal arrangement, any data item would be entered onto the system only once. It would then be accessed by who ever needed it, provided that they were suitably authorised. Disputes about whose data were correct, between planners and accountants for example, became a thing of the past but there was no guarantee that the common information was correct.

1.1.6 The development of MRPII

During the 1970s a basic logic for manufacturing control was developed primarily in the USA by control experts such as Joseph Orlicky, George Plossl and Oliver Wight who promoted and developed their ideas by working with the American Production and Inventory Control Society (APICS). Initially the approach was named 'Material Requirements Planning' or MRP and later, as the logic became more comprehensive, 'Manufacturing Resources Planning' or MRPII (see Chapter 2). Successful use of such systems became limited not by the functionality of the computer systems, but by the training and discipline of the human users.

Early MRPII enthusiasts believed that it was suitable for almost all kinds of production, and certainly with a few bespoke additions, it has been successfully implemented in almost all types of industry. However, the fact that it can be used does not mean that it should be used. MRPII is complicated to install and maintain and the expenditure on education and training needed to create the right culture for MRPII is considerable. During the late 1980s, it was recognised that if simpler approaches were adequate for a particular environment, they should be used in preference to MRPII.

1.1.7 Japanese developments

Japanese manufacturers developed an interest in using computers for manufacturing much later than western manufacturers. This may have been partly because until the early 1980s, computers using Japanese script were not readily available, but it may also be because, shortly after the Second World War the Japanese, faced with very limited resources, including space for factories or warehouses, recognised with the help of American consultants, that if businesses could be sufficiently simplified, simple control systems were adequate. The most widely publicised system was 'Kanban', which is a form of mechanical Order Point.

When Japanese motor cars were first marketed in the West, many features such as sun-roofs, heated mirrors and fog-lamps, regarded as extras by European producers, were standard on Japanese models. This was seen as a marketing exercise, but in reality it was an update of Henry Ford's view on car colour: the more standard the product, the higher the productivity and the easier the planning and control of manufacture.

The Japanese regarded computers as products to be made for export to the West. It is at least theoretically possible that a product, planned and controlled in the West using a Japanese computer, was out-sold by a Japanese product with lower overheads because production was controlled by Kanban.

Interestingly, however, Japanese manufacturers are starting to install MRPII, just as western companies are realising that Kanban can replace MRPII in some environments or, more commonly, be used alongside MRPII.

1.2 Types of manufacturing business

1.2.1 The planning compromises

Planning any manufacturing business involves a series of compromises. A salesman who is trying to meet his customer's requirements immediately and in full, will be in favour of having as many different products as possible on the company's range and of keeping generous stocks of all of them.

No doubt Henry Ford's salesmen honestly believed that they could increase sales if they could offer models in dark blue or green. However, as Henry understood, a large range increases stock levels and decreases productivity.

Production managers favour long runs of the same product, since this saves machine set ups and gives them the opportunity to tune the

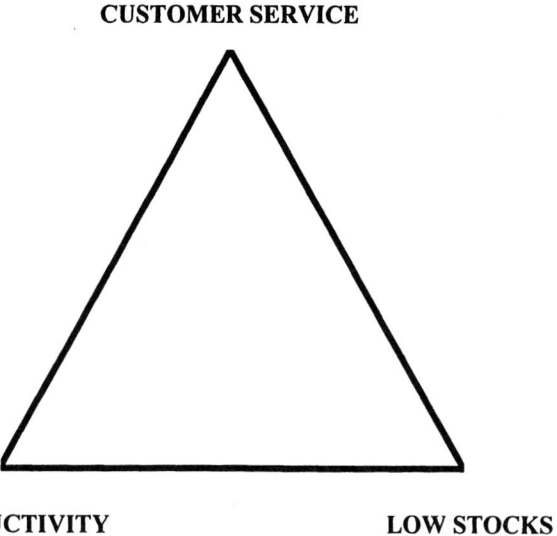

1.1 The three-cornered planning compromise.

equipment to its highest output rate. Accountants, however, frown on long production runs because they increase total stocks. Holding stocks costs money both in terms of original investment and additional costs of insurance, pilferage, storage, counting and obsolescence.

Long production runs can also decrease customer service, because to a shop floor supervisor whose performance is measured by volume of output, it does not seem worth interrupting a machine which is running superbly on one item, just because another one is out of stock and a customer wants one immediately. High machine utilisation contributes to productivity, but reduces flexibility.

None of these views is incorrect or totally valid. It is the job of management, and in particular the production planners, to find the correct compromise between the three extremes. This is illustrated in Fig. 1.1 and 1.2.

All businesses face this same compromise, but obviously the chosen operating position will depend on the pressures on the business. For example, for a pharmaceutical company with a life saving drug, failure to supply could literally be a matter of life and death for a patient. The high level of customer service required may well be achieved in part by accepting higher stocks and lower productivity than some other businesses.

THE MANUFACTURING CONTROL PROBLEM

1.2 The planning compromises.

Commodities such as sugar, salt, soda-ash, nuts and bolts, dyestuffs, light bulbs, etc are effectively identical irrespective of source. Customers tend to choose a supplier for the lowest price or the most convenient location. If the preferred supplier is out of stock for a period, they will temporarily buy elsewhere and possibly pay a higher price, but will return to the original supplier when he has product available, provided that he still offers the best deal. For such manufacturers, it will be advantageous to minimise costs by achieving maximum productivity and low stock levels, even if customer service suffers as a result.

Demand for consumer goods such as radios, personal stereos, training shoes or toasters, for example, depends very much on fashion and can be very volatile and, to a degree, price insensitive. Very short development lead times are essential. Stocks of specific models or components must be kept low because of the danger of being left with unusable stocks of obsolescent products or components. Manufacturers of fashion-influenced consumer goods will see flexibility, design and speed of response as key objectives, and some productivity penalty may be acceptable if it is necessary to achieve these objectives.

All the above types of company have to face the same compromises, but the optimum positions which they choose between the extremes may be very different and will depend both upon the environment in which they operate and their internal resources.

1.2.2 The real differences between businesses

Managers in most businesses tend to believe that their problems are unique. At first sight, this seems obvious. For example, would one expect to find similarities between producing small electronic items such as intruder alarms or hearing aids, packing pharmaceuticals or making items of clothing? In fact the key operation for all three is assembly, and this must be preceded by buying or making the correct quantities of all components at the required time. In one case resistors, capacitors, chips, fuses, circuit boards, etc are being assembled, whilst in the case of pharmaceutical packing the components are the medicine, a container, a cap, labels, a carton, a leaflet, etc. In garment manufacture, cut pieces of cloth, sewing thread, labels, buttons, trimmings, hangers, etc are assembled into the finished garment. The basic planning logic is very similar for all three.

A pottery making a range of china items and a steel producer which rolls its steel into a variety of sheets or girders at first appear to be fundamentally different, but both have a single important raw material – china clay in the one case and iron ore or perhaps pig iron in the other.

They then turn the raw material into a large number of different end products such as cups, saucers and bowls in the one case and steel girders or sheets of different sizes and hardness in the other. The planning approaches for the steel mill and the pottery are almost identical but are both very different from the approach needed by assembly industries.

Continuous process industries such as oil refineries have very different control problems. They run for 24 hours per day with the same feedstock, e.g. crude oil, and produce continuously a range of products such as ethylene, petrol, paraffin or tar oils in a ratio which is fixed or at best can be varied only slightly by changing the operating conditions. Another industry with this problem is chlorine production by electrolysis of brine. For every tonne of chlorine made, 1.14 tonnes of sodium hydroxide are produced. The ratio is fixed by the chemistry and cannot be changed. The control problem is more one of managing the demand of each product to equal the supply, rather than controlling supply to meet demand. This type of control problem tends to be very specialised and will not be discussed further in this book.

1.2.3 The need for a manufacturing strategy

In more conventional manufacturing, the planning systems and logic required depend more on the business environment within which the company operates than they do on the products being manufactured. Companies in the second half of the 1990s work in an environment very different from that of the 1950s. Gone are the queues of customers' vehicles waiting for their share of the output. Most companies are engaged in continuing international competition for their market share. Successful companies have identified a business strategy and, from that, a manufacturing strategy. Production planning and control systems must support these strategies.

Strategy development should start by looking at the business from the customer's view point. What are his needs? What aspects of our business must be improved if we are to meet his needs? In marketing terminology, what unique selling points (USPs) must we develop to win and keep his business? Amongst the possibilities are:

- Competitive prices.
- Exceptional quality and reliability.
- Short delivery lead times.
- Security of supply.
- Responsiveness to design change.

- Reliability of delivery promise dates.
- One-off designs or quick and effective bespoke modifications to standard products.

The strategy for manufacturing and manufacturing control should define policy with respect to quality, make or buy and customer service objectives. It must also cover policy on health, safety and the environment but these areas are outside the scope of this text.

1.2.4 Elements of a manufacturing strategy

1.2.4.1 Quality

High quality no longer gives a competitive advantage. Adequate quality has become a norm, without which a company will not even get to the starting line of the competition. Use of the word adequate however avoids some difficult questions. How adequate is adequate? There is little point in a manufacturer of bulldozers spending money to emulate the quality of paint finish achieved at considerable expense by Rolls Royce Motors. Once the machine has started working it will rapidly become marked and dented, but significant quality failures, such as paint runs or rusty patches, on a bulldozer at an exhibition or when first delivered to a customer, will suggest that other aspects of quality not so easily seen are also poor and may well influence the choice of supplier next time.

The manufacturing strategy document must give some general guidance on quality targets. Do we want to be the best irrespective of fitness for purpose? If so, how large a premium are we prepared to pay? Alternatively, given that fitness for purpose defines a minimum standard, are we content merely to meet this standard or should we aim to be in the middle of the range set by the competition?

1.2.4.2 Make or buy?

It is perfectly possible to run a business whilst subcontracting all manufacture. Many famous names do this, particularly in the electronics industry. Reasons for contracting out all or some of manufacturing may be cost saving, flexibility, unfamiliar technology or capacity shortage.

1.2.4.3 Cost savings

A supplier with particular expertise in an area and operating at high volumes with specialist equipment, or a small, flexible, owner-managed business may well be able to supply at a lower cost than in-house manufacture, but care must be taken when comparing internal and external costs. A frequent mistake is to compare the cost charged by a contractor for an item with an internal cost which includes a contribution to overheads as well as material and labour costs, and then to subcontract the job even though capacity is available in house, because the contractor appears to be cheaper. Overheads are likely to remain largely the same whether the work is done in house or not, and so should be eliminated from this comparison. If, as a result of subcontracting, internal labour would be temporarily under occupied but still paid, the cost of this payment must be added to contractor costs before making the comparison.

Before taking a decision to cease internal manufacture and contract out all component production for cost reasons, it is important to ensure that overhead costs associated with in-house manufacture can be eliminated. If not, and the company continues to pay its own overheads whilst contributing to the suppliers through the contract price, the saving from subcontracting may be less than originally calculated or in the worst case negative.

1.2.4.4 Flexibility

A large company suffering from the bureaucracy which is common in large organisations, may well find that small, local suppliers can provide shorter lead times and greater flexibility than can be achieved internally. Although the medium term solution must be to simplify the business processes and devolve authority and responsibility to managers of 'mini businesses' within the large company, a short term solution may be the use of small subcontractors, where typically an owner manager and key staff may be prepared to work all night to meet a deadline, in a way which would be difficult to organise and possibly illegal in a large company.

1.2.4.5 Unfamiliar technology

If a new product requires technology in which the company is inexperienced, either because the technology represents state of the art (e.g. vacuum welding, laser cutting or rapid prototyping using laser beams and light curing resins) or conventional well established processes which are new to the company (e.g. the manufacture of tissues or fancy containers for a toiletries manufacturer), it may be desirable to subcontract the manufacture to experts, at least initially until volumes grow sufficiently to support new investment in training, people or equipment.

1.2.4.6 Capacity shortage

Subcontractors can provide additional capacity either temporarily or more permanently. A company may choose to run say a machine shop, with only 80% of the average number of operators required. Provided that demand does not fall by more than 20% below average, the machine shop works steadily with the operators fully occupied. The remaining load is passed on to subcontractors, who absorb all the fluctuations in demand.

However a high technology company may prefer to keep manufacture in house even if contracting out would be cheaper, in order to avoid the risk of revealing valuable process technology to a potential competitor. If partial contracting out is essential for capacity reasons, it will be wise to send out straightforward tasks and keep confidential know-how in house.

If subcontracting is regular practice, the manufacturing strategy should specify the procedures for selecting and approving contract manufacturers. A strategy document cannot legislate for specific cases but it can lay down the guidelines to be followed.

1.2.5 Customer service policy and type of manufacture

The length of time the customer is prepared to wait between placing his order and taking delivery, compared with the total manufacturing lead time, is one of the key influences on manufacturing control policy. This is illustrated in Fig. 1.3. The lower part of the bar chart illustrates the major activities which are involved in meeting a manufacturing order, starting with design and finishing with delivery. The upper part indicates how different customer service requirements influence the processes which can be carried out after receipt of the customer's order.

1.2.5.1 Make to Order

If the customer is prepared to wait months or even years, as is the case with a large capital item such as a power station, the supplier is able to wait until a firm customer order is received before starting design work and placing orders for raw materials and components. This mode of operation is called Make to Order or MTO. True design and make to order situations are relatively rare. In many cases, the customer may supply the design, or the manufacturer may already have a standard design which can be easily modified. The manufacturer may choose to hold stocks of multipurpose materials especially if they have a long supply lead time.

THE MANUFACTURING CONTROL PROBLEM

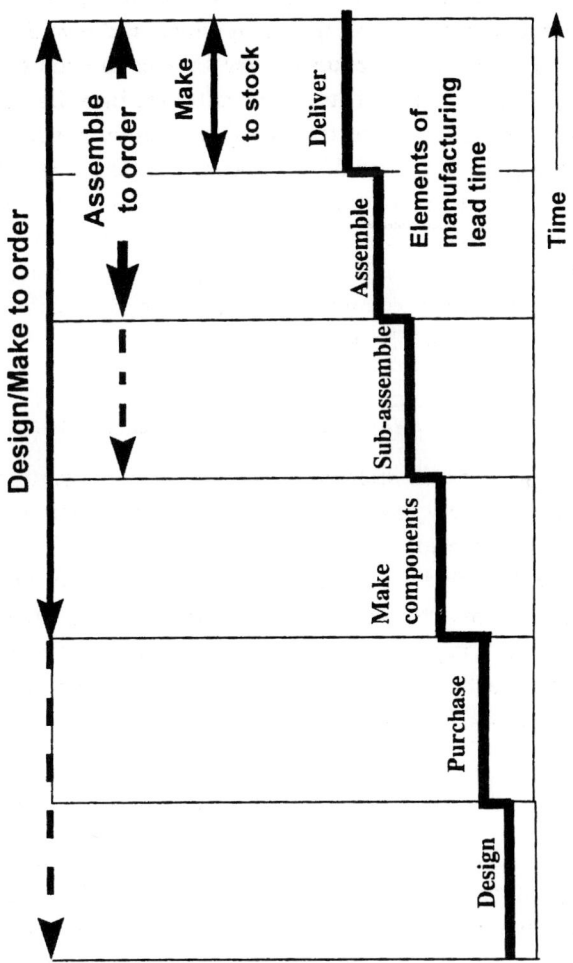

1.3 Relationship between customer and manufacturing lead times.

1.2.5.2 Make to Stock

In many cases the customer requires immediate delivery, or at least delivery in a time very much shorter than a typical manufacturing lead time. The life saving drug mentioned earlier is an extreme example, but even with much less emotive products such as paint, for example, if a retail customer finds his favourite brand not in stock, he will probably take a rival brand rather than wait for delivery of new stock. The manufacturer supplying the retailer must therefore offer almost immediate replenishment either to avoid the original stock-out or to minimise the loss of sales, and he may well choose to do this by holding stocks of finished product. This form of manufacture is called Make to Stock or MTS.

1.2.5.3 Assemble to Order

With a large product range, holding stock of all finished products may be unacceptably expensive. In some cases it may be possible to hold stocks of a relatively small number of multipurpose sub-assemblies and components and then assemble them quickly after the customer's order is received and the product specification is known. Personal computers are often built in this way. The supplier will stock chassis and a variety of circuit boards, disk drives, modems, etc. The relevant items are then easily assembled by plugging them together after the customer's order is received. High volume motor car manufacturers use similar techniques in order to give customers a wide choice of options and features, with competitive delivery promises. This mode of operation is known as Assemble to Order.

Many companies find that they operate in all three areas, depending on the product. It is important to define clearly which products are to be subject to each approach, since there are differences in the planning approach and possibly in the equipment required in each case.

Exercises

1.1 List the items you would expect to be covered in a statement of manufacturing strategy.

1.2 List the advantages of operating a Make to Stock rather than a Make to Order business.

1.3 A company manufactures brass valves (stopcocks) for both domestic and industrial use. The valves are offered in a range of sizes, all of which are manufactured in house. The first operation is to cast the brass bodies in the foundry. The second operation is to cut threads on the inlet and outlet, in the machine shop. One operator can machine 30 000 valves per year, more or less regardless of size. Demand is increasing steadily but is still comfortably within the capacity of both the foundry and machine shop. The production director has been looking ahead and if the growth continues there will be a problem two years from now. A small but enterprising local machining company has already offered to take over his machining operations and has quoted a price of £0.43 per valve for the 15 mm size. The company accountant provides the following figures for the current standard cost of the 15 mm valve:

	Casting		Machining	
Materials	0.15	(brass)	0.75	(cast body)
Direct labour	0.25		0.33	
Local overhead	0.20		0.20	Supervision, cleaning, safety, etc
General overhead	0.15		0.15	Planning, inspection, etc
TOTAL	0.75		1.43	

Demand for the 15 mm size is about 20 000 per year.

The production director notices that excluding the £0.75 for the cast body, the standard cost for machining one body is £0.68, or £0.25 more than the contractor's quote of £0.43 for the same operation. Sending out all the 15 mm castings for machining would yield a saving of 20 000 × £0.25 or £5 000 per year. He decides to send all future machining of the 15 mm valve to the contractors in order to make this saving. Is this a wise decision, given the information available?

1.4 (a) List all the factors which contribute to the cost of holding stocks. Some will be directly related to the value of the stock, others may be a fixed cost per year. For a business with which you are familiar, make estimates of the total cost of holding stock, expressed as a per cent per annum of the stock value. Make reasonable guesses for information which is not to hand. (If you are not familiar with a particular business, consider an assembler of an electrical consumer product such as a toaster, who makes to stock and purchases all components.)

(b) What do you think are the activities involved in changing over (or setting up) an automated bottle filling plant to handle a different liquid and a different bottle size? Make rough estimates of the cost of each major activity. Assume that the line is not 100% occupied, so that if it were not being changed over it would be standing idle for the corresponding time.

What additional costs should be included if the plant is fully occupied?

2

Achieving control of the business

In this chapter we will consider what must be done to achieve the correct balance between the three conflicting objectives of high customer service, low stocks and high manufacturing productivity and will show that for most companies this is primarily a matter of materials control. Some of the tools and techniques which can be used for control will be introduced.

2.1 A model of a manufacturing business

In most businesses production planning is a low profile, back room activity. Often only the planners themselves or people who work closely with them recognise the nature and complexity of the business control problem. The uninvolved can reveal their limited understanding with questions such as 'Why don't businesses merely make what the customer wants? If stocks are too high why don't you just buy or make less? If productivity is low, shouldn't the operators work harder?' Here we consider the difficulties faced by production controllers, and some of the tools and techniques which are available to overcome these difficulties.

The simplest model of a manufacturing business is a box. Raw materials are put in at one end and finished goods emerge from the other (see Fig. 2.1).

Although undoubtedly correct, this model is too simple to be of much use. A refinement is to recognise the specific stocking points at which materials are held. For example, raw materials will probably go into a store, from which, after quality clearance, they will be issued for use in specific production orders. Similarly, finished product may be stored before being issued to a customer's order (see Fig. 2.2).

Even this model is far too simple, however, because in practice there are likely to be multiple production stages with products having to be planned and monitored through each stage (see Fig. 2.3). If the hundreds or even thousands of different products, involving possibly tens of thousands of

ACHIEVING CONTROL OF THE BUSINESS 17

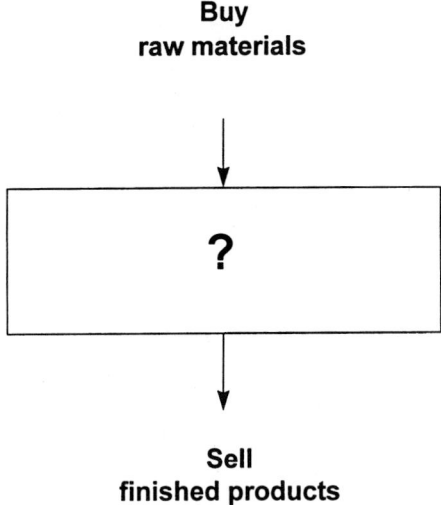

2.1 What is a manufacturing business (1)?

different materials are taken into account, the magnitude of the control problem becomes clear even before taking into account complications caused by machine breakdowns, quality rejections or failure to deliver on time by suppliers.

Control is simplest in businesses which manufacture a few simple products continuously, but since such businesses often operate in a very competitive environment, high standards of control are required to minimise costs. In food or pharmaceuticals, for example, most products follow standard routes with only three or four operations per route and typically less than ten components per stage. In contrast the engineering industry may have thousands of components used to build, say, a high speed colour printing press and each may take a different route through stages such as drilling, turning, milling, shaping, etc. A diagram tracking the flow of each item through the workshop can easily look like a plate of spaghetti.

However, even in a complicated environment production control breaks down into two questions which are simple to ask but more difficult to answer. These are:

- How do we buy and make the right things at the right time?
- How do we ensure that we have the resources available to do so?

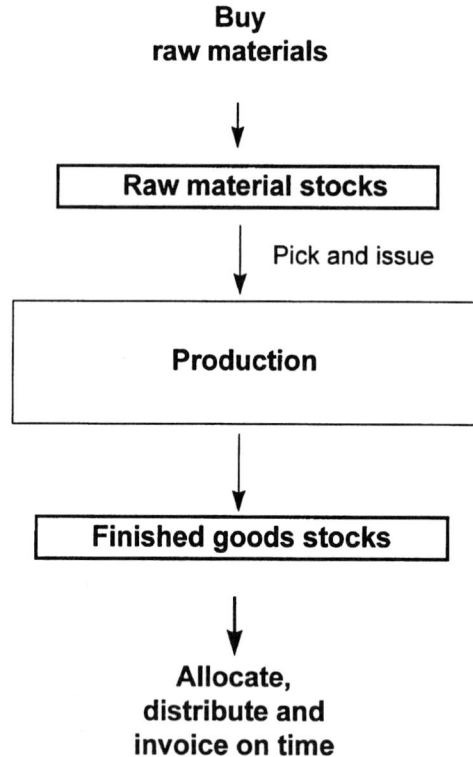

2.2 What is a manufacturing business (2)?

Much of the remainder of this book will be devoted to attempts to answer these simple questions.

2.2 Materials control

Probably the most common method of deciding when to order more material is to wait until something is needed and then look in all the places where it ought to be kept to see if any can be found. If the search proves fruitless an order is placed. This works very well for items which can be obtained almost instantly from a supplier near the factory gate. Fast foods for lunch or nuts and bolts from a hardware shop are typical of the few

What is a manufacturing business?

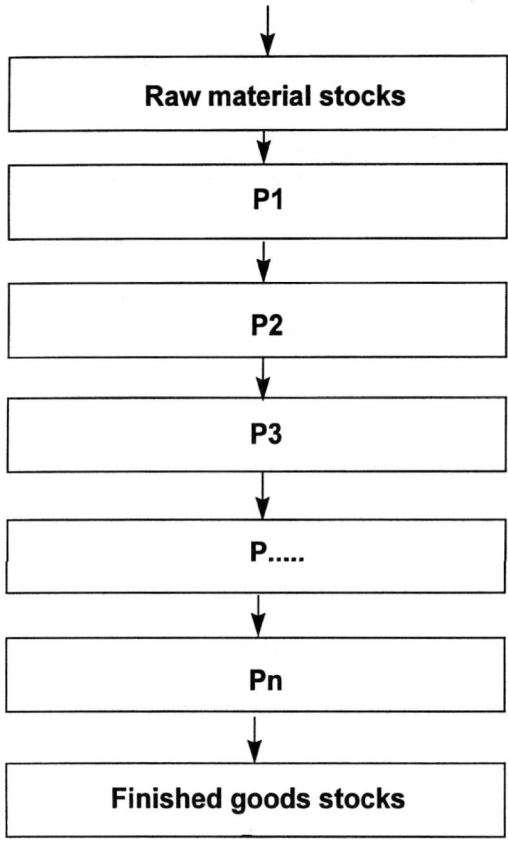

2.3 What is a manufacturing business (3)?

items for which this technique works well. In other cases, the time delay between recognising the need and receiving delivery either by purchase or by manufacture will be days, weeks or months and this 'react when there is a problem' approach is unacceptable.

2.2.1 Order Point

The period between placing a manufacturing or purchase order and receiving delivery is called the **lead time**. To maintain supply, an order must be placed when there is still enough material in stock to last throughout the lead time. In the Order Point method of control, a critical

Re-order when the stock falls below the order point

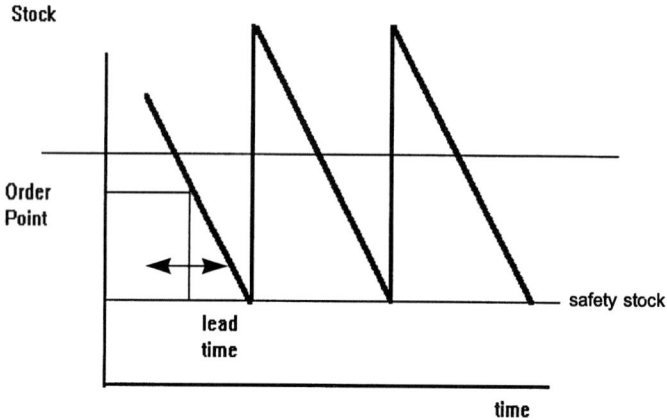

Order Point = safety stock + usage during lead time - quantity on order

2.4 Order Point.

stock level for each item is defined. If the stock falls below this level a replenishment order is placed. If demand consists of many small requirements, it may be regarded as continuous, and a plot of stock against time will follow a sawtooth pattern as in Fig. 2.4. The stock level falls linearly until a replenishment is received and then rises suddenly by the quantity delivered. Ideally a delivery should arrive just as the stock level falls to zero or, if we need to allow for unexpected usage or delivery delays, to a specified safety stock level. The order must be placed at the time when the stock exceeds the safety stock by the amount we expect to use during the lead time. Allowance must be made for any material on order but not yet delivered.

Effective operation of an Order Point system requires stock levels to be monitored continuously so that a replenishment order is placed immediately the stock falls below the order point level. This is particularly easy if the stock and order records are maintained on a computer, which can be programmed to print a daily list of items with stock less than order point. Since the order point level takes into account items ordered but not yet received, an item disappears from the daily list as soon as an order is placed.

Order Point makes the assumption that past demand is a good indication of the future. For example, if demand over the past year has been 520 (i.e. the average usage per week is 10) and the supply lead time is 6 weeks, the demand that must be met before the next delivery is 60 (i.e. 6 weeks at 10 per week). A new order should be placed if the stock plus any material on order is found to be below 60 plus safety stock.

A particularly simple version of Order Point is the **two bin system**. Each material or item is stored in two bins or locations. The second one contains a quantity equal to the order point but it is sealed to prevent use. Material is taken preferentially from the first, and a new order is placed whenever it is necessary to unseal and access the second bin.

2.2.2 Periodic Review

With Order Point, each material is monitored continuously and an order placed when necessary. Typically the **order quantity** is fixed and the **interval** between orders varies with demand.

An alternative is the Periodic Review method, in which stocks of a group of products are reviewed at regular intervals. A sufficient quantity is ordered so that stocks will fall to safety stock by the delivery after the next review (see Fig. 2.5) i.e. the interval between orders is fixed, and the order quantity varies with demand.

Periodic Review does not require a stock record to be maintained and also has the advantage that items purchased from the same supplier can be checked and ordered at the same time. If a review date is missed, however, shortages can arise for a whole group of items.

Order Point type techniques work well only if demand is continuous and steady. If demand fluctuates, large safety stocks are required to cover for uncertainty. Order Point can be effective for the control of a regularly used item such as a multipurpose fastening or a mature product no longer growing and sold to many customers, but it would not be very effective for an item used only every quarter (see Fig. 2.6). The order point level would be breached as stocks fell sharply following the issue to manufacturing of the requirements for the quarterly manufacturing order. The next delivery would arrive a lead time later even though it would not be required until the next manufacturing campaign.

2.2.3 Stock Projection

Order Point assumes that the usage of an item in the future will be similar to past usage. It is therefore unsuited to products or items which are

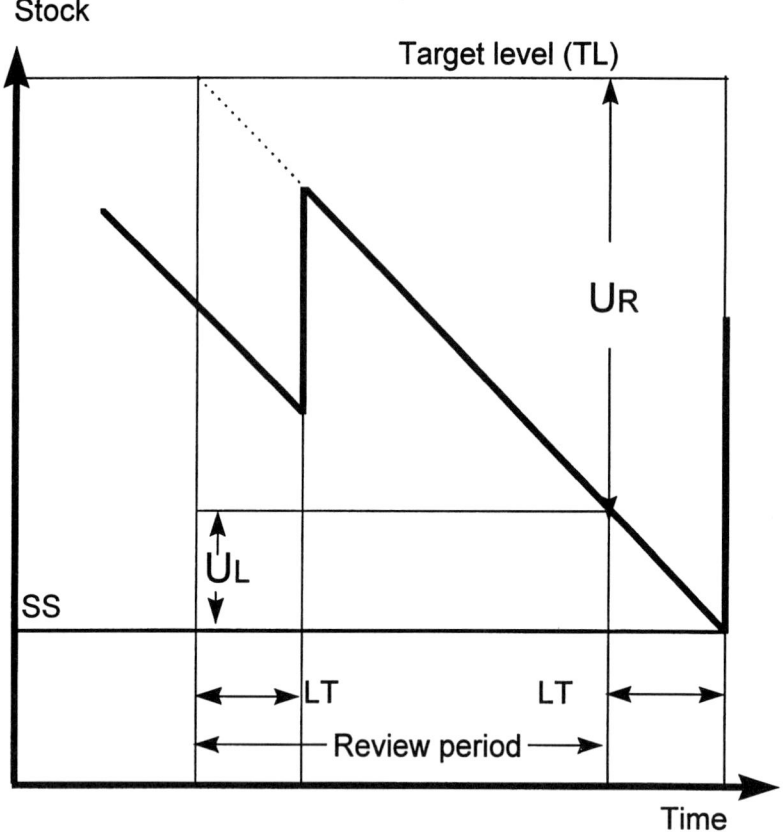

Target level (TL) = usage during review period + usage during LT + SS

$$TL = U_R + U_L + SS$$

Order quantity = TL - current stock - quantity on order

2.5 Periodic Review.

growing or declining rapidly unless they are very cheap, easy to store items, and a large safety stock can be held. On some occasions Order Point is used in non-ideal situations because there is no satisfactory alternative. Control of maintenance spares for which it is difficult if not impossible to predict future requirements is a case in point, as is the control of stationery items which are used intermittently.

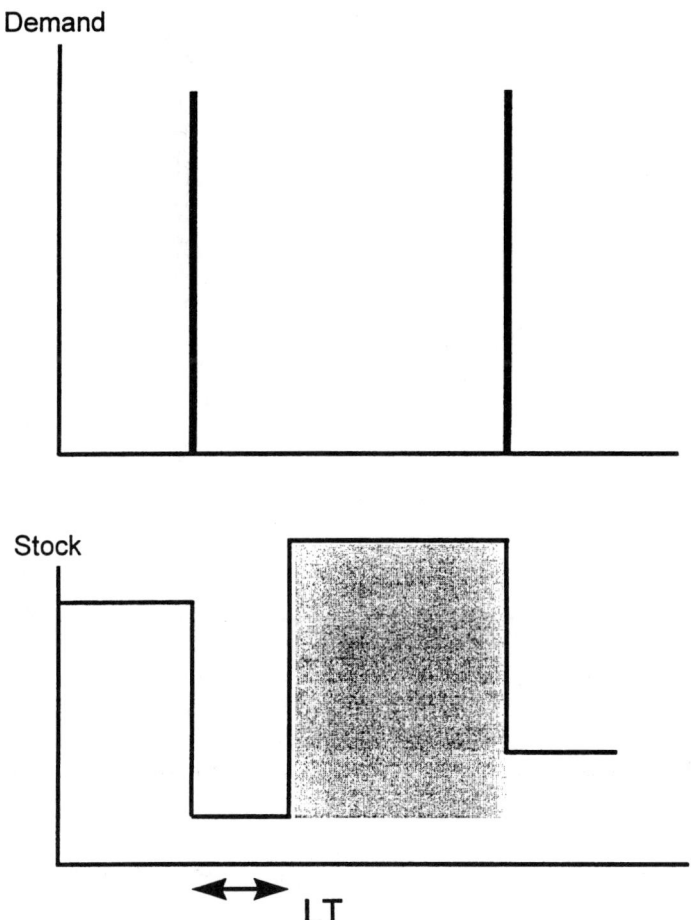

2.6 Order Point and discrete (or lumpy) demand.

If, however, a forecast of future usage can be made, projected stock levels can be calculated and the date when stock will fall below zero can be predicted. A replenishment order must then be placed a lead time before this date. Provided that they can be forecast, periods of zero demand, growth or decline can be taken into account. For obvious reasons, this stock projection technique is sometimes called Time Phased Order Point.

Consider the example in Fig. 2.7. Superlem is a very successful soft drink sold in various bottle sizes. For this example only the popular 500 ml packs will be considered. Sales are growing steadily and the product manager has provided the sales forecast by period as shown on line 1 of

LEMO1, Superlem drink 500 ml glass bottle

| | Opening stock | 85 | | | Order quantity | | 60 | | | |
| | Lead time | | | | | | 2 weeks | | | |

	Period	1	2	3	4	5	6	7	8	9	10
1	Sales forecast		20	21	22	22	24	25	25	26	28	30
2	Projected stock 85		65	44	22	0	36	11	46	20	52	22
3	Manufacturing order receipts						60		60		60	
4	Manufacturing order releases				60	60	60					

2.7 Stock projection for LEMO1 Superlem drink.

Fig. 2.7. In this case the periods are weeks. For simplicity low numbers are used for sales and stocks, etc. In practice, pack quantities would be much higher. It may be helpful to think of the units as thousands of bottles.

The current (or opening) stock is 85 packs. This is shown on line 2 of the figure. If the sales during week 1 are 20 as forecast, the closing stock for week 1 will be $85-20 = 65$. This projection can be continued to give the anticipated closing stocks for weeks 2–4, as shown on line 2 of Fig. 2.7.

After the requirement for 22 in week 4 is satisfied the projected stock falls to zero and will go negative during week 5 if no action is taken. In order to prevent this, a manufacturing order must be completed by the beginning of week 5. The manufacturing order quantity for filling is 60 and the order is required to be in stock by the beginning of week 5. This is shown as a **manufacturing order receipt** on line 3.

The closing stock for week 5 is now predicted to be 36, but with the expected sale of 25 in week 6 this will fall to 11 by the end of the week. Another manufacturing order receipt for 60 is needed by the beginning of week 7 if a stock-out is to be avoided. The projected closing stock for week 7 will then be 46 which will satisfy requirements for week 8. Continuation of the projection shows that a further order for 60 is required by the beginning of week 9.

LEMO1, Superlem drink 500 ml glass bottle

| Opening stock | 85 | Order quantity | 60 |
| Safety stock | 40 | Lead time | 2 weeks |

	Period		1	2	3	4	5	6	7	8	9	10
1	Sales forecast		20	21	22	22	24	25	25	26	28	30
2	Projected stock	85	65	44	82	60	96	71	46	80	52	82
3	Manufacturing order receipts				60		60			60		60
4	Manufacturing order releases		60		60			60		60		

2.8 Plan for LEMO1 with safety stock of 40.

Note that the convention used in the example is that when an order quantity is shown as being received in a period, it is assumed to be available for use from the beginning of that period. It is perfectly feasible to adopt a different convention in which it is assumed that a quantity shown as being received in a period is only available for use by the end of the period (in effect the beginning of the next period). This latter convention tends to be favoured when the planning periods are days and are identified not by period number but by date.

In the Superlem example, the lead time for a bottle filling order is two weeks, so orders to be received in weeks 5, 7 and 9 must be released to production two weeks previously, that is at the beginning of weeks 3, 5 and 7.

In the example, the projected stock is allowed to fall to zero in week 4. This presents no problem provided that everything goes to plan, but if demand for the Superlem 500 ml pack proved to be greater than forecast, there would be a stock-out in week 4. In an industry in which good customer service is particularly important, management may well choose to hold a safety stock of finished packs to provide protection against errors in the sales forecast. Figure 2.8 shows a revised plan for Superlem 500 ml (LEM01) in which a safety stock of 40 packs is maintained.

A manufacturing order receipt is planned not when the projected stock falls below zero, but when it falls below safety stock. Not surprisingly, an additional manufacturing order receipt is required for week 3 to build the extra stock. For the purposes of further planning, the data in Fig. 2.7 with no safety stock held, will be taken as the real plan for LEM01, with Fig. 2.8 only indicating how a safety stock would have been incorporated had it been deemed necessary.

2.2.4 Comparison of Order Point and Stock Projection

If the sales forecast is flat and exactly equal to past sales, the Stock Projection technique gives exactly the same result as the Order Point method. However, trying to control stock by Order Point has been likened to driving a car forward whilst looking out only through the back window. With a straight clear road ahead, it would be relatively easy to learn to steer using only rear vision, but uncharted bends in the road would impose impossible problems.

Order Point only looks backwards, but sales forecasts or advance customer orders in conjunction with Stock Projection enable planners to look forwards. Whilst looking out through the windscreen is not a perfect approach to driving a car (the screen may be smeared or unexpected bends can cause problems), it is clearly better than looking backwards all the time. Sales forecasts will not always be accurate, but in the worst case, they can be set equal to past sales, and Stock Projection will do as well as Order Point. If market intelligence and extrapolation techniques are used to refine the forecasts for growing or declining products, Stock Projection will out perform Order Point significantly.

A further advantage of Stock Projection is that by looking forward, all the orders likely to be required up to the planning horizon can be predicted. Advance preparation for these orders can be made and component requirements obtained by use of the MRP technique.

2.3 Material Requirements Planning

In the Superlem example, the lead time for filling the 500 ml bottles was 2 weeks. This was used to step back from the **receipt date** or **due date** for each manufacturing order to determine the order **release date**. This is the date when the job tickets, component requisitions and other paperwork authorising the order should be released to production. It is also the latest date at which the bulk drink and all the package components must be available. There is little point in the production supervisor being authorised to start filling bottles if everything necessary is not available.

In order to calculate what components and intermediates are required to make the Superlem 500 ml packs, a recipe or in engineering terms a **bill of materials** is needed. Different industries use different names such as 'packing instruction' or 'parts list', but these are simply lists of everything needed to make one unit of product. The term bill of materials will be used in this text.

The MRP technique involves lengthy calculations and usually requires computer assistance. Computer systems require codes to identify products and materials. In practice material codes should be unstructured, or retain only a minimum of meaningful structure, and should not be longer than five or six characters. Although people find meaningful codes much easier to interpret than a string of random numbers and letters, if computer systems depend on the structure, and the structure has to be changed for any reason, reprogramming can be a lengthy and costly exercise.

In the interests of both simplicity and clarity, this advice will be ignored in the remainder of this book, and simple codes of five characters or less with some meaningful structure will be used. For example:

LEM01, LEM02, etc for sales items, intermediates or raw materials
B1, B2, etc for bottles, C1, C2, etc for caps and L1, L2, etc for labels

Thus the bill of materials for one bottle of Superlem 500 ml might be:

LEM01 Superlem 500 ml glass bottle

Code	Description	Qty per
LEM00	Lemon squash (bulk)	0.5 L
B1	Bottle 500 ml glass	1
C1	Cap	1
L1	Label	1

The quantity shown against each component in a bill of materials is known as the 'quantity per' and specifies how much of the component is required to make one unit of the parent item (one Superlem 500 ml pack in this case).

Thus to fill 60 of the 500 ml bottle requires 60 × 0.5 litres = 30 litres of bulk drink, 60 bottles, 60 caps and 60 labels. In practice, allowance would have to be made for an expected wastage of bulk drink or packaging materials during filling but this complication will be ignored for the time being. For the filling of Superlem 500 ml bottles, Fig. 2.7 shows that these materials will be required in the specified quantities at the beginning of periods 3, 5 and 7.

LEM02, Superlem drink 1 litre glass bottle

| | Opening stock | | 85 | | | Order quantity | | 80 | | |
| | Safety stock | | 0 | | | Lead time | | 1 week | | |

	Period		1	2	3	4	5	6	7	8	9	10
1	Sales forecast		5	20	0	0	50	0	0	10	50	10
2	Customer orders		0	30	20	10	20	0	0	0	0	0
3	Total requirements		5	50	20	10	70	0	0	10	50	10
4	Projected stock	85	80	30	10	0	10	10	10	0	30	20
5	Manufacturing order receipts						80				80	
6	Manufacturing order releases					80				80		

2.9 Plan for LEM02 with forecasts and orders.

2.3.1 Customer orders and sales forecasts

The above calculations for the filling of LEM01 assumed that sales forecasts were the only source of demand. This is rarely the case. If customers are prepared to place firm orders a significant time ahead of requirement date, the customer orders are more significant indicators of future demand than sales forecasts. This point is illustrated by plans for LEM02, a 1 litre glass bottle of Superlem, as shown Fig. 2.9. The planning grid has been extended to include customer orders and total requirements lines.

In this example, the total requirement is obtained by adding the sales forecast and customer orders for each period. This simple treatment is only valid if the forecast is reduced as an expected (or normal) order is entered to the system. It is clearly important that no demand is counted both as forecast and order. This technique, known as Forecast Consumption will be considered in more detail in the discussion of Master Production Scheduling in Chapter 3.

The bulk drink and package component requirements for LEM02 can be calculated in the same way as for LEM01.

LEM02 Superlem 1 litre glass bottle

Code	Description	Qty per
LEM00	Lemon squash (bulk)	1.0 L
B2	Bottle 1 litre glass	1
C1	Cap	1
L2	Label	1

Note that the bulk drink and the cap C1 are common to both LEM01 and LEM02.

To fill 80 of the 1 litre bottle requires $80 \times 1.0 = 80$ litres of bulk drink, 80 bottles, 80 caps and 80 labels. The plan for LEM02 in Fig. 2.9 shows manufacturing order releases of 80 packs in weeks 4 and 8. Thus 80 litres of LEM00 the bulk drink and all the other package components are required at the beginning of weeks 4 and 8.

This information is a starting point for planning the total requirements for both bulk drink and package components but before this can be done all other requirements for bulk Superlem or common components must be determined. For the purposes of this exercise, the only other pack using the Superlem bulk drink is LEM03, a 3 litre plastic container of Superlem. Calculation of the requirements for bulk Superlem for filling into LEM03 is part of Exercise 2.3. Readers are recommended to do Exercise 2.3 at this point. The calculated results should agree with the data for LEM03 in line 3 of Fig. 2.10.

Identical logic to that used for calculating the total requirements for bulk Superlem can be used to calculate requirements for all the package components used. In the case of multipurpose components such as the cap C1, it is important to ensure that the demands from all the packs using these components have been included in the total requirements.

Since predictions of forward requirements are now available, the stock of each component can be projected forwards to determine when orders must be received and released. In the case of purchased package components, these will be purchase orders rather than manufacturing orders, and the lead times will be purchase lead times but the principles are exactly the same. The process of projecting stocks forward to determine when orders are required, followed by multiplication of the quantity per for each item by the order quantity to calculate the number of components needed for each order (a process known as 'exploding' the order through the bill of materials) can be continued downwards through

(Units = litres)

	Period	1	2	3	4	5	6	7	8	9	10
1	From LEM01			30		30		30			
2	From LEM02				80				80		
3	From LEM03	240			240		240		240		
4	TOTAL	240		30	320	30	240	30	320		

2.10 Requirements for LEM00 Superlem drink.

all the levels of the bill of materials until purchased items are reached. The total requirements for each purchased item are calculated and if necessary purchase orders, specifying quantity and planned receipt date, are generated. At this point the process stops. Purchased items do not have a bill of materials and responsibility for meeting the purchase orders lies with the supplier.

2.3.2 Independent and dependent demand

For sales items such as LEM01 and LEM02, the demand comes from wholesalers or retailers who will normally be third parties independent of the manufacturer. Such demand coming from outside the planned system is referred to as 'independent' demand, because it is independent of any plans of the manufacturer. It is not normally possible to calculate future independent demand definitively and if advance information is required, it must be forecast.

Demand which originates within the company, for example the demand for bulk Superlem drink or for bottles, is known as 'dependent' demand because the size of the demand depends on in-company activities or plans and can normally be calculated by using the bill of materials and planned order releases for higher level items, just as the requirements for LEM00 were calculated above. Dependent demand is normally for internal production use, whereas independent demand is for sales items.

	Period	1	2	3	4	5	6	7	8	9	10
1	Sales forecast										
2	Customer orders										
3	For internal use										
4	Total requirements										
5	Projected stock										
6	Manufacturing order receipts										
7	Manufacturing order releases										

2.11 A multipurpose planning grid.

In practice, any particular item may be subject to both independent and dependent demand. For example, although LEM01 is a sales item subject to independent demand coming from outside the planned system, it is possible that it could also be used internally, for example in a special promotion pack in which a lemon drink and an orange drink are packed together and sold at a reduced price. The demand for LEM01 for internal use is dependent demand because it depends on the manufacturing plan for the special pack. In an engineering environment, a sub-assembly or even a purchased component which is normally used for assembly of the final product (dependent demand) could be sold as a spare (independent demand).

Since, in principle, any item can be subject to sales forecasts, customer orders and demand for internal use, a general purpose planning grid requires an extra row as indicated in Fig. 2.11.

Although useful concepts in terms of understanding demand, the distinction between independent and dependent demand is becoming increasingly arbitrary as more and more companies recognise the advantages of sharing information between supplier and customer in so called supplier partnerships. In the simplest case, the manufacturer

| Opening stock | 0 | | | | Order quantity | | | 400 | | |
| Safety stock | 0 | | | | Lead time | | | 1 week | | |

	Period	1	2	3	4	5	6	7	8	9	10
1	Total requirements	240	0	30	320	30	240	30	320	–	–
2	Projected stock 0	160	160	130	210	180	340	310	390		
3	Manufacturing order receipts	400			400		400		400		
4	Manufacturing order releases			400		400		400			

2.12 Plan for LEM00 Superlem drink.

makes available to the supplier the output from his MRP system covering planned purchase order releases, and this serves as demand for the supplier's planning. In effect, what used to be independent demand has become very close to being dependent. Similar effects can be achieved by linking a distribution planning system to the manufacturing planning system. What used to be independent demand for the manufacturer now becomes dependent on the distribution plans.

2.3.3 Planning bulk drink manufacture

The MRP process can be used to cover all the items on the bill of materials as explained above. For simplicity, however, only the planning of the manufacture of the bulk drink, LEM00 will be considered in detail. Total demand has been calculated as shown in Fig. 2.10 and this demand has been incorporated into the plan in Fig. 2.12. Current stocks are zero. The manufacturing order quantity is 400 litres with a lead time of one week. An open manufacturing order for 400 litres is due for completion imminently. No safety stock of bulk drink is held and the manufacturing lead time is one week. (Again small numbers are being used for convenience. In order to relate to typical quantities for soft drink manufacture, the quantities should be mentally scaled up by perhaps a thousand times.)

There is no opening stock but the open order due for receipt early in week 1 will meet the requirements for filling in week 1 and provide sufficient stock to cover requirements up to the beginning of week 4, when a further receipt of 400 litres is required. Continuing the projection shows that further receipts are needed in weeks 6 and 8. With a lead time for manufacture of one week, these orders must be released in weeks 3, 5 and 7.

Using a fixed order quantity of 400 with a demand that does not exceed 320 per week but is erratic, is not an ideal arrangement and results in the holding of high stocks which are not immediately needed. It would be better if the bulk drink manufacturing orders could be matched in both quantity and timing with the filling plans. This would require variable manufacturing order quantities. The possibility of doing this will be considered later, but for the moment, the assumption is that equipment constraints preclude this.

The bulk drink LEM00 also has a bill of materials as follows:

LEM00 bulk Superlem drink (units = litres)

Code	Description	Qty per
LEM99	Lemon juice concentrate	0.1 L
E123	Citric acid	0.05 kg
E124	Preservative	0.002 kg
(W1	Water	0.91 L)

It is sometimes not convenient to express the quantities as those required for one unit of the product, i.e. 1 litre in this case. For example, a small quantity ingredient such as the preservative in this case, may require more decimal places than the computer system permits, if expressed as per litre of the bulk drink. In such cases, it is more convenient to express the bill of materials as the quantities required for one batch of the product, and the bill of materials must include an extra item of information, which is the quantity made by the recipe, expressed in the chosen units of measure. This is sometimes called an explosion factor, and is used by the computer to keep the calculations consistent even though quantities are specified in units convenient for the user.

By exploding the manufacturing order quantity through the bill of materials we find that the three manufacturing campaigns of 400 litres planned to start in periods 3, 5 and 7, each require 40 litres of lemon juice concentrate, 20 kg of citric acid and 0.8 kg of preservative E124. The requirement for water is shown in brackets on the bill of materials because if it is available straight from the tap, planning ahead is unnecessary. If, however, the water requires pre-treatment such as de-ionisation or filtering, it may be necessary to make water a planned item to ensure that supplies are adequate.

MRP will repeat this process of aggregating total requirements, projecting the stocks forward to plan new orders, and then exploding the order quantity through the bill of materials for each manufacturing stage, until purchased materials are reached.

2.4 Inadequacies of MRP

The MRP system as described so far, is a logical process of starting with the requirements for the end item, producing a manufacturing plan for that item, and then using a bill of materials to calculate requirements on previous stages and so on, until the acquisitions of all purchased items have been planned. In the early 1970s many companies adopted MRP enthusiastically but the results were almost invariably disappointing. In some cases, poor results could be attributed to inaccurate data. If stock figures are incorrect, if there are errors in bills of materials or lead times are unrealistic, MRP cannot be expected to produce sensible plans, but even in well managed systems, with accurate data, the expected benefits were not often achieved. It is now recognised that simple mechanistic MRP suffers from inherent weaknesses, of which the most important are described below.

2.4.1 Sales forecasts are often wrong

In the Superlem example, the MRP is driven directly from the sales forecasts. If either the forecasts are changed or in any period sales do not equal forecast, MRP at the next run replans down through the levels. Plans can change faster than those responsible for releasing orders can respond. The result is likely to be chaos, with little synchronisation between plans at different stages.

2.4.2 Plans are not necessarily realistic: no capacity planning

An MRP system is driven by materials needs. It takes no account of whether production capacity is available to meet the plan, or whether suppliers can provide what is needed by the required date. Unrealistic plans lead to poor customer service because product is not available when expected. Conversely stocks of intermediates and components become excessive because they were procured to support a level of usage which was never achieved. Badly managed MRP systems without capacity planning frequently show large numbers of orders over-due. What is the purpose of planning to make something yesterday, last week or last month? This cannot be a sensible basis for planning.

2.4.3 Production does not follow the plan: no feedback

Many MRP implementations are initiated by the planning department or even worse the data processing department with little involvement by the production department. The result is that production personnel feel little commitment to achieving the plans even if they are realistic. In those few cases where realistic plans are offered and the production department is committed there could still be unexpected events like machine breakdowns or quality rejections. Unless there is a feedback mechanism and plans are adjusted to allow for both positive and negative deviations, orders quickly become overdue and the plans of little relevance.

2.5 Improvements to MRP: the development of MRPII

During the 1970s and 1980s, additional features such as Master Production Scheduling, Capacity Planning and Production Activity Control were added to MRP systems in order to overcome the listed problems.

Master Production Scheduling sits between the sales forecasts and MRP. Its prime purpose is to exert control over changes to the plan so that changing customer requirements are met as far as possible, whilst keeping disruption, both on the factory floor and in MRP, to a level which can be accommodated.

Capacity Planning uses data about production rates, change-over times and machine and labour efficiency to calculate how much manufacturing resource (machines and people) is required to achieve the plan. Traditionally MRP systems make no attempt to modify the plans to fit the capacity available, but having identified the underloads and overloads, leave solving the problems to the human planner.

Production Activity Control calculates a target completion date for every operation, and provides facilities for progress to be recorded. An operation is the activity required at any one work centre (a resource such as a group of similar machines or a group of operators with similar skills). A manufacturing order can go through several operations. Any delays which threaten the achievement of the final order completion date must be fed back to the planner.

With these refinements, it was realised that MRP could be used not only to plan materials requirements but also machine and labour requirements. Simple additional modification made it possible to predict

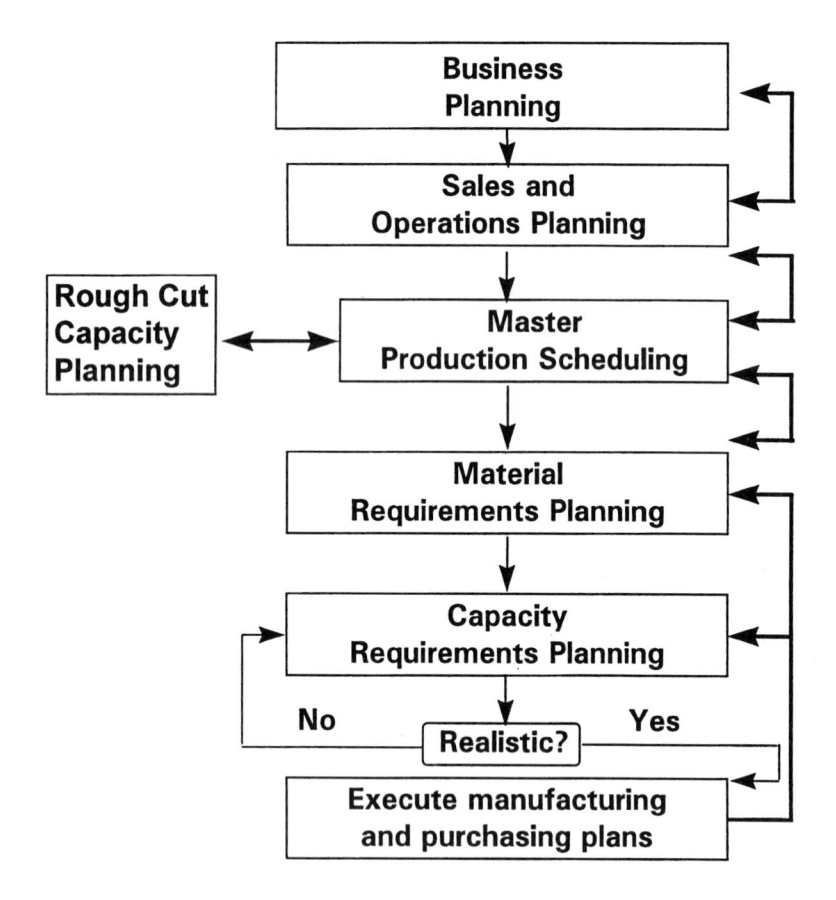

```
                    ┌──────────────────┐
                    │     Business     │◄──┐
                    │     Planning     │   │
                    └────────┬─────────┘   │
                             ▼             │
                    ┌──────────────────┐   │
                    │     Sales and    │◄──┤
                    │Operations Planning│  │
                    └────────┬─────────┘   │
                             ▼             │
┌───────────┐       ┌──────────────────┐   │
│ Rough Cut │◄─────►│      Master      │◄──┤
│ Capacity  │       │Production        │   │
│ Planning  │       │  Scheduling      │   │
└───────────┘       └────────┬─────────┘   │
                             ▼             │
                    ┌──────────────────┐   │
                    │     Material     │◄──┤
                    │Requirements      │   │
                    │     Planning     │   │
                    └────────┬─────────┘   │
                             ▼             │
                    ┌──────────────────┐   │
           ┌───────►│     Capacity     │◄──┤
           │        │Requirements      │   │
           │        │     Planning     │   │
           │        └────────┬─────────┘   │
           │                 ▼             │
           │   No   ┌──────────────┐  Yes  │
           └────────┤  Realistic?  ├───────┤
                    └──────────────┘       │
                    ┌──────────────────┐   │
                    │Execute manufacturing│◄┘
                    │ and purchasing plans│
                    └──────────────────┘
```

2.13 Main elements of MRPII.

the need for other resources such as warehouse space or finance. To indicate this increased capability the name 'Manufacturing Resources Planning' was adopted. This also has initials MRP and so, to distinguish it from the original Material Requirements Planning, it became known as MRP the Second, or MRPII, a confusing name but one which is now so widely adopted that changing it would be very difficult.

Probably the most significant difference between MRP and MRPII, however, is the culture needed to operate it. The plans must be based on accurate data and kept up to date. They must always be realistic and production management must be committed to achieving the plan.

The education required to achieve this new culture is a major part of the effort needed to implement MRPII. Figure 2.13 shows the major elements of an MRPII system. Material Requirements Planning has already been described in detail and Master Production Scheduling, Capacity Planning and Production Activity Control described briefly.

Business Planning is the top level planning process of the business which covers long term sales forecasting, including plans for the introduction of new products, and the implications of these forecasts for production, including if appropriate, the need for new factories and equipment over a five to ten year time scale. In order to minimise the quantity of data involved, business plans are normally made for broad groups of products rather than individual items and are usually expressed in financial terms.

Sales and Operations Planning, which is known in some texts by its old but confusing name of Production Planning, provides senior management with a control lever for the planning process. Data are summarised by product family and by period (usually months) and then for each family, the Sales and Operations Planning meeting reviews past sales against forecast, actual production against forecast, actual production against plan and actual stocks against planned stocks. The future plans are then reviewed in the light of recent past experience.

Later chapters will look in detail at each of the major components of MRPII.

Exercises

2.1 The 15 mm high tensile bolt, B1 is used in small quantities in almost every product made in the factory. It is controlled by Order Point. The purchasing lead time is 4 weeks and the total usage in the past 12 months was 104 000 bolts. It is ordered in 20 000 lots, but nothing is currently on order. Experience has shown that a safety stock of 5 000 is desirable. Calculate the order point level.

Could there be a situation in which the stock of B1 in stores was 12 000 but it was inappropriate to place an order?

2.2 In a soft drinks manufacturing business, average usage of a general purpose 500 ml bottle is 1.2 million per year. A safety stock of 50 000 bottles is held. Stocks are reviewed and replenishment orders placed every 4 weeks. The delivery lead time is 2 weeks. You are carrying out the review and find a stock of 80 000 bottles. How many should you order? Assume for simplicity that the factory works a 48 week year.

2.3 LEM03 is a 3 litre plastic container of Superlem drink which is part of the range of soft drinks discussed in Chapter 2. This is a newly launched pack and because of the uncertainty of demand, it has been agreed that a safety stock of 50 packs will be held. Given the information in the table below, calculate the manufacturing orders for filling which are needed if the forecast demands for the pack are to be met. Calculate also the quantities and dates of the requirements of bulk Superlem drink for filling. Your answer should agree with line 3 of Fig. 2.10 on page 30.

LEMO3, Superlem drink 3 litre plastic container

Opening stock   85   Order quantity   80
Safety stock   50   Lead time   1 week

	Period	1	2	3	4	5	6	7	8	9	10
1	Sales forecast	5	0	20	0	40	20	70	0	70	10
2	Customer orders	20	40	10	10	30	0	10	0	0	0
3	Total requirements										
4	Projected stock 85										
5	Manufacturing order receipts										
6	Manufacturing order releases										

2.4 Magnetics PLC assembles a range of micro-computers for process control and data logging. Magnetics' preferred policy is to buy all components and only carry out assembly in house, but when the range was first developed, hard disk drives with suitable high capacity and sufficiently rugged to operate in hostile environments such as chemical plants, were not available, and so they developed two drives of their own. The MD 200 has a capacity of 200 megabytes and the MD 500 has 500 megabytes. Both are highly successful and in addition to using them in their own assemblies, Magnetics has flourishing sales to other computer assemblers. The popularity is partly due to the performance and reliability of the drives but also to the excellent customer service offered. This is achieved by a combination of careful sales forecasting and holding a small safety stock. Magnetics' aim is to supply from stock, but because of daily fluctuations in the rate of arrival of orders and the lean manning of the packing and dispatch unit, customer orders can wait for up to three days before dispatch. Once they are dispatched they are invoiced and deleted from the planning records. The stock record is simultaneously reduced by the quantity dispatched.

(a) Calculate when additional order releases are required for MD 200, given the following planning information:

Demand for MD 200

Opening stock   18   Order quantity   30
Safety stock   5   Lead time   1 week

An open manufacturing order for 30 is due in week 2

	Period	1	2	3	4	5	6	7	8	9	10
1	Sales forecast	2	6	7	8	8	9	9	10	10	10
2	Customer orders	4									
3	For internal use	4	4	4	4	4	4	4	4	4	4
4											

40 PLANNING AND CONTROL OF MANUFACTURING OPERATIONS

(b) The assembly plan for all computers incorporating the MD 500 disk drive is:

Planned manufacturing order receipts for all computers incorporating the MD 500 disk drive

Assembly lead time = 1 week

	Period	1	2	3	4	5	6	7	8	9	10
1	Manufacturing order receipts	(O) 10	(O) 12	12	12	16	16	20	20	20	20
2											
3											
4											

(o) indicates open order. There is 1 MD 500 drive per unit

Note that the assembly order quantity is not fixed. The policy is to assemble the requirements for the week by the beginning of the week.

Planning information covering external sales of MD 500 is:

External demand for MD 500

Opening stock 20   Order quantity 40

Safety stock   10   Lead time   1 week

	Period	1	2	3	4	5	6	7	8	9	10
1	Sales forecast	8	10	10	10	10	10	10	10	10	10
2	Customer orders	2									
3											
4											

Calculate the total requirements for the MD 500 and plan the manufacturing order releases and receipts required for the MD 500 in the next ten weeks.

(c) One of the key components in both sizes of disk drive is a vibration free bearing, VFB10, which is a purchased item. There are two bearings per disk. The bearing is used only in the manufacture of the MD 200 and MD 500.

- Purchase lead time is 3 weeks.
- Safety stock is zero.
- Opening stock is 90.
- Order quantity is 80.

Calculate the purchase orders for bearings required during the next ten weeks. Make any estimates necessary to complete the calculation. Explain why these estimates are necessary.

2.5 Although MRP is an effective way of calculating the materials requirements needed to meet a particular sales forecast or set of sales orders, it does not prove to be an effective way of controlling a manufacturing business. List the reasons why.

3

Master Production Scheduling

This chapter will describe the principles of Master Production Scheduling, in particular with respect to achieving a balance between stability and responsiveness, and the role of Master Production Scheduling in customer order management and the provision of realistic delivery promises.

3.1 Introduction

As Chapter 2 showed, driving the MRP calculation directly from sales forecasts proved unsatisfactory, partly because of the large number of changes introduced into the MRP system. If a particular order was received a week earlier than forecast, it would appear that sales were exceeding forecast and MRP would react by increasing production. Subsequently in the week of the forecast, sales would now appear to be below forecast because the expected order had already been received in a previous week, and MRP would reverse the previous changes, much to the chagrin of the shop floor, where operators and supervisors may well have been making a special effort to meet the increased demand of the previous week. Master Production Scheduling leaves control in the hands of the planner, but the power of the computer can be used to draw his attention to possible changes.

For a typical 'Make to Stock' company, the format of a Master Production Schedule (MPS) is very similar to that of stock projection in MRP.

On the planning grid, rows are provided for both sales forecasts and customer orders (see Fig. 3.1).

For the moment the total requirements row will be regarded as the sum of sales forecasts and orders. The opening stock level is projected forward exactly as in MRP, taking account of any existing manufacturing orders. However, should stock fall below the safety stock level, a manufacturing order is not automatically created or moved, but a suitable message is

	Period	1	2	3	4	5	6	7	8	9	10
1	Sales forecast										
2	Customer orders										
3	Total requirements										
4	Projected stock										
5	MPS order receipts										
6	MPS order releases										
7	Available to promise										

3.1 A Master Production Schedule planning grid.

generated for the planner, who can then assess the significance of the change and above all determine whether it is feasible, before accepting or rejecting it.

This point can be illustrated by reference to the plan for LEM01, the 500 ml glass bottle pack of Superlem, originally derived in Fig. 2.8. Figure 3.2 shows the situation after time has moved on by one week, so that period 2 in Fig. 2.8 is now period 1 and so on.

An additional sales forecast of 30 has been added for the new period 10. However in the previous week 1, actual sales were 25 compared to the sales forecast of 20. Thus the opening stock for the new week 1 is now 60 rather than the previously projected 65, and the forecast sales of 21 in the new week 1 cause it to drop to 39 which is below the safety stock level of 40. Thus, according to the rule that safety stock should not normally be penetrated, the open MPS order (or manufacturing order) for 60 due in week 2 should be brought forward to week 1. However, this may not be possible or desirable, since with a 2 week lead time, the order should have been started a week ago. The MPS system will provide a message suggesting that the order be brought forward. In this particular case the planner would probably reject it since the stock is only one below safety stock.

LEM01, Superlem drink 500 ml bottle

| Opening stock | 60 | Order quantity | 60 |
| Safety stock | 40 | Lead time | 2 weeks |

	Period	1	2	3	4	5	6	7	8	9	10
1	Sales forecast	21	22	22	24	25	25	26	28	30	30
2	Customer orders										
3	Total requirements	21	22	22	24	25	25	26	28	30	30
4	Projected stock 60	39	77	55	91	66	41	75	47	77	47
5	Manufacturing order receipts		(o) 60		60			60		60	
6	Manufacturing order releases	60		60		60					

3.2 Planning grid showing firm planned orders and breach of safety stock.

3.2 Exception messages

The warning messages which prompt the planner to investigate a potential imbalance between supply and demand are usually referred to as **exception messages**. Common types of exception messages are:

- Reschedule in (i.e. make sooner).
- Reschedule out (make later).
- Increase quantity.
- Decrease quantity.
- Create order.
- Cancel order.

3.3 The firm planned fence

In some MPS systems all manufacturing orders are under manual control.

MASTER PRODUCTION SCHEDULING

Firm planned fence

| Firm planned region under manual control | Planned region under computer control |

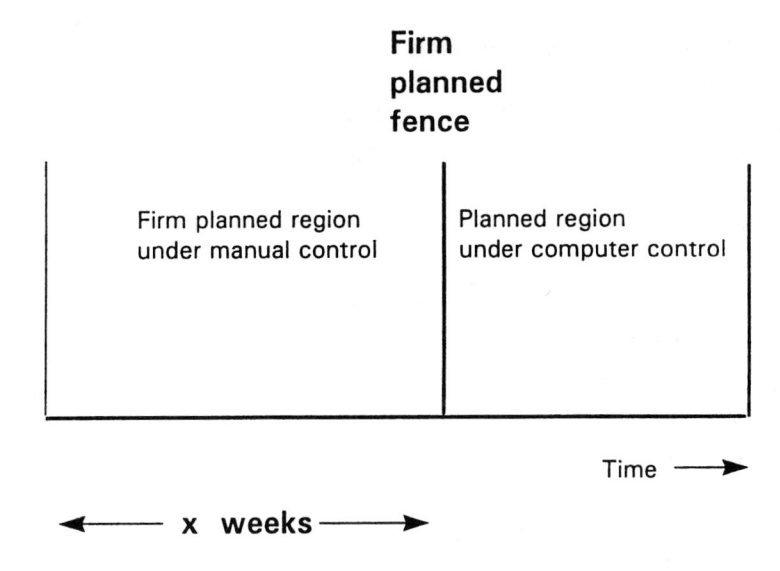

Time ⟶

⟵ x weeks ⟶

x equals cumulative lead time plus planning time

3.3 The firm planning concept.

However, if an order is so far ahead that no preparation has started (no purchase orders for raw materials have been placed, for example) then changes can be safely left to the computer. Many systems therefore permit a 'fence' to be specified x weeks ahead (see Fig. 3.3).

Orders outside the fence are under computer control since this saves work. Inside the fence, orders are under manual control with the system making recommendations (x weeks should be equal to the cumulative lead time for the product plus a planning allowance). Cumulative lead time is the time taken to carry out all the activities ranging from the purchase of the raw materials to the assembly of the finished product ready for dispatch (see Fig. 1.3). Planning allowance is the time taken by the planner to consider and react to the exception messages.

Although 'planned order' and 'firm planned order' are the terms recommended by the American Production and Inventory Control Society and the IOM, some MPS and MRP software achieves a similar purpose by having 'suggested works orders' and 'works orders'. The latter are entirely under manual control, whilst a new suggested orders list will be generated every time the MPS or MRP runs.

In most systems it is also possible to designate individual orders outside the firm planned fence as 'firm planned' and therefore under manual control. This feature can be used in special circumstances, for example to prevent orders being planned during a future period of planned machine maintenance. In most systems also, firm planning can be applied to both MPS and MRP orders.

3.4 Master Production Scheduling policies

Some of the policies necessary for effective master scheduling are discussed below.

3.4.1 The MPS should attempt to balance supply with demand

In a Make to Stock company such as a typical pharmaceutical manufacturer, high levels of customer service are extremely important. The first Master Production Scheduling objective is therefore to ensure that supply is in balance with demand and safety stocks are maintained. The master scheduler must cooperate very closely with the sales function so that he is aware of initiatives and understands the latest priorities. The sales department must be kept fully informed about actual or potential supply problems.

3.4.2 The MPS must be realistic

Although meeting the customers' requirements is the first objective, there is little point in having an MPS which is not achievable, either because some of the materials or components required for assembly cannot be made available in time, or because the production resources of equipment and operators will be overloaded.

When a proposed MPS is passed to MRP any material shortages should be highlighted to the materials planner by an exception message. If the materials planner, in spite of his best efforts, cannot remedy the shortage (and keep his own plans realistic) he must inform the master scheduler, who must then adjust his schedule even if this means failing to meet some customers' requirements.

In a well run Make to Stock company, with judicious use of safety stocks, failure to supply on time should be rare, but when it does happen the master scheduler must give as much notice as possible to his sales and marketing colleagues who in turn must inform the customer. Bad news is never welcome but giving advance warning accompanied by a realistic new promise date will in the long term earn more respect than defaulting without warning.

Master Production Scheduling in a company which makes to order from a limited product range can be much simpler than for a Make to

Stock company. As orders are received they are provisionally loaded onto the customer order row of the MPS planning grid, the appropriate cumulative lead time ahead. Two checks are needed before the promise date can be confirmed to the customer. Firstly, is there adequate production capacity available to meet the proposed completion date? Secondly, are all the components and sub-assemblies either in stock or available in the lead times assumed when the cumulative lead time was calculated?

Essentially in a Make to Order environment, customer orders are loaded onto the MPS in the first slot at which adequate capacity is available. If the production capacity needed for the order can be easily determined, the MPS process and the associated giving of a delivery promise to the customer are relatively simple. Consider, for example, a manufacturer of a range of control panels for electric motors. Voltage and power requirements will vary between customers, but each panel takes the same time to assemble. The production manager knows that he can supply 12 panels per week. As customer orders are received they are slotted into the MPS in the earliest week after the recognised lead time, which does not have 12 panels already planned (see Fig. 3.4).

For a small company, this process can be so simple that the MPS consists only of a piece of analysis paper with a hand drawn planning grid for each product family. An order clerk with access to the MPS can give a reliable delivery promise to a customer whilst answering the initial telephone enquiry. If there is more than one order clerk, it is important that both can access common data so that the same capacity slot is not promised to two customers. In many cases a simple spread sheet accessed via a network of personal computers may be all that is required.

If the items being scheduled are very different in terms of specification and the load on production, it will not be possible to specify the available capacity per week in terms of the number of units and a more sophisticated analysis will be necessary before an order can be placed into the MPS and a promise date given to the customer. Typically the load resulting from each order must be determined in common units such as man-hours or machine-hours and the production capacity must be expressed in the same units. Orders are then loaded into the MPS to 'consume' the first free slot of capacity.

In a business which designs products to order, or assembles products to order from a specified range of features and options, the calculation of loads and the consumption of capacity can be very complicated. In extreme cases a considerable amount of design work will be needed before a new order can be slotted into the MPS and a reliable promise date given.

Motor control panels family

Production capacity is 12 panels per period

New orders are slotted into earliest period with free capacity after the required by date. Units are control panels.

	Period	1	2	3	4	5	6	7	8	9	10
1	Maximum capacity per period	12	12	12	12	12	12	12	12	12	12
2	Customer orders	12	12	11	3						
3	Spare capacity available to promise	0	0	1	9	12	12	12	12	12	12
4											

3.4 Order slotting for a Make to Order company.

Such situations and the software support available in the form of Rough Cut Capacity Planning and Option Planning are discussed in more detail in Chapter 9 and Chapter 7 respectively.

A frequent cause of poor materials management is to have an overstated MPS, i.e. a wish list which calls for more output than production can achieve. This leads to two problems. The obvious one is that there will be a failure to supply customers by the dates planned but, more subtly, if MRP's recommendations for buying components and making intermediates or sub-assemblies to support an inflated and unrealistic MPS are achieved, there will be a build up of raw materials and in-process stocks, since these will be generated faster than they are actually consumed.

A realistic MPS is a clear indication of priorities. Consider an example in which eleven identical manufacturing orders are loaded into an MPS period for which there is only capacity for ten. Assume also that each order requires ten items and the supply chain is only capable of meeting the requirements for ten orders. In such a situation, the priority must be that all ten components are made available for the ten most urgent orders and none for the lower priority eleventh. With no clear indication of priorities, the overloaded supply chain might deliver nine components for each of the eleven orders, but the required ten for none of them, with the result that nothing could be made.

Although the above is an extreme example, the cry that component stores are overloaded but we do not have all of what we need for any job, is one which is frequently heard. With a realistic MPS the eleventh and least urgent order would have been moved to a later date and the requirement date for its components similarly delayed. The MRP system would then give the materials planners and all other sections of the business a clear indication of priorities, and attention would be focused only on the 100 components needed in the period.

3.4.3 Planning to demonstrated capacity

Even in well organised companies it is not unusual for production management genuinely to believe that they can achieve a certain level of output, say 500 000 items per month, and to insist that plans are laid accordingly. Typically, at the end of the first month actual output may be only 420 000 but a credible explanation such as higher than expected sickness amongst operators is available and management insists that the plan must again be for 500 000 next month. At the end of the second month there will be another perfectly good reason, such as component shortages, why planned output was not achieved, and so on. In the meantime processing and purchasing plans will be under continuous revision as allowance is made for the unconsumed materials and the re-adjustment of the MPS. Giving attention to these changes may overwhelm the materials planner or at least divert him or her from the important task of ensuring that everything is available for the revised and realistic MPS. This in turn can exacerbate the failure to meet the plan and a vicious spiral develops. The only safe way is to base plans on **demonstrated capacity**, which means output actually achieved, measured by averaging over a period of say six months and allowing for any periods of planned shutdown.

Frequently, after several months of planning with the load not exceeding demonstrated capacity, the improved coordination between purchasing, processing and packing is such that output rises, and demonstrated capacity increases.

Although the effectiveness and wisdom of planning to demonstrated capacity only has been proven many times, it is not always supported by production managers who quite reasonably have a desire to increase output and beat targets. The argument that if we do not plan for improvement, we are unlikely to achieve it appears compelling. In practice, however, there is rarely a problem because in a typical company where lead times have been set largely by experience, the quoted lead time for an activity will normally be considerably longer than the actual time taken on the equipment, e.g. an operation lead time might be quoted as one week, when the line running time is 15 hours. This means that there is usually a queue of components awaiting assembly which may be eaten into if output exceeds plan.

If more output is needed from any resource which is already fully occupied, that resource is a potential bottleneck limiting production. Any time lost on a bottleneck is lost permanently, since there is no spare capacity available to replace the lost production. The schedules for a bottleneck work centre should aim to maintain a buffer or queue of work in front of the work centre, to ensure that time is never lost because of the non-availability of the next job.

If increased output is required, and a work centre's output is improving, it will slowly be eating into the protective queue and increasing the risk of running out of work. In such a situation demonstrated capacity should be based on actual achievement over a shorter period than six months. As in many other areas of master scheduling, judgement is required by both production management and the master scheduler.

3.4.4 The MPS must be stable

Section 3.1 demonstrated the importance of keeping the MPS under manual control to prevent spurious changes being fed to MRP. The master production scheduler will clearly not react to trivial changes, but there will frequently be perfectly good marketing reasons for changing the master schedule. For example, in the pharmaceutical industry, an epidemic may result in a large unforecast increase in demand for a particular drug, or a manufacturer of roofing materials may experience a dramatic but unexpected increase in business after a hurricane. In other industries the withdrawal of a competitive product may present a marketing opportunity which must be seized. All the above are good reasons for considering a change to the MPS, but the feasibility of the change must be assessed before it is accepted. The availability of both materials and machine capacity must be checked. If the best efforts of planning, purchasing and production cannot get a reliable promise for delivery of the required components, or if the necessary production capacity cannot be made available by replanning, the use of contractors or by delaying less important jobs, the change should not be considered further, no matter how desirable it may be.

However, the fact that a change is highly desirable and ultimately feasible, does not make it easier to handle. Too many changes will swamp the system. The planner may not have time to find answers to all the queries which arise and whenever one job is expedited, at least one other is put back. The number of exception messages can become too great for a planner to handle before the next MPS or MRP run is due. As a result things which are not required may be made or purchased whilst urgently required items are not planned.

If the managing director insists that a particular order must be achieved in a quarter of the normal lead time and thumps the table hard enough and often enough, it will almost certainly be achieved. What may also happen, but it may not be visible to the managing director, is that ten other orders may be delayed and ten other customers displeased.

Each company must develop an agreed policy on MPS changes. The first rule is simple:

A change can only be made when it has been demonstrated that production capacity and materials are or can be made available.

The master scheduler will have to liaise carefully with the materials and capacity planning function to check the feasibility of a change.

Even if a change has proved to be feasible it is still necessary to decide if making it is the best option. In principle the criterion for this decision is also simple:

A change is made when the cost to the business of not making it exceeds the cost of the change.

In practice however these costs can rarely be quantified and by default the decision is often left to the judgement of the master production scheduler who is probably being lobbied furiously by all interested parties.

It has been suggested that master production schedulers should be responsible directly to the managing director in order to maintain independence from the accountancy, sales or production functions, but few if any companies have adopted this radical but enlightened suggestion. In practice the master scheduler needs support so that when necessary he can resist insistent demands for change either from senior sales managers who understandably put the interests of their customers first, or from senior production managers keen to maximise output, possibly at the expense of difficult to make but urgently needed products.

The necessary support is achieved by having a formal change approval mechanism. The seniority of the approval needed depends on the timescale. For example, the following authorisation zones might apply:

Period	Approval by
0-1 week	Production and marketing directors
1-4 weeks	Production and marketing managers
4-6 weeks	Planning manager
6 weeks to firm planned fence	Master production scheduler

Beyond the firm planned fence the system makes the change automatically.

The periods given above are illustrative only. Each company must develop its own rules and periods which may vary from hours to months, depending on supply lead times and the response required by the market.

3.5 Sales orders, sales forecasts and Available to Promise

In section 3.1 the 'total requirements' row in the MPS grid was calculated as the sum of sales forecast and customer orders. This is an acceptable approach provided that the forecast is **consumed** as customer orders are received. Forecast consumption is best explained with an example. If originally the forecast for a period is ten items with no orders yet received, the total requirement is ten. If an order for four is received from a regular customer whose business was expected when the forecast was made, the total expected requirement does not increase to fourteen but remains at ten, i.e. the order for four plus a remaining forecast of six. The order for four has consumed four of the forecast. A forecast consumption mechanism of this sort is essential if the routine arrival of an expected order is not going to change the requirements on the MPS.

Occasionally an order may be received from a new customer who was not considered as a possibility at the time the forecast was made. Whether or not such an order should be accepted and a delivery promise offered are matters of commercial judgement. If such an **abnormal order** is accepted, it should not consume forecast since it is additional to the requirement expected when the forecast was made. Accepting such an additional requirement will throw the MPS out of balance and if large enough will generate an exception message. The possibility that accepting the abnormal order will result in a failure to supply regular customers is one of the points to be considered in deciding whether to accept the order for the requested date or not.

A useful feature of the MPS for a company which aims to make to stock, but is constrained by manufacturing batch size, is that it provides

MASTER PRODUCTION SCHEDULING

MX01 Mixed fruit drink 500 ml bottle

Opening stock 18 Order quantity 30
Safety stock 0

	Period		1	2	3	4	5	6	7	8	9	10
1	Sales forecast		10	10	10	10	10	10	10	10	10	10
2	Customer orders											
3	Total requirements		10	10	10	10	10	10	10	10	10	10
4	Projected stock	18	8	28	18	8	28	18	8	28	18	8
5	MPS order receipts			30			30			30		
6	MPS order releases											
7	Available to promise		18	30			30			30		

3.5 Available to Promise for a Make to Stock company.

information about how much stock is available to promise to a customer. Typically an additional row is provided on an MPS display as in Fig. 3.5. The **Available to Promise** (or ATP) row indicates how much actual or planned stock will be available to promise to a customer on a specified date, without jeopardising other promised orders. Since in this example there are currently no customer orders, 18 packs can be promised to a customer immediately, and a further 30 in period 2 when the manufacturing order for 30 is received into stock and a further 30 in each of periods 5 and 8.

Receipt of a normal order must consume both the ATP and the sales forecast. If, for example, a normal order for four items is received for immediate delivery, both the ATP and sales forecast in period 1 must be consumed (see Fig. 3.6).

If, however, a large order were to be received from a new customer for

MX01   Mixed fruit drink 500 ml bottle

Opening stock: 18
Safety stock: 0
Order quantity: 30

	Period		1	2	3	4	5	6	7	8	9	10
1	Sales forecast		6 ~~10~~	10	10	10	10	10	10	10	10	10
2	Customer orders		4									
3	Total requirements		10	10	10	10	10	10	10	10	10	10
4	Projected stock	18	8	28	18	8	28	18	8	28	18	8
5	MPS order receipts			30			30			30		
6	MPS order releases											
7	Available to promise		14 ~~18~~	30			30			30		

3.6 Receipt of normal order.

nine items in period 6, and the sales department deemed it abnormal but agreed to accept it, it should only consume ATP (in period 5) leaving the sales forecast unchanged (see Fig. 3.7).

The best use is made of actual and planned stock if each customer's order is supplied from the latest manufacture which will be available in time, i.e. the 30 in period 5. This leaves the 14 ATP in period 1 and the 30 due in period 2 available for other customer orders which may be received for earlier delivery and preserves maximum flexibility.

Accepting the abnormal order for nine has resulted in a change in total requirement and hence a change in projected stock. The next run of MPS will generate an exception message for the MPS order in period 8. If this cannot be brought forward, a stock-out will occur if sales for periods 5, 6 and 7 are in line with or greater than forecast. It will not be possible to accept some orders from regular customers for the requested delivery dates.

MX01 Mixed fruit drink 500 ml bottle

Opening stock   18   Order quantity   30
Safety stock   0

	Period	1	2	3	4	5	6	7	8	9	10
1	Sales forecast	6 ~~10~~	10	10	10	10	10	10	10	10	10
2	Customer orders	(n) 4					(a) 9				
3	Total requirements	10	10	10	10	10	19 ~~10~~	10	10	10	10
4	Projected stock 18	8	28	18	8	28	9 ~~18~~	-1 ~~8~~	19 ~~28~~	9 ~~18~~	-1 ~~8~~
5	MPS order receipts		30			30			30		
6	MPS order releases										
7	Available to promise	14 ~~18~~	30			21 ~~30~~			30		

3.7 Receipt of abnormal order.

Accepting an abnormal order from a new but potentially important customer may be a correct commercial decision, even if service to some existing customers is jeopardised. Such consequences should have been taken into account when deciding whether to accept the abnormal order. Good liaison between the master scheduler and the sales function is essential.

Problems arise with this simple approach to consuming forecast when there is a slight timing error in the forecast and the customer orders received in a period, although all deemed normal, exceed the forecast. The ideal approach is to determine when each order was expected and consume the appropriate forecast. In practice, however, this can be difficult and few commercially available MPS systems provide this facility. A practical approach is to assume that an excess of orders over forecast in any period is attributable to an order being early, and to consume the excess from the next latest period.

Normal orders for 14 arrive for period 4
(4 are assumed to be early from period 5)

MX01   Mixed fruit drink 500 ml bottle

Opening stock	18	Order quantity	30
Safety stock	0		

	Period	1	2	3	4	5	6	7	8	9	10
1	Sales forecast	6	10	10	0 ~~10~~	6 ~~10~~	10	10	10	10	10
2	Customer orders	(n) 4			(n) 14		(a) 9				
3	Total requirements	10	10	10	14 ~~10~~	6 ~~10~~	19	10	10	10	10
4	Projected stock 18	8	28	18	4 ~~8~~	28	9	-1	19	9	-1
5	MPS order receipts		30			30			30		
6	MPS order releases										
7	Available to promise	14	16 ~~30~~			21			30		

3.8 Receipt of excess of orders over forecast.

For example, with the situation as in Fig. 3.7, additional orders totalling 14 are received for period 4. All the forecast in period 4 is consumed, plus four of the forecast in period 5. There is a temporary change to the projected stock in period 4 but this is corrected in period 5. There are no changes to the MPS orders (see Fig. 3.8).

Some systems avoid this problem by the simple expedient of not consuming forecast and taking whichever is the greater of sales forecast or customer orders as the total requirements figure. This effectively treats any orders in excess of forecast as abnormal. It has the merit of simplicity but can result in a significant increase in exception messages and changes to plan.

A particular problem arises if the orders received in period 1 are less than forecast by the end of the period. When the MPS is rerun, the new opening stock will be higher than expected and exception messages may be generated to reduce or defer the MPS. If the deficit is merely because a customer order is later than forecast, stability can be preserved by rolling forward the unconsumed part of the forecast into the new period 1. This will of course be an incorrect response if there is a genuine shortfall of sales against forecast, in which case some adjustment of the MPS may be appropriate. The most convenient arrangement is to roll forward automatically any unconsumed forecast and preserve stability. The quantity rolled must be reported to the master scheduler who can then intervene if appropriate.

3.6 Formats for the Master Production Schedule

The formats adopted so far to illustrate MPS and MRP, with time running horizontally, were the ones used with the early MRP systems. The periods were months and it was convenient to look forward for one year and have twelve columns across a page. Modern systems, however, tend to use time periods of a day or, at most, a week. A format with time running vertically rather like a bank statement proves more convenient (see Fig. 3.9). Transactions which reduce stock, e.g. sales forecasts and customer orders are on the left, manufacturing orders which increase stock on the right. The projected stock figure is the equivalent of the running balance in the account.

In practice, additional columns are usually incorporated to show information such as order number, order status or codes alongside an order, indicating that an exception report applies. Similar formats can be used for MRP displays in which dependent demands are not aggregated even if they fall on the same day. Each can be labelled with the order number from which it originates, which makes it very easy to identify the origin of demand. Available to Promise can be shown either in an additional column or in a separate report.

However the traditional horizontal display, with the date relating directly to the displacement to the right, is easier to understand on first acquaintance and is almost universally used in text books and other teaching materials.

MX01 Mixed fruit drink 1 litre bottle

Safety stock 0   Order quantity 2 000

Date	Sales forecasts & orders	Stock	Manufacturing orders
	Opening stock 2 500		-
1/1	800	1 700	-
1/2	800	900	-
1/3	800	100	-
1/4	800	-700	-
1/4	-	1 300	2 000
1/5	800	500	-
30/5	-	2 500	2 000
1/6	800	1 700	-
30/6	-	3 700	2 000
1/7	800	2 900	-
1/8	800	2 100	-
1/9	800	1 300	-
1/10	800	500	-

3.9 Master Production Schedule with vertical time display.

3.7 Summary

The MPS is a statement of what the company expects to manufacture. For most companies it will cover the final stage of manufacture, but for Assemble to Order (ATO) companies, particularly when the customer is offered a wide choice of optional extra features, the MPS may be for the assembly of a fictitious part number representing a product family. The master schedule for the family is used to reserve capacity and is passed to MRP to initiate the acquisition of components. The real product is not assembled until a customer's order with a full specification has been received. This approach, called Option Planning, is described in more detail in Chapter 7, as already mentioned.

The MPS attempts to balance demand with supply but must always be

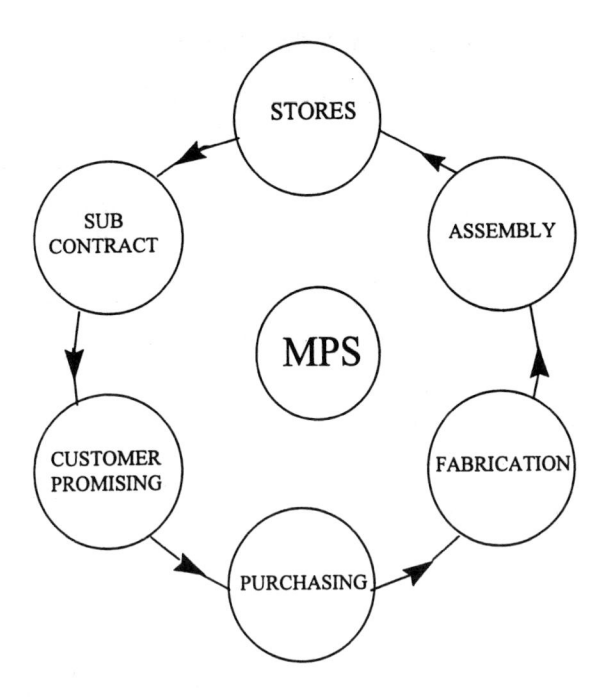

3.10 Master Production Schedule as the sun at the centre of the MRPII universe.

realistic. Both sales and production must agree any compromises necessary to ensure that the MPS is achievable. The MPS not only provides the information for making customer promises but is the basis of plans for all the other manufacturing activities. The MPS may be regarded as the sun at the centre of the manufacturing business, as illustrated in Fig. 3.10.

All activities are synchronised with respect to both quantity and timing with the master schedule, which in turn is designed to ensure that customer orders are supplied on time and in full.

Once established, control of the MPS is the control of change. An appropriate compromise must be established between reacting to the requirements of the market and providing the stability needed for effective production.

Exercises

3.1 (a) The sales forecast for the grapefruit drink 500 ml pack has just been revised. The manufacturing orders and other details in the MPS are as overleaf. Complete the table to show the output you would expect from an

MPS run. What messages would you expect and what judgemental decision would the planner have to make?

Grapefruit drink 500 ml

Opening stock	79	Lead time	2 periods
Safety stock	40	Firm planned fence	6 periods
Order quantity	50		

	Period	1	2	3	4	5	6	7	8	9	10
1	Sales forecast	7	10	17	23	23	24	24	24	29	30
2	Customer orders	15	10	5							
3	Total requirements										
4	Projected stock										
5	MPS order receipts		(FP) 50	(FP) 50					(P) 50		
6	MPS order releases										

(FP) indicates firm planned order, i.e. under human control.
(P) indicates planned order, i.e. under computer control.

(b) Had the opening stock been only 72, what differences in output would you expect?

3.2 A work station, manned by a single operator winds and assembles low voltage transformers. All products are made to order with a lead time of one week. The promise date given to the customer is to the week, irrespective of whether the order is planned to be completed on a Monday or a Friday.

The ATP sheet used by the company is shown opposite. However, this sheet has not been updated for some time and a number of new orders have been received since the last update. The existing order book, in priority order, is also shown.

Order slotting exercise

Low voltage transformer family

Production capacity is 40 operator-hours per period. Lead time 1 period.
Capacity unit is operator-hours.
The equipment, manned by one operator can make all the transformers in the range, but the time taken depends on the voltage and power rating.

	Period	1	2	3	4	5	6	7	8	9	10
1	Maximum capacity per period	40	40	40	40	40	40	40	40	40	40
2	Customer orders	41									
3	Spare capacity available to promise	-1									
4											

Order no	Model	Quantity	Hours/item	Promise week
101	A	10	2	1
102	C	3	5	1
103	D	6	1	1
104	G	5	2	2
105	K	9	1	2
106	L	5	3	2
107	C	1	5	?
108	M	17	1	?
109	A	5	2	?
110	G	6	2	?
111	G	10	2	?
112	D	10	1	?
113	K	10	1	?
114	L	6	3	?

Calculate a promise date, to the nearest week, for the orders which do not yet have one and update the ATP sheet.

3.3 A group of multipurpose packing lines packs a large number of different but broadly similar products. Experience has shown that the total number of packs produced is a reliable measure of work load. A summary of actual production achieved in the past six months and the plans for the next six are as follows:

Actual and planned output (000 of packs)

Month	-6	-5	-4	-3	-2	-1
Actual output	98	84	92	87	90	95
Month	1	2	3	4	5	6
Planned output	90	88	70	70	110	115

The number of operators on the group of lines will be the same as in the past. The lines have been fully occupied during the past six months and on occasion it has been necessary to use sub-contractors to meet demand. Sub-contract output is not included in the data above. The increase in work load in months 5 and 6 results from a new product launch. The packing line manager is confident that he can meet this work load and strongly opposes any plans to use sub-contractors. MRP shows no supply problems.

Are these plans satisfactory? If not, what action might you the master production scheduler take?

3.4 List the costs which may result from a change in the production schedule and some of the costs which may arise from not making the change.

3.5 Which exception message would you expect from the situation shown in the table on page 63, which is based on Fig. 3.8? The projected stock in period 7 is now negative. Does this mean that the MPS is unrealistic? What are the implications of the negative value?

MX01   Mixed fruit drink 500 ml bottle

Opening stock   18   Order quantity   30
Safety stock   0

	Period	1	2	3	4	5	6	7	8	9	10
1	Sales forecast	6	10	10	10	10	10	10	10	10	10
2	Customer orders	(n) 4					(a) 9				
3	Total requirements	10	10	10	10	10	19	10	10	10	10
4	Projected stock 18	8	28	18	8	28	9	-1	19	9	-1
5	MPS order receipts		30			30			30		
6	MPS order releases										
7	Available to promise	14	30			21			30		

3.6 This exercise also refers to the MPS shown in the table in Exercise 3.5. A request is received to supply eight in period 2 from a regular customer whose requirements were taken into account when making the forecast. Can and should the order be accepted? If it is accepted, what changes should be made to the data in the table?

3.7 The following is part of the MPS for a drink pack, shown in a 'time runs vertically' format:

| Safety stock | 100 | Order quantity | 250 |
| Opening stock | 225 | | |

Requirement	Qty	Date	Mfg order receipts	Qty	Stock balance
		31/12			225
Sales forecast	100	1/1			125
		7/1	MO123	250	375
P9 customer order	150	9/1			225
		27/1	MO124	250	475
Sales forecast	200	1/2			275
		25/2	MO124	250	525
Sales forecast	200	1/3			325
Sales forecast	200	1/4			___
Sales forecast	200	1/5			___
Sales forecast	200	1/6			___

Continue the projection of the stock and calculate the due dates of the next two manufacturing orders. Comment on anything which appears sub-optimum about this plan.

4

Manufacturing orders

This chapter will describe some of the activities associated with the creation and execution of a manufacturing order and the interaction with materials planning.

4.1 The order life cycle

Previous chapters have shown how the output of the materials planning and control process, using either Order Point or MPS/MRP is a series of manufacturing and purchase orders. The minimum information needed to define an order is the material code (sometimes called part number or item number), the quantity and the due date, which is the date by which delivery of the ordered item should be complete. The lead time for the material specifies how long before the due date the order must be placed. Stepping backwards in time from the due date by the lead time defines the latest planned start date for the order. The discussion of the mechanism of MRP in Chapter 2 showed how MRP assumes that the materials needed to produce a manufacturing order will be required at the start date. In an MRP environment, the order was probably first created with a due date far into the future and given a 'planned' status. As the due date crosses the firm planned fence the status changes to 'firm planned'.

It is convenient to define a 'release' date, normally a few days earlier than the start date. This is the date when the planner should start to prepare the paper work and carry out a final check that everything is available as planned. Such an order has a 'ready for release' status. The order should be 'opened' (or 'released' depending on the terminology preferred) by the start date. An opened (or released) order is a licence for production to manufacture and the planner should only open a manufacturing order if all requirements for the order are or will be available at the required time. The planner must only open and issue paper work for an order with a shortage with the prior agreement of the

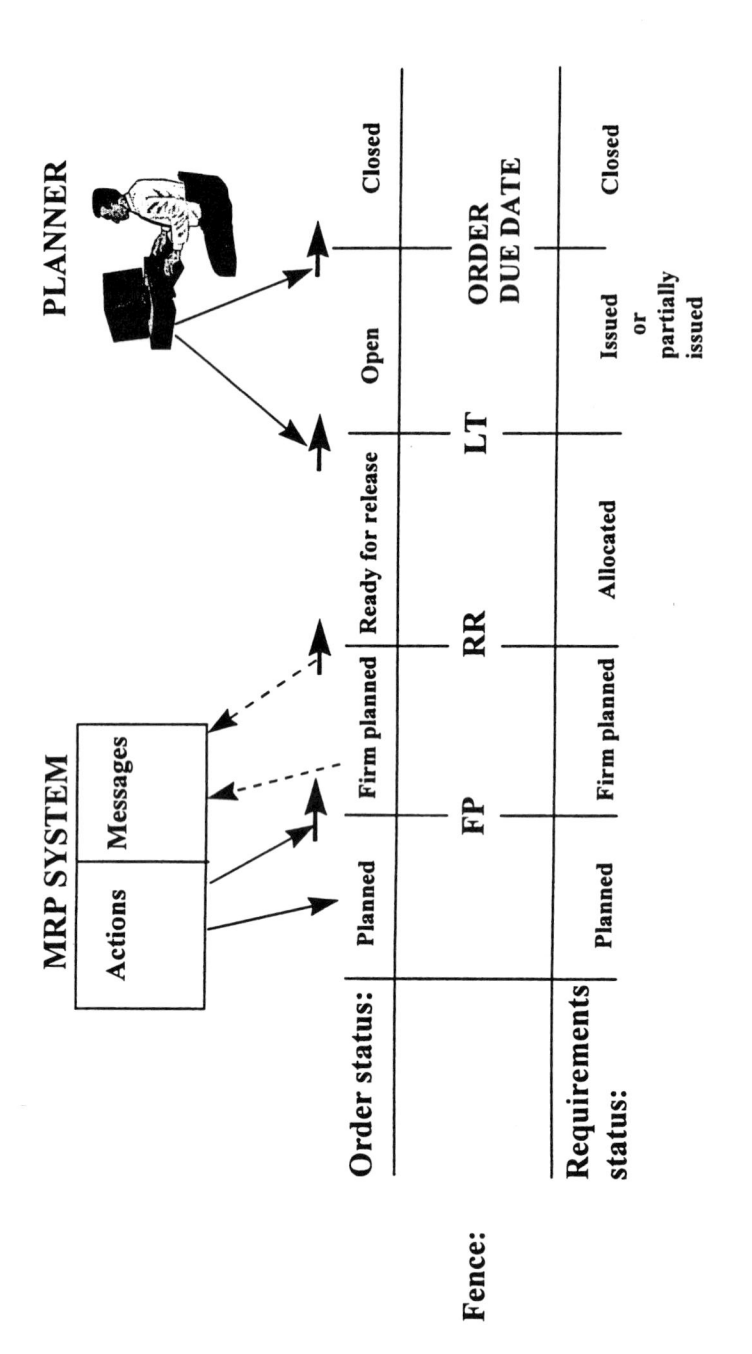

4.1 Order ageing statuses.

production supervisor. In other cases, if the supervisor has the paper work for an order he should be able to be confident that everything needed to produce the order is available. Finally, when production is complete, all the issues have been recorded and all the product has been received into stock, the order is 'closed'.

This progression is represented in Fig. 4.1. Some software systems use different names or miss out some of the statuses defined here, but the principles of progression through the stages are similar.

4.2 Requirements

The process of 'exploding' the order through the bill of materials for the product to determine the intermediates and raw materials required by the order was described in Chapter 2, Section 2.1.

In most systems the requirements are permanently recorded against the order, once the order status becomes firm planned. After this point the bill of materials may be changed without affecting the order, or the requirements on the order may be modified if the order is special in any way. For example, an alternative bottle cap for the lemon drink LEM01 could be substituted, should the original be unavailable.

Making such a change to the requirements of a 'planned' order would be a waste of time, since it would be re-exploded through the bill of materials in the next MRP run. If such a change is needed on an order with a due date beyond the firm planned fence, the order status must be manually changed to 'firm planned'. In some industries the planners can be allowed to make such changes with only minimal formality, but in industries such as pharmaceuticals or defence electronics, good manufacturing practice requires that any such modification must be carefully controlled and documented. Only authorised persons can have access to the routines which change requirements.

The requirements for all manufacturing orders, when suitably sorted and aggregated, become the dependent demand used by MRP in planning the manufacture of intermediates and the purchase of raw materials.

The next significant event in the history of a requirement is the issue transaction, when material is issued from stores for use on the order and the requirement is said to be satisfied. With an integrated stock recording and planning system, the same transaction can decrease both the stock record and the requirement on the order. In this way the stocks and requirement records are kept synchronised and there is little danger of showing the stock as still in stores and the requirement satisfied or vice

Table 4.1 Order transactions for a manufacturing order for filling of 1000 × 100 ml packs of Argento silver polish

Stocks of finished packs	Stock of bulk polish	Activity	Order quantity, packs	Quantity of bulk polish required	Order status
200	150 L	Order approaches ready for release date	1000	100 L	FP
200	150 L	Order ready for release	1000	100 L	RR
200	150 L	Paperwork prepared. Order opened	1000	100 L	OP
200	50 L	100 l of polish issued	1000	0	OP
500	50 L	Order part complete (300 packs received)	700	0	OP
1200	50 L	Order complete (700 packs received)	0	0	OP
1200	50 L	Paperwork checked etc.	0	0	CL

versa, as could happen with manual stock records and planning systems, if great care was not taken.

4.3 Receipts

Perhaps the most important event in the history of a manufacturing order is its completion, and the taking into stock of the product. Again with an integrated system there should be a single receipt transaction which simultaneously increases the stock record and decreases the quantity on order.

Table 4.1 illustrates the transactions required as a manufacturing order for 1000 × 100 ml packs of Argento, a popular liquid silver polish, progresses from the firm planned stage to completion. For simplicity only the requirement for the bulk polish is considered. The 150 litres in stock more than meets the requirement of 100 litres for the order. There is also an existing finished goods stock of 200 packs before stock is received from the order.

4.4 Nomenclature

Different industries use different terminologies. For example, in engineering companies MRP plans sub-assemblies and parts or components, but in a process industry such as the soft drink producer exemplified in Chapter 2, the terminology is more likely to be intermediates (or bulk drink), raw materials and package components such as bottles and caps. The names may be different but the planning processes and the treatment of manufacturing orders are very similar if not identical. Differences in the planning process depend much more on factors such as whether manufacturing is repetitive or batch or whether the company makes to order or makes to stock, than on the type of product or business area.

There is no doubt, however, that initially people feel more comfortable if a new computer system uses their standard terminology and some modern manufacturing control packages provide facilities for tailoring screens and reports to use the user's preferred nomenclature. If this feature is not available, it is usually simpler to conform to the terminology of the package. With explanation and training, staff quickly adapt to new names and jargon.

In the days before on-line computer systems in which all terminals have access to the same data which is updated in real time, stores records would either be manual or perhaps a computer record would be updated by batch input of transactions at the end of the day. The planners probably did not have convenient access to the up-to-date manual stores records and this caused problems with reordering or whilst checking component availability prior to release of an order. These difficulties were minimised by using the concept of 'physical', 'free' and 'allocated' stocks.

Typically the stores would record only physical stock, i.e. stock which was there and could be seen and counted. The physical stock increased when materials were received and put away, and decreased when materials were issued. This record was of little use to a planner attempting to check whether all the necessary components were available for an order due for opening. If, for example, he needed 50 of a component and the record showed 100 to be in stock, the simple conclusion would be that there was no problem. However this conclusion would be unreliable because no account was being taken of other possible open orders for which the requirements had not yet been withdrawn from stores. If the open but unsatisfied requirements were for more than 50, adequate stock would not be available for both the existing and proposed new open orders.

This problem was overcome by holding a separate stock record on cards or in a ledger in the planning office. This held both free and allocated records. The sum of these two for an item gave the physical stock. A component would be available for an order if the free stock figure was greater than the new requirement. When all the component requirements of the order had been checked and found to be available, the free stocks were decreased and the allocated stocks increased by the relevant quantities. Later, after the requirements had been physically issued by the stores, a copy of the transaction note was passed to the planners and the allocated stock figures were reduced. Provided that all transactions were accurately recorded, this system worked well, but if errors occurred, reconciliation of the two records could be extremely difficult. With on-line records and MRP, an exception message should have been produced for any shortage and the MRP stock projection screen will show the physical stock and all unsatisfied requirements for the component in date order. The full picture is available to the planner without the need to record free and allocated stocks, although some modern MRP software still records an allocated stock figure. However the definition does not always agree with that above.

Similarly, without an on-line order record, a manufacturing order could be represented by ledger entries in planning and production control, and by order documents and an entry on a schedule on the plant. The concept of an order status becomes meaningless in such situations because keeping the order status up to date on all the records is virtually impossible.

To overcome this problem the original MRP logic, developed under the auspices of APICS, introduced the concept of a **scheduled receipt**, which is a manufacturing order which has been opened and released to production or purchasing. When a firm planned or sometimes a planned order is converted into a scheduled receipt, the component requirements for the order are deemed to be allocated or satisfied and are not taken into account by the total requirements calculation of MRP. The allocated stock record for each component is increased by the quantity required. When MRP carries out the stock projection exercise for the component, the total allocated stock quantity of each component is subtracted from the opening balance (the physical stock) before the projection process in MRP starts. As in manual systems both the physical and allocated stock figures are decreased when the component issue transaction is recorded.

Scheduled receipts are normally shown on a separate row of the standard MRP planning grid. They are taken into account when planning the parent item of the order but are ignored by MRP when firm planned and planned orders are exploded through the bill of materials to calculate component requirements.

Scheduled receipts and allocated stock records were essential when stock records and component requirements for orders could not be updated simultaneously and in real time. With modern on-line systems, however, they are unnecessary and serve only to complicate further the already complicated logic of MRP.

The terms production and inventory control, production and inventory management, operations management and resource management mean different things to different people. Undoubtedly there is a core of activities and nomenclature which is common to all four and APICS publishes a useful, and frequently updated dictionary (the *APICS Dictionary*) of resource management terms. Unfortunately, Churchill's famous comment about two nations divided by a common language applies to these areas. Some APICS terms can be confusing to speakers of UK English, and no doubt the reverse applies. At the time of writing, a draft British Standard, BS 5191, is in the final stages of checking for publication. It will be interesting to see how many nomenclature difficulties it helps resolve.

In the meantime, there follows a summary of the problems with nomenclature and definition of terms associated with manufacturing and purchase orders. Some of the APICS terms have been translated into what might be called their 'common sense English equivalents', which the author has tried to use in this text:

- **Master Production Schedule (MPS)**
  Not a schedule at all, but a medium term production plan, usually expressed in terms of sales items, but sometimes in terms of a product family.
- **Opening an order/Releasing an order**
  The two terms are identical in meaning and refer to both manufacturing and purchase orders. In the latter case a formal order is placed with the supplier. For manufacturing orders, opening or releasing means the process of checking that all the items (sub-assemblies, components, etc) needed for the order are available, printing the documents needed to define the order and passing these to production. The documents represent a licence to produce.
- **Open order/Released order**
  An order which is active. It has been released to production, or in the case of a purchase order to the supplier.
- **Ready for release**
  The status of a manufacturing or purchase order which is within a time specified by the ready for release fence of its planned release date. The ready for release fence represents the time required to check the availability of components, etc, to print the documents needed and to pass to production or the supplier. The fence is typically set at one to three days. The MRP system will provide an action message to remind the planner to open the order by the planned date.

- **Scheduled receipt**
  An open manufacturing or purchase order. All the component requirements for this order are considered to have been allocated. Scheduled receipts are ignored by the MRP explosion calculation. With modern on-line computer systems a scheduled receipt is an unnecessary concept.
- **Projected available balance**
  Planned stock or projected stock. A projection forward of the current stock of a planned item or material, taking into account all forecast orders or calculated requirements and all expected receipts from all manufacturing or purchase orders.
- **Projected on-hand**
  A projection forward of the existing stock of an item, taking account of all known or calculated requirements, but considering receipts into stock only from scheduled receipts. Stock expected to be received from firm planned or planned orders is ignored. An outdated concept for which the original purpose is obscure.
- **Allocated stock**
  Stock of an item reserved for issue to a particular manufacturing or sales order but not yet recorded as having been issued from stores. Allocated stock records are not needed provided that stock records and the size of a requirement can be down-dated simultaneously and in real time by a single issue transaction.

4.5 Summary

Disciplined and correct recording of the planning and progress of an order is a key element of an effective planning system. Transactions must be based on accurate up-to-date information. It is essential that everyone involved realises that although recording may appear dull and routine, it is the foundation upon which effective control rests. Two key parameters associated with an order are the order quantity and lead time. Effective planning and control depends on the setting of correct values for these two parameters and for safety stock which is associated with the item rather than the order.

Chapters 5 and 6 will discuss the setting of appropriate values for these three parameters.

Exercises

4.1 An order for 10 000 items is due on Friday 28 February. The lead time is 20 working days and the planner is allowed two days to prepare the paperwork and open the order. The company works a five day week. Calculate the ready for release date and the planned start date for this order.

4.2 The bill of materials for Argento, the liquid silver polish, 100 ml pack is:

Code	Description	Quantity per	Units
M19	Argento polish bulk	0.1	L
C09	Bottle 100 ml printed	1	Each
C21	Cap – child resistant	1	Each
C29	Carton – printed	1	Each
C32	Outer	0.1	Each

(a) Calculate the requirements for an order to fill and pack 10 000 packs of the polish. Production losses are negligible with this product.

(b) How many bottles are placed in each outer?

5

Order policies

Whilst considering the mechanisms of manufacturing control, values of parameters such as order quantities, lead times and safety stocks have been stated and taken for granted. This chapter and Chapter 6 will look in more detail at how values may be set for these parameters and at the effect the values have on the overall control performance.

5.1 Order quantities

In all the examples used so far, a fixed order quantity has been assumed. That is, whenever a need to make or buy an item has been identified, an order has been raised for the specified fixed quantity. Although this is the most commonly used and simplest order policy, it is by no means the only one. Most MRP systems offer several options.

Considerations on order policies apply equally well to master production scheduling and to MRP. The examples used will consider only a total requirement irrespective of whether this is the sum of sales forecasts and customer orders as in master production scheduling, or obtained by aggregating dependent demand from manufacturing orders at a higher level, as in MRP.

5.1.1 Fixed period order policy

With a fixed period order policy, whenever an order is needed, the quantity ordered is sufficient to cover the requirements for a fixed number of days or weeks ahead. Consider the following example:

>   Opening stock   12   Order policy: Fixed period 3 weeks
>   Safety stock   0

ORDER POLICIES

Weeks	1	2	3	4	5	6	7	8	9	10
Total requirement	10	5	0	12	3	2	4	14	8	4
Projected stock 12	2	12	12	0	6	4	0	12	4	0
Order receipts		15			9			26		

Projecting the stock forward shows it falling to minus three in week 2. Therefore a new order must be received in week 2. With a fixed period policy of three weeks, the order must just cover the net requirement of three in week 2 plus the requirements for weeks 3 and 4, a total of 15. A second order is required to be received at the beginning of week 5, for a quantity sufficient to cover the requirements for weeks 5, 6 and 7, and so on.

A feature of a fixed period policy is that it plans to have no stock residues at the end of a period so large quantities of stock are not carried over periods of low demand. The projected stock of two at the end of week 1 shows that actual usage has differed from predicted requirements since the previous order was placed. A disadvantage of the fixed period policy is that it can place orders which are unrealistically large or small if requirements are very erratic. This can be avoided by incorporating an order modifier facility which specifies a minimum quantity, a maximum quantity and in some cases a 'multiple'. The multiple factor would be applied if, for example, an item was always purchased in boxes of 12, or if there is a fixed manufacturing lot size and an order must be for a whole number of lots.

If a minimum of 10, a maximum of 20 and a multiple of 5 are set, the orders created in the example would be modified as follows:

Opening stock 12 Order policy: Fixed period 3 weeks
Safety stock 0   Min 10
                  Max 20
                  Multiple 5

Weeks	1	2	3	4	5	6	7	8	9	10
Total requirement	10	5	0	12	3	2	4	14	8	4
Projected stock 12	2	12	12	0	7	5	1	7	−1	
Order receipts		15			10			20	?	

The maximum condition restricts the order for week 8 to 20. An additional order is then required for week 9 but its quantity cannot be determined until the requirement for week 11 becomes visible.

Once modifiers are applied, period-end residues can no longer be avoided, so one of the advantages of the fixed period policy over the fixed quantity policy is lost. There are also some advantages to keeping production orders a fixed size which will be discussed later in this chapter, so in most manufacturing situations the simple fixed quantity is the preferred policy.

The fixed period policy is probably most useful for purchased items where the price is not sensitive to order size. Orders will then be generated at regular intervals. In some ways a fixed period order policy bears the same relationship to a fixed quantity policy as the periodic review method of stock control does to Order Point (see Chapter 2, Section 2.2).

5.1.2 Lot for lot order policy

A special case of the fixed period order policy is when the number of periods is always one, i.e. one day, one week, etc.

Thus, what is required in a period is what is made in the period. This is called the **lot for lot** (or L4L) policy.

In a lot for lot operation there should be no opening stock unless usage in the previous period was less than expected (or if a safety stock is held). If the first example from Section 5.1.1 is reconsidered, but with a lot for lot order policy and no opening stock, the plan becomes:

Opening stock   0   Order policy: Lot for lot
Safety stock   0

Weeks	1	2	3	4	5	6	7	8	9	10
Total requirement	10	5	0	12	3	2	4	14	8	4
Projected stock 0	0	0	0	0	0	0	0	0	0	0
Order receipts	10	5	0	12	3	2	4	14	8	4

The order quantity is always equal to the total requirement for the period. The period end stock is always planned to be zero. Should there be a small opening stock this is planned away at the first opportunity.

A lot for lot order policy permits operation with minimum stocks since everything is planned to be produced just before it is needed. It is particularly appropriate either for very expensive or very bulky items, or for items which involve very little machine change-over time or other ordering cost.

5.2 Setting order quantities

Section 1.2.1 of Chapter 1 showed that one of the objectives of production planning is to find a compromise between holding too high a stock, which costs money, or reducing productivity by having too many set-ups (or change-overs), which also costs money. Setting sensible order policies is one of the key steps to achieving this compromise.

Several approaches are possible, as described below.

5.2.1 Economic Order Quantity

If a product effectively has continuous sales and stock is replenished at regular intervals just before it falls to zero, a plot of stock against time will be the familiar saw-tooth as in Fig. 5.1(a). If the order quantity is N, the average stock if no safety stock is carried will be N/2. The shaded triangle above the N/2 average line is exactly equal in area to the shaded triangle below the line. Stocks and hence stock holding costs increase linearly with N, as in Fig. 5.1(b).

However, the larger N, the fewer the number of orders needed each year and the fewer the number of equipment set-ups required. Therefore the total set-up cost varies inversely with N (see Fig. 5.1 (c)). It is not difficult to see that the total cost of set-up and stock holding will be the sum of these two effects and will be a curve with a minimum at a particular order size as in Fig. 5.2. This order quantity is known as the 'Economic Order Quantity' or EOQ. A straightforward calculation using simple calculus shows that the Economic Order Quantity is given by:

$$EOQ = \sqrt{\frac{2RS}{Ci}}$$

Where R is the annual requirement
S is the cost of one set-up
C is the cost of one item in £
i is the cost in £ of holding £1 worth of stock for one year
e.g. interest on borrowed money, warehouse costs, etc
expressed as a decimal fraction of the stock value

For reasons which will become obvious, the derivation of the EOQ formula will not be considered in detail. It is a straightforward piece of

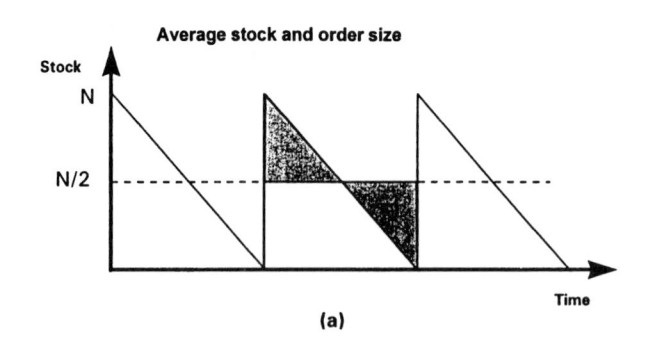

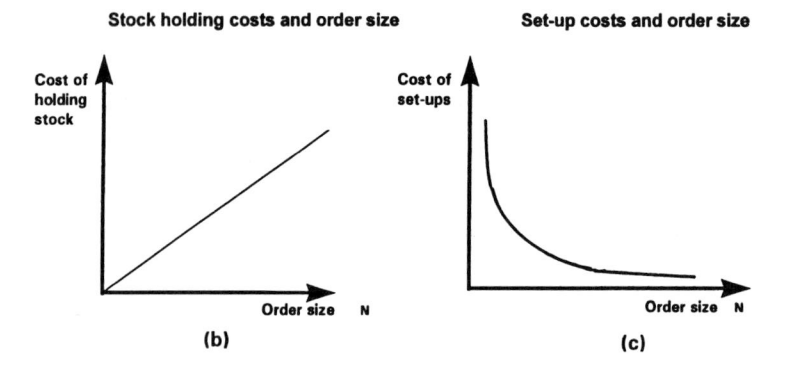

5.1 Calculating order quantities.

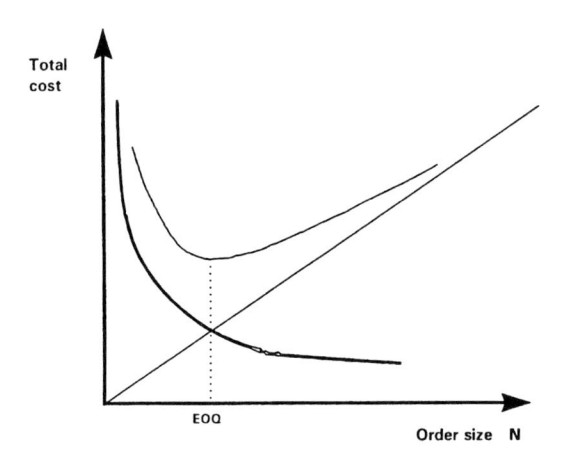

5.2 Economic order quantity.

calculus, covered in most standard texts (see, for example, *Production and Inventory Management*, by Fogarty & Hoffman, published by South-Western Publishing Company). The important point to understand is that the formula attempts to balance stock holding costs against set-up costs to find the minimum total cost.

Although very elegant the EOQ formula is of limited use in practice. It makes the assumption that off-take is linear, that set-up costs can be sensibly defined, and that stock holding costs are a constant fraction of stock value.

The first assumption can be very wrong if there are a few large off-take orders rather than many small ones. Certainly at first sight the more set-ups there are to be done, the higher the cost, but if the fitter carrying out the work and the equipment being set-up would otherwise have been idle, is there a real cost? Alternatively, if this particular set-up is the one that persuades management to employ an extra fitter or buy a new machine, it could be a very expensive set-up indeed. In practice, set-up times can also depend on the previous product and this too adds complications.

Similarly with the cost of stock holding, the interest on capital tied up varies linearly with stock value, but the additional warehousing cost of putting one extra pallet into a part-full warehouse is negligible. However, if that pallet is the one that convinces management that a new and bigger warehouse is required, it too could have a very high cost.

The apparently attractive Economic Order Quantity formula involves at least two parameters which cannot be calculated as constants independent of the business circumstances, and this severely limits its usefulness. However the principle that the total cost is a combination of stock holding and set-up costs, and that the minimum will depend on order size is still valid. Unfortunately the preferred order quantity cannot be easily determined.

5.2.2 Sophisticated order policies

Techniques have been developed to determine order quantities without making the assumption of linear off-take. Techniques called Part Period Balancing and Least Total Cost use the actual requirements pattern specified in the MRP data to calculate stock holding costs, but they still make the assumption that there is a single cost per set-up and that stock holding cost per period is a fixed percentage of value. Because these doubtful assumptions limit their value, they will not be discussed further here. Descriptions can be found in standard texts such as Fogarty and Hoffman's book quoted above. Many other sophisticated formulae have been developed but it is doubtful if any of them have practical benefits which justify the complication of the calculation.

5.2.3 A practical approach to order quantities

Work with simulation models has shown that small order sizes have advantages other than in reducing finished goods stocks. They are easier to schedule effectively, assist flow through plant, reduce lead times and increase the flexibility of response to changes in demand and there is evidence that the EOQ formula, which ignores these additional benefits, overestimates the optimum size.

It has to be recognised that calculating order sizes is far from being an exact science. Two practical approaches with only empirical justification are:

- Divide the EOQ quantity by a factor of 2 or 3. For very bulky items the factor should be 3 whilst for small easy to store items it can be 2.
- Work to a given set-up to run ratio.

Given the minimum average set-up time for the equipment, the order size is set to make the run time several times as long as the set-up time. For expensive or bulky items the factor may be 1 or 2 (e.g. one day set-up followed by one or two days' run), whilst for cheap easy to store items the factor would be 4 or 5. If there are several stages to the manufacture, the ratio applies to the total run and total set-up times for all stages.

When operating a fixed period order policy, the period must be chosen such that the average demand during the period is equal to the preferred order size (however this is determined).

With all the unknowns and lack of precision in this area it is not surprising that there are many adherents to the 'NRN' approach. NRN stands for 'nice round number'.

There is one indisputable fact. The faster and easier the set-up, the smaller is the optimum order size and the less the total cost. Every opportunity must be taken to reduce set-up times either by choosing appropriate equipment or by efficient working during the set-up.

When drawing up a specification for new equipment, there is a tendency to concentrate on the performance required whilst the equipment is running, i.e. to choose on the basis of run speed or reliability and hence maximum output per day. In practice the set-up time is at least as important as production rate.

A machining centre capable of producing 100 items per hour should easily complete packing an order for 600 in one day (assuming six standard hours worth of output per day), but if the set-up time is two days the total time for the order is three days. A less sophisticated machine capable of only 50 items per hour, but less prone to temporary problems and hence achieving seven standard hours per day and a set-up time of half a day, would take 2.25 days for the same order. A full economic comparison must take into account the capital cost of each piece of equipment and the operator requirements of each. The assumption 'The faster the better' can be a dangerous one.

Exercises

5.1 (a) Given the following information about a general purpose hydraulic valve, which is a purchased item for a fork lift truck manufacturer, project the stock forward and determine what purchase orders are needed.

Opening stock   21   Order policy: Fixed period 2 weeks, no modifiers
Safety stock   0   Lead time   1 week

Week	1	2	3	4	5	6	7	8	9	10
Total requirements	7	13	9	5	4	3	12	18	7	6
Projected stock 21	14	1								
Order receipts										

(b) Calculate the purchase order receipts required if a decision is made to operate with a safety stock of six and to impose a minimum order quantity of ten.

5.2 Plan the order receipts for the following item working on a lot for lot order policy and maintaining a safety stock of five:

Opening stock   7   Order policy: Lot for lot
Safety stock   5

Week	1	2	3	4	5	6	7	8	9	10
Total requirements	8	0	4	11	6	5	7	2	9	10
Projected stock 7										
Order receipts										

5.3 A household disinfectant with annual sales of 2 000 000 1 litre packs is produced on a shared automated filling line which for set-up requires four operator hours for cleaning and six fitter hours. The cost of one pack is £0.5. The fitters and operators have plenty of other work to do but the line is on average only 60% occupied. Only one fitter can work on the line at any one time so the elapsed time for set-up is six hours.

Stock holding costs are estimated at 25% of the value per annum.
Operators cost £20 per hour.
Fitters cost £25 per hour.

Calculate the EOQ using the standard formula.

5.4 (a) The requirement for the disinfectant in Exercise 5.3 remains at 2 000 000 packs per year, but other products sharing the line grow, so that some of the other products have to be packed at a contractor, which costs £50 per hour more than packing in house. How would this change the estimated cost of set-up and the EOQ calculation?

(b) The contractor reports that he is approaching full capacity and cannot accept more work. Marketing have recognised a new opportunity for disinfectant and would like 20% additional output.

You are asked to explore whether the company should invest in a new packing line or get more output from the existing line by increasing order quantities to reduce the time spent on set-up and accepting the increased stock holding costs.

A packing line and its associated services have a capital value of £1.0 million and an expected working life of ten years. The line is available for use for eight hours per day for 250 days per year. Borrowing capital costs 15% per annum.

What would be a reasonable way to modify the set-up costs in this situation?

If when using the revised order quantities from the EOQ formula your capacity calculations show that the decision is evenly balanced, which decision would you favour?

6

Lead times and safety stocks

This chapter will consider how to set values for lead times and safety stocks.

In Chapter 2 the lead time for an item was defined as the time between the release of an order and receipt of the material. This definition applies to both purchase orders and manufacturing orders. If lead times are set too short, orders may not be completed on time but setting them too long means that orders are released sooner than they need to be, leading to congestion on the shopfloor and increased levels of work in progress.

6.1 Setting purchasing lead times

Setting purchasing lead times is usually straightforward since the supplier will quote his lead time for supply, to which must be added an allowance for the buyer to react to the MRP message and place the order, plus any time required to inspect the goods on receipt and to locate them in the stores. Unfortunately, suppliers' lead times tend to increase when they are busy and decrease when they are not so busy. A good buyer will therefore monitor lead times continuously and check with the supplier if a change looks likely. The relationships between buyers and suppliers will be discussed further in Chapter 10.

6.2 Setting manufacturing lead times

At first sight it might be expected that the major elements of a manufacturing lead time would be the actual manufacturing time for the order plus the time taken to change over or set up the equipment before starting. If this were the case, however, the lead time for producing 10 000 items on equipment achieving 3000 items per hour with a set-up time of half a day would be about one day.

In practice very few companies would react this quickly. In most companies, a typical lead time for a manufacturing order involving only one manufacturing operation would be at least a week.

How can the difference be explained? Part of the explanation is that manufacturing lead times must include an allowance for other activities such as:

- Getting materials out of stores.
- Transporting finished goods to the sales warehouse.
- Quality control tests.

However, even the addition of generous allowances for these activities does not give the length of lead time quoted by typical non-repetitive (or job shop) manufacturers.

The differences can be explained by considering what happens if an extra job arrives at a multipurpose piece of equipment which is already 80% occupied. Probably the plant is already working on another order. Indeed there may be several other jobs queuing and the new job joins the back of the queue. In most companies which have not had a special programme to reduce lead times, queuing time is usually the major constituent of lead time and can often account for 90% of the total. The new job could be given a high priority and put straight to the front of the queue but this merely lengthens the queue for the other jobs and the average queue time is unchanged.

A well known motor manufacturer carried out an investigation and found that it was taking six months to turn a casting into a crankshaft, but that the total machining time was only 15 minutes. Transport within or between factories accounted for about ten days and all the rest of the six months was spent queuing. Such results are not extreme. A major pharmaceutical company carried out an investigation and found that for one of its key products, the time required to take raw materials through multiple chemical and purification stages to a pure drug was one year. Analysis revealed that each batch spent only five days actually undergoing processing, eight days being transported and ten days awaiting the results of quality control tests. The remaining 340 days were spent queuing.

Figure 6.1 shows the main elements of most purchasing and manufacturing lead times, although not necessarily to scale.

As with order quantities, there is no simple theoretical way of determining what manufacturing lead times should be. A simple, empirical but practical approach is to set the planned lead times equal to the observed lead times and then reduce the planned lead times slowly over a period of months until significant problems arise. The planned lead times can then be increased just enough to alleviate the problem.

LEAD TIMES AND SAFETY STOCKS

PURCHASE LEAD TIME

| Planning time | Supplier lead time | Receive and inspect |

MANUFACTURING LEAD TIME

| Planning and component assembly | Queue | Set up | Run | Move |

.... Repeat for each operation ....

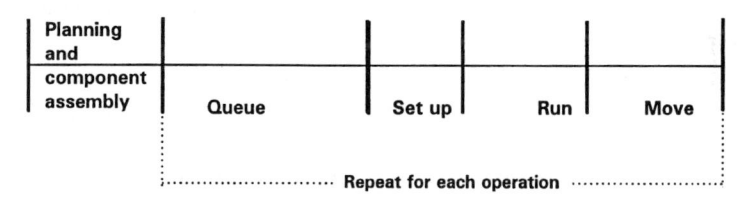

6.1 Elements of purchasing and manufacturing lead times.

An alternative but more complicated approach is to assign a value to each element of the lead time shown in Fig. 6.1 and set the lead time equal to the sum of the times for all the individual elements. Objective values can be measured for planning, component assembly, set-up, move and inspect times. The run time can be calculated for a typical order size. This leaves queue times to be estimated for each operation and this is the difficult part of the exercise. Some trial and error may be necessary but, unlike the approach discussed above in which the whole lead time is adjusted by trial and error, in this case only the queuing element needs to be set and adjusted empirically.

Rules of thumb for setting queue times initially are:

Occupation of work centre	Average queue time allowance
Heavily occupied	4 or 5 times average set-up and run time
Moderately occupied	2 or 3 times average set-up and run time
Lightly occupied	0 or 1 times average set-up and run time

These rules are unfortunately very crude. If a work centre is not heavily occupied, but problems of late delivery persist, the queuing allowance should be increased slowly. Conversely if deliveries are on time, the allowance should be reduced slowly until pain is felt and then increased slightly to alleviate the pain.

The origin of queues and the relationship between average queue length and the occupation of the work centre will be considered further in Chapter 9, Section 9.7.

6.3 Consequences of incorrectly set lead times

The flow of work through a plant can be likened to liquid flowing through a cylindrical funnel, as in Fig. 6.2. The plant capacity is represented by the cross sectional area of the neck of the funnel, and the average lead time through the plant is represented by the average time for a 'molecule' of the liquid to pass through the funnel. This is given by the volume of liquid in the funnel divided by the output rate, e.g. if there are six litres of liquid in the funnel and the rate of flow is one litre per day, the average through-put time (or lead time) is six days.

Provided that the input rate equals the output rate the observed through-put time will be constant. If, however, input exceeds output, the volume of liquid in the funnel will increase, and the through-put time will increase.

A real plant behaves similarly. If the volume of work in progress remains constant, the average lead time will be constant at, say, six weeks, but if the work input exceeds output, the average lead time will increase to, say, seven weeks, and if plans are based on a six week lead time, orders will be completed late. An instinctive reaction is to increase the planned lead time on the assumption that if it is now taking seven weeks, each order must be allowed seven weeks. However in this case instinct proves to be unreliable. The planning system which has been releasing each week all the orders required for completion in week 6, now releases everything required by the end of week 6 and the end of week 7. In terms of the funnel analogy, twice as much liquid as normal is poured into the funnel for a week, but the outflow remains constant. The volume of liquid in the funnel increases leading to a one week increase in through-put time.

Exactly the same process can happen in a factory using MRP. Immediately after the increase of the planned lead time MRP recommends the release of an extra week's work into the system. If this recommendation is followed and output is not increased, the work in progress will increase by a week and the lead time will increase to eight weeks. If the planning system responds to this second increase in lead time by releasing orders even earlier, the control system enters a vicious spiral from which the only way out is to increase output or decrease input.

This escalation of lead times is frequently observed with purchase lead times during an upturn in the business cycle. The supplier receives more business than he expected, his backlog grows so he announces an increased

Lead times and capacity

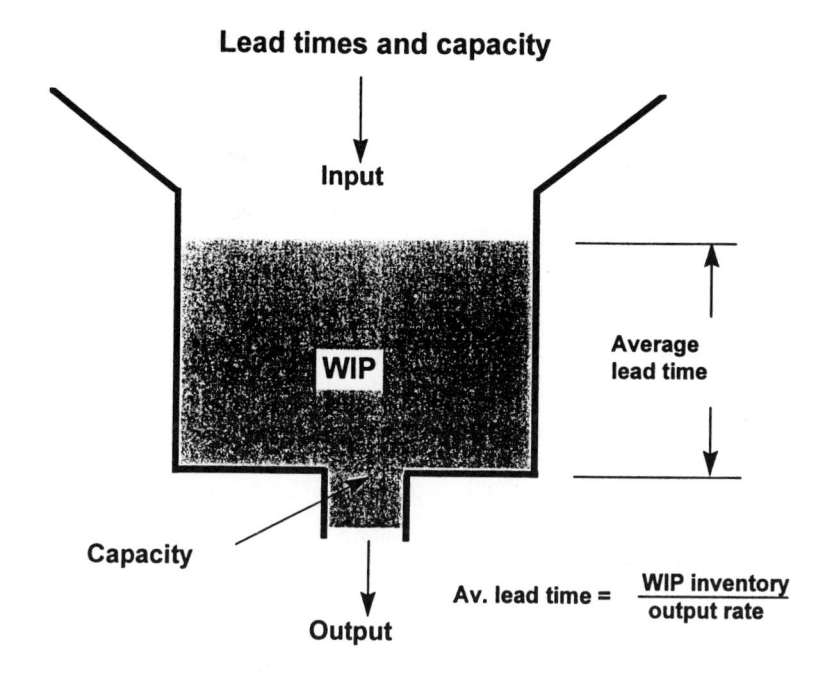

$$\text{Av. lead time} = \frac{\text{WIP inventory}}{\text{output rate}}$$

6.2 Flow of work.

lead time. His customers react by ordering to cover their requirements further ahead and the supplier receives even more orders and feels obliged to announce a further increase in lead time, and so on. When the inevitable down-turn in the economy is reached, the opposite effect occurs. An announcement of a decrease in lead time means that customers delay placing orders, with the result that lead times fall even further.

The author remembers well the painful experience of watching the lead time for the purchase of printed cartons increase from eight weeks to nine months in only a few weeks, as a result of expectations of serious industrial unrest in the printing industry. Buyers were attempting to build up stocks to provide protection against supply failure. When the expectations proved unfounded, all the extra orders which were no longer required were cancelled and the suppliers' lead times collapsed dramatically to four weeks.

For purchased items, bought in the traditional way, there is little that purchasers can do to avoid such difficulties, but an alternative approach to the control of purchasing, discussed in Chapter 11, Section 11.7 can alleviate the problems.

For internally planned manufacture, the problem can be controlled. Consider the simple representation of a paper clip manufacturing facility

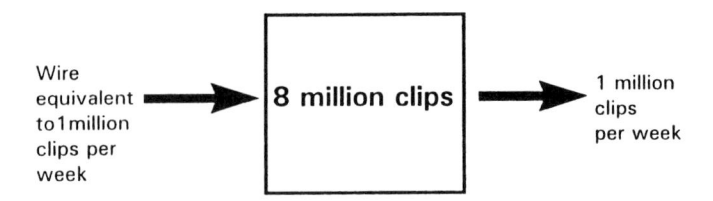

```
Wire
equivalent  ──▶  ┌─────────────────┐  ──▶  1 million
to 1 million      │  8 million clips │        clips
clips per         └─────────────────┘        per week
week
```

6.3 Paper clip manufacturing facility.

shown in Fig. 6.3 and used in Exercise 6.1. (Readers are recommended to undertake Exercise 6.1 at this point.) The company has had a good record of delivering customers' orders on time, with plans based on an eight week lead time but an investigation shows that the actual time required, including reasonable queuing time, is only six weeks. If the planned lead time were to be reduced from eight to six weeks, no raw materials would be released into production for two weeks. The initial manufacturing stage would cease working for two weeks but when it started up again new orders would find shorter queues ahead, would flow through in six weeks and emerge on time. Reducing a planned lead time which was greater than the actual lead time would reduce the work in process from eight million clips to six million with no adverse effects.

If, however, the planned lead time had been reduced to six weeks when the actual lead time was seven weeks, i.e. it actually took seven weeks, including reasonable queuing time, to convert wire into clips, then there would be two weeks with no input, and one week with no output. The in-process stock would fall only to seven million clips and subsequent output would be consistently a week late. Increasing the planned lead time back to seven weeks would not solve the problem. Two weeks' worth of wire would be released into the plant, but only one million clips would be produced in the week. The actual lead time would increase to eight weeks because of an extra week's queuing, and output would continue to be one week late on average.

The only way to correct a situation like this is to increase capacity temporarily, in order to drive an extra week of product out of the system as the planned lead time is increased. Increasing the planned lead time from six to seven weeks releases an extra week of work, but the extra capacity delivers an extra one million clips. The work in progress is $7 + 2 - 2 = 7$, so the planned lead time equals actual and product is delivered on time.

If these somewhat complicated arguments are difficult to follow, referring to the funnel analogy may be helpful. If there is too much liquid in the funnel, and the output capacity remains fixed as shown, the only way to reduce the volume in the funnel is to reduce the input, but if the input is determined by demand from the customer, all that is achieved is to transfer some of the backlog from the factory to the planner's desk. The customer sees no difference between waiting whilst his order queues on the planner's desk or whilst it queues in an overloaded factory.

The only solution to problems of arrears or too much work in progress is to increase capacity. In the case of the funnel, the diameter of the output pipe must be increased. In real life, increased working hours or the use of supplementary resources may provide the solution.

6.4 Safety stocks

Chapter 2 described the use of safety stocks of sales product to provide protection against demand temporarily exceeding forecast in a Make to Stock business. Good customer service is important for many companies, and without it they would not be competitive. Part of the service to be provided is the constant ability to fill orders as quickly as possible. This is where safety stocks can really give a company a competitive edge.

If excellent sales forecasts were always available, covering for example the next six months, most companies would have little need for safety stocks, but in real life sales forecasting can be difficult particularly for products with unpredictable peaks in demand, such as ice cream or soft drink sales in a heat wave, or drugs used to treat epidemics or seasonal diseases, so safety stocks tend to be much used. In addition to providing protection against excessive demand, a safety stock of finished product also provides some protection against delays in the replenishment supply from production.

Some companies also maintain safety stocks of key raw materials to protect production against delivery failure or rejection. In fact safety stocks may be held at any stage in production, e.g. raw materials, components, sub-assemblies, semi-finished products awaiting a customer's order, etc. The closer they are to the customer the more sure the protection provided to that customer, but the earlier in the production chain the stock is held, the more flexible is the cover provided. For example, a stock of intermediates ready to be converted into a range of final products provides greater flexibility and cover than does the equivalent quantity of finished items specific to markets or customers.

It is sometimes forgotten that safety stocks only provide protection against timing errors in demand or supply. Protection ceases once the stock has been consumed. Safety stocks cannot protect a product from the effects of sales consistently exceeding forecast. They can however 'buy time' to enable production to be increased.

The undoubted benefits from holding safety stocks have to be weighed against the costs. These are the normal costs of holding any stocks, e.g. cost of capital, space, insurance, pilferage, damage and obsolescence. In the case of sales items with expiry dates and limited lives, the increased risk of obsolescence caused by holding sales safety stocks can be significant. For example, it is unlikely that a baker specialising in oven fresh bread will choose to hold a large safety stock of baked loaves, which have a shelf life measured in hours and would have to be thrown away if not sold.

In such cases, provided that the raw materials have a longer shelf life than the finished product, it may be appropriate to hold stocks of raw materials and to keep spare production capacity available, so that the raw materials can be turned quickly into finished product to meet temporary increases in demand. The baker, for example, may choose to hold stocks of flour and spare processing capacity. The flour has a shelf life of weeks or months, but takes a relatively long time to process. Possibly the higher than expected sales trend identified at 2.00 pm will not have been maintained when the new loaves become available and it may be that much of the new production has to be thrown away.

In the UK, the traditional baker did not have the resources necessary for this approach, nor was he normally prepared to take this risk. He chose to bake a fixed quantity early in the day and if that was all sold by 3.30 pm, the disappointed customers understood that this was part of the price to be paid for enjoying fresh produce and made a note to get to the shop earlier in future. However, the 1980s saw the growth of bakery chains or in-store bakeries in supermarkets. These are stocked with specially formulated, uncooked dough from a central plant and only the final baking is done in the store. Small quantities of each type of bread can be baked as required and, if necessary, surplus dough can be kept under refrigeration for the few hours before the store opens again the next morning. In this case, the safety stock is held as an intermediate with the result that the lead time to produce additional finished product is very much reduced and customer service greatly improved. Traditional bakeries have found it difficult to compete with this combination of safety stock policy and new technology.

6.5 Setting safety stock levels

Considerable attention has been given to calculating safety stock levels for a particular degree of forecast accuracy which are sufficiently high to minimise the number of stock-outs but not so high as to incur unnecessary

Probability of forecast error

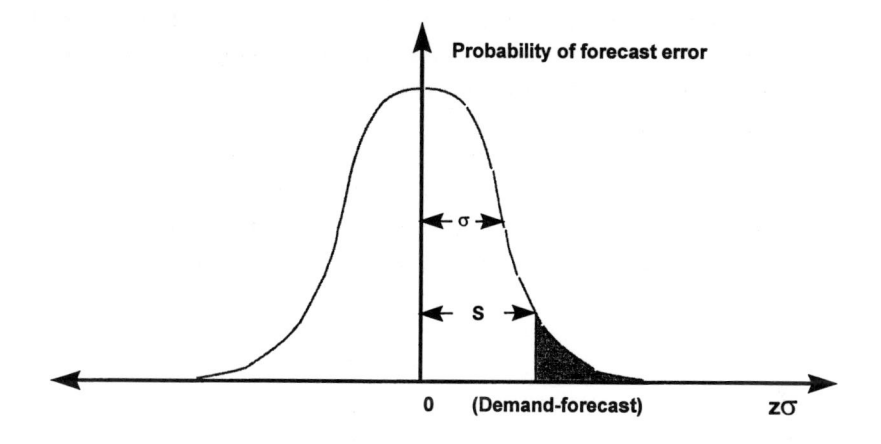

z	0.5	1.0	1.5	2.0	2.5	3.0
Cumulative area	0.692	0.841	0.933	0.977	0.994	0.999

6.4 Safety stock and variability of demand.

stock holding costs. Obviously the more accurate the sales forecasts, the lower the safety stock required to achieve a specified level of customer service.

If the error between forecast and demand is random, the actual demand in a forecasting period would be expected to follow a normal distribution about the forecast, i.e. there is a reasonable probability that the demand will be close to forecast and a very low probability that demand will be very much greater or very much less than the forecast (see Fig. 6.4).

The width of the curve is a measure of the average forecast error. If the forecasts are highly inaccurate, the curve will be wide. If forecasts are always 100% accurate, the curve collapses to a spike. If the distribution is truly 'normal' the average error can be measured by a parameter called the standard deviation or σ. Readers for whom a standard deviation is a new concept, may find it helpful to think of σ as a measure of the width of the curve at half of the maximum height. σ can be calculated by comparing demand with forecast over a range of past periods. The formula is:

$$\sigma = \sqrt{\frac{\Sigma_i (F_i - D_i)^2}{n}}$$

where F_i and D_i are the forecast and demand for period i and n is the number of periods considered.

The formula for σ may look daunting to readers unfamiliar with mathematical symbols, but all it means is that for each past forecasting period (say for each month), the error between forecast and actual demand is calculated and squared. The squares are then averaged over the number of periods being considered σ is obtained by taking the square root of the average. Fortunately nowadays, the calculations can usually be left to the computer and all that the user needs to know is that the standard deviation, σ, is a measure of forecast accuracy.

S in Fig. 6.4 is the safety stock held. If demand in a period, exceeds forecast by a quantity greater than S in Fig. 6.4 a stock-out will occur. The probability of this happening is given by the ratio of the shaded area to the total area under the curve, or if the total area is normalised to unity, by the shaded area. Thus a safety stock of S will give protection against stock-out during the period with a probability equal to the ratio of the unshaded area to the total area under the curve. This depends on how many standard deviations S represents, i.e. on Z, where:

$$Z = S/\sigma$$

Z is a factor characteristic of a normal distribution, and the value of Z required to give a particular service level can be looked up in a table such as that in Fig. 6.4. Thus the safety stock required to give, say, 98% customer service performance can be determined by looking up the value of Z corresponding to 0.98 and using the formula:

$$\text{Safety stock} = Z\sigma$$

With the information shown, the nearest value to 0.98 is 0.977, which corresponds to a Z value of 2. Thus a safety stock equal to two standard deviations of sales from forecast will give a 97.7% customer service level.

If the replenishment lead time is not equal to the forecast period it is necessary to apply a correction of the square root of m, where m is the number of forecast periods in the replenishment lead time:

$$\text{Safety stock} = Z\sigma \sqrt{m}$$

Further details of such calculations can be found in, for example, Fogarty & Hoffmann, *Production and Inventory Management* (South-Western, 1983), or R G Brown, *Decision Rules and Inventory Management* (Holt, Rinehart and Winston, 1967).

Calculating a standard deviation manually is laborious since every deviation must be squared and then the square root of the mean deviation taken. Squaring eliminates minus signs from the cases where forecast exceeds demand. Many texts describe an alternative approach based on the mean absolute deviation or MAD which, as the name implies, is the average value of the deviation between forecast and demand irrespective of sign. The formula is:

$$\text{MAD} = (\Sigma_i \mid F_i - D_i \mid)/n$$

where the | | sign indicates 'absolute value of' (i.e. ignore negative signs).
For a normal distribution:

$$\sigma = 1.25 \text{ MAD, approximately.}$$

Therefore:

$$\text{Safety stock} = 1.25 \text{ MAD } Z \sqrt{m}$$

However, with the widespread availability of personal computers and powerful electronic calculators, there is no longer any justification for using the approximate formula and it will not be considered further.

Although the statistical safety stock calculation is mathematically very elegant, it suffers from two major weaknesses:

- It considers only problems resulting from demand exceeding forecast. Stock-outs can also be caused if replenishment production orders are late or fail to arrive at all.
- A normal distribution of forecast errors is only likely if there are many customers and demand is effectively continuous. The analysis is not valid if demand is 'lumpy'.

The formula can only be sensibly applied if demand is continuous and the supply of items from either purchasing or manufacture is very reliable. A simpler and frequently more effective approach is to set safety stocks empirically by plotting the minimum stock level experienced each day or week over a past period of, say, one year. Outstanding customer orders count as negative stock. It is then obvious by inspection what level of safety stock would have been necessary over that period just to prevent stocks going negative. Individual planners may choose to hold some additional stock to allow for the fact that future periods may be more erratic than the period monitored. Like setting order quantities and lead times, setting safety stocks is not an exact science.

If safety stocks are expressed in terms of weeks' cover (i.e. how many weeks of sales they equal) a rough and ready approach is to give similar items a safety stock of the appropriate weeks' cover without investigating their detailed past history.

In some ways the need for safety stocks indicates a failure of the planning and control systems. Ideally the uncertainties which cause the need for safety stocks should be eliminated or reduced by better sales forecasting, more dialogue with customers, shortening internal lead times and discussions with suppliers, etc. Safety stocks should be used only temporarily whilst implementing less expensive approaches to improving customer service, or as a last resort after attempts to reduce uncertainty have failed.

Whatever the method of setting a safety stock, it is important that the values are reviewed regularly, e.g. annually, to correct for sales growth, changes in the uncertainty of sales or for any past failure to provide the desired cover.

Exercises

6.1 The paper clip bending facility represented in Fig. 6.3 on page 88, produces one million clips per week in a variety of sizes. Each week sufficient wire for one million clips is received from the supplier and passed to the first manufacturing stage. These particular lots of wire emerge as finished clips a lead time later. A stock-take shows that the in-process stocks are equivalent to eight million clips. What is the average lead time?

6.2 All materials or components received from suppliers are routinely tested. Five working days are allowed for this, the Purchasing Group arranges for deliveries to be at least five days before items are required for production so that clearance can be received before use.

During the period before the summer examinations a number of the younger inspectors are given study leave. This reduces the inspection capacity and the testing arrears increase to ten days' work. Items are frequently not cleared when required for use. A priority system is introduced but this prevents the inspectors handling the work in the order which gives greatest efficiency, and the backlog increases slightly.

To avoid further embarrassment the section manager requests Purchasing to ensure that all purchased items are delivered 15 days before needed, to give his staff time to react.

Will this action solve the problem? What is likely to happen?

6.3 The actual sales compared with lead time forecasts for an electric tooth brush in the UK for the past 12 months are:

Month	Forecast	Actual sales
1	100	85
2	100	105
3	100	110
4	110	115
5	110	105
6	110	112
7	120	110
8	120	128
9	120	121
10	130	125
11	130	125
12	130	139

The units are 'items'. Assume that the above represents a normal distribution.

The production lead time is two months.

The product manager wishes to be 98% certain that he does not go out of stock in any month. Calculate the necessary safety stock level.

NB: The lead time forecast means the forecast made a lead time ahead of the sale. Once production has started the quantity of that order cannot be increased. Therefore the safety stock must cover the deviation between sales and forecast over the lead time.

7

Bills of materials

The use of a bill of materials or recipe to 'explode' the requirements of one level of manufacture down to the next was described in Chapter 2. This chapter will examine some of the features of bills of materials, which are of use not only for basic MRP calculations but also as part of Option Planning (a way of achieving benefit by reducing uncertainty) and for management reporting.

7.1 Yields and shrinkages

The bill of materials for LEM01, the 500 ml glass bottle of the soft drink Superlem used in Chapter 2 showed a requirement of 500 ml of the bulk drink and one bottle, cap and label for each bottle of the finished product. This implies that 2000 litres of the bulk drink and 4000 of each package component would yield 4000 of the finished packs. In practice, however, as every production manager or operator knows, this is very unlikely to be the case. Some of the drink may be spilled on the floor during setting up, some may be left in the pipes at the end of the run or, more importantly, because the quantity supplied by the filling head is slightly variable, the volume required for each bottle may have been set at say 505 ml in order to safeguard against under-filled packs and a possible risk of prosecution for supplying short weight.

Similarly, a small percentage of the bottles may be broken when being handled, or filled bottles may be rejected because the label is not applied correctly.

Although such losses should be eliminated as far as possible by, for example, good equipment design and the use of well thought out standard operating procedures, there will usually be a residual loss which cannot be eliminated cost effectively, but which can be allowed for by applying a yield factor to the bill of materials. If an order for 4000 bottles of LEM01 actually produces 3800 instead of the nominal 4000, the yield is 0.95. This factor must be applied to the order quantity to determine the expected output of the order. The planned stock is only increased by the expected output, not the nominal order quantity. If a specific quantity for an order must be achieved, possibly because the customer will only accept the precise quantity ordered, the required quantity must be divided by the yield to determine a planned order quantity such that the desired quantity will actually be produced.

Some systems prefer to specify the amount lost or shrinkage in which case:

$$\text{Shrinkage} = 1 - \text{yield}$$

Such a yield, which assumes the loss of equal quantities of all ingredients, is referred to as the parent yield, because it is applied to the order quantity of the parent item.

In some cases a particular component may be lost preferentially. For example, when packing toothpaste on an automated line, a number of cartons may be destroyed in setting up the cartonner. The loss of cartons may therefore be greater than for other components. It is desirable therefore to be able to specify a shrinkage against each component so that MRP will order a correspondingly greater quantity of that component. It is more conventional to specify component shrinkages rather than yields but the net result is the same.

In the case of components lost in setting up the equipment, the quantity lost is independent of the order size. An ideal system would permit the specification of both a fixed quantity and a proportional quantity lost, but few systems are this sophisticated and it is usually necessary to base the proportional loss on a typical order size. Careful equipment design can minimise both the planning complication and the cost of losses.

Some people find it confusing to be planning for an order of 10 000 but to find that the projected stock is shown to increase by only 9500 because there is an overall yield of 0.95. An alternative is to set the parent yield to 1 and increase the component shrinkage by 0.05 on every component. Thus the component requirements are increased so that the eventual yield is equal to the nominal order quantity. Both approaches are effective. The choice is a matter of preference.

A bill of materials corresponds to one or more manufacturing stages covered by a single manufacturing order. For example, the choice might be to have an order to make bulk Superlem drink from its ingredients followed by one or more orders to fill the drink into finished packs. Bills of materials for both stages are shown overleaf.

Bill of materials (single stage)

LEM00 bulk Superlem drink (units = litres) (Yield = 0.97)

Code	Description	Quantity per	
LEM99	Lemon juice concentrate	0.1	litres
E123	Citric acid	0.05	kg
E124	Preservative	0.002	kg
(W1	Water	0.99	litres)

Bill of materials (single stage)

LEM01 Superlem 500 ml glass bottle (Yield = 0.95)

Code	Description	Quantity per
LEM00	Lemon squash (bulk)	0.5 litres
B1	Bottle 500 ml glass	1
C1	Cap	1
L1	Label	1
etc		

Alternatively it is possible to have a single order and single bill of materials to make filled packs from ingredients – lemon juice concentrate, citric acid, etc – and package components as shown below.

Bill of materials (multiple stage)

LEM01 Superlem 500 ml glass bottle (Yield = 0.92)

Code	Description	Quantity per	
B1	Bottle 500 ml glass	1	
C1	Cap	1	
L1	Label	1	
LEM99	Lemon juice concentrate	0.05	litres
E123	Citric acid	0.025	kg
E124	Preservative	0.001	kg
(W1	Water	0.45	litres)

The 'quantity per' is the quantity nominally required to make one unit of the finished product, a 500 ml bottle in this case. Bulk Superlem drink does not appear on this bill of materials and in this case may not even be a recognised intermediate material. The yield for the combined stage is the product of the yields of the individual stages.

Having a single bill and manufacturing order covering multiple manufacturing stages reduces the amount of paper work and reporting, but is only feasible if all the product from each stage goes to the same next stage. In the above example all the bulk Superlem produced is filled into LEM01, the 500 ml pack. If at any point in the manufacturing chain there is branching, for example if a single batch of bulk Superlem drink is filled into more than one finished pack, separate orders and bills of materials are needed for each stage. The MRP system will work its way down through all the levels and recommend manufacturing orders for each stage. Bulk Superlem will be a recognised material which is taken into stock and then issued back to manufacturing when needed.

If it is feasible, it is far simpler to treat the whole of manufacturing as a single stage. Intermediates do not need to be recognised materials but are regarded as work in progress. As will be seen in Chapter 9, each manufacturing activity such as bulk drink manufacture or filling, becomes an operation on the routing for the manufacture of the finished drink pack.

Working with single orders covering many stages increases control and reduces the possibility that stocks of intermediates such as bulk drink will be left accidentally to sit out their shelf life in stores.

7.2 Phantom bills of materials

Because of the way that products are designed and developed, it may well be that the bill of materials structure preferred by the developers and production engineers is not the same as the structure needed by the planners. The latter usually find it preferable to have as many multi-stage bills as possible, in order to minimise the number of manufacturing orders and part numbers needed. Developers and production engineers tend to design one stage at a time, with a bill of materials corresponding to each stage. This can be achieved whilst still enjoying the benefits of single orders by designating intermediates such as bulk drink as phantom parts. A phantom has a bill of materials just like a normal part but MRP does not plan a phantom. It 'blows through' the requirements to the next level down until it finds a real part. In most MRP systems stock can be recorded against a phantom should it arise for any reason. The MRP system should take it into account and use it, but MRP will never plan to create stocks of phantom parts.

7.3 Planning bills of materials

Sometimes it is convenient to group items together purely for planning purposes, and a special type of bill of materials can be used to do this.

Perhaps the simplest case is to assist the preparation of summary reports for management. For example, if management requires a report of the total sales, in packs, of all items in the Superlem drinks family, a planning or family bill could be defined as follows:

FAM01	**Superlem drinks family**	**(Unit = packs)**
Code	*Description*	*Quantity per*
LEM01	Superlem 500 ml	1
LEM02	Superlem 1 litre	1
LEM03	Superlem 3 litre plastic	1

This bill would be used by a special programme which recognised FAM01 as a family part and aggregated data such as sales forecasts, actual sales, actual production, planned production and stocks to the family level.

Calculating the aggregate figures in packs may not always give the most useful information, since adding 500 ml packs to 3 litre packs could be deceptive, but if this is the case, an alternative family bill FAM02 can be created with the 'quantity per' defining, for example, cost, bulk drink content or whatever unit of aggregation provides the most useful management information.

A special use of a planning bill is to break down a forecast made at family level over the members of a family, based on past sales data.

For example, Marketing may prefer to forecast the sales of the Superlem family in total, irrespective of the pack size which is sold. A bill of materials with quantities per based on past sales would then enable MRP to divide the forecast amongst the packs. This significantly reduces the forecasting work load and, as will be shown in Chapter 8, probably makes the forecasts more accurate, but does require periodic monitoring of the quantities per.

FAM03	**Superlem drinks family**	**(Unit = litres)**
Code	*Description*	*Quantity per*
LEM01	Superlem 500 ml	—
LEM02	Superlem 1 litre	—
LEM03	Superlem 3 litre plastic	—

In this example the forecast is made in litres.

The quantity per needs careful thought. It is the number of packs of the appropriate size sold per litre of total drink sold. If the proportion of bulk drink sold by pack is:

0.5 litre	1 litre	3 litre
0.30	0.45	0.25

i.e. 30% of Superlem by volume is sold as 0.5 litre packs. Therefore for every litre of bulk drink sold, 0.3 litres go into 500 ml packs, giving a quantity per of 0.6 packs, 0.45 litres go into 1 litre packs, giving 0.45 of a pack and 0.25 litres go into 3 litre packs, giving 0.083 of a pack.

If sales for a period, measured in total litres were 10 000 litres, this would be made up of 3000 litres as 500 ml (6000 packs), 4500 litres as 1 litre packs (4500 packs) and 2500 litres as 3 litre packs (833 packs)

7.4 Option Planning

A special case of the use of a planning bill is to plan a product which has many different options. A motor car is a good example, where some of the options on a particular model (code named Model Z), available to the customer are listed below.

Model Z options
2 door
4 door
1600 cc
2 000 cc
Manual
Auto
ABS
Red
Green
   20 colours
etc
VHF radio

The total number of variants is 2 × 2 × 2 × 2 × 2 × 20 = 640 (without allowing for hatch/saloon, central locking and heated mirrors, etc.) It is impossible to forecast accurately each variant.

Even with the limited list of options shown, there are 640 different combinations of engine size, body, colour and accessories. It is clearly impossible to forecast separately the sales of each variant but relatively easy to determine the percentage of the total which have a particular option, e.g. 85% of the total have the 1600 cc engine, irrespective of body, colour, etc (see over).

Model Z options	%
2 door	10
4 door	90
1600 cc	85
2 000 cc	15
Manual	80
Auto	20
ABS	17
Red	5
Green	17
20 colours	
etc	
VHF radio	95

But each option can be forecast as a percentage of the whole. For example, 2 door models make up 10% of all Model Zs sold, but we have no information on the other features or options on this 10%.

By using a planning bill for a dummy or pseudo-item called 'Model Z', planning can start with only a forecast of the total number of cars to be sold and the percentages for each option, based on historical sales. Then MRP will use the planning bill to break down the forecast and order the correct mix of components (see Fig. 7.1). Of course the combinations in which the parts have to be assembled are not known until the orders are received from the customers, but assembly can take place much more quickly than if all the components and sub-assemblies had to be planned and procured after receipt of the customers' orders.

Some of the parts in the planning bill in Fig. 7.1 are not real items but are groups of parts it is convenient to plan together, even though in practice they are never assembled into a recognisable sub-assembly. Such items are called pseudo-items. The bill of materials for the pseudo-item defines the members of the group. Pseudo-items or parts must exist on the MRP data base but require much less supporting information than do real or phantom items.

Many process industries face the situation where a particular pack is sold in many markets each requiring specific labelling, instruction leaflets and printed cartons. In such cases it is relatively easy to forecast the total number of items to be sold, but much more difficult to predict the requirements from individual markets. With an Assemble to Order policy, the appropriate quantities of bulk product, plain containers and caps, etc, would be obtained in advance, in line with the total forecast. The specific

BILLS OF MATERIALS   103

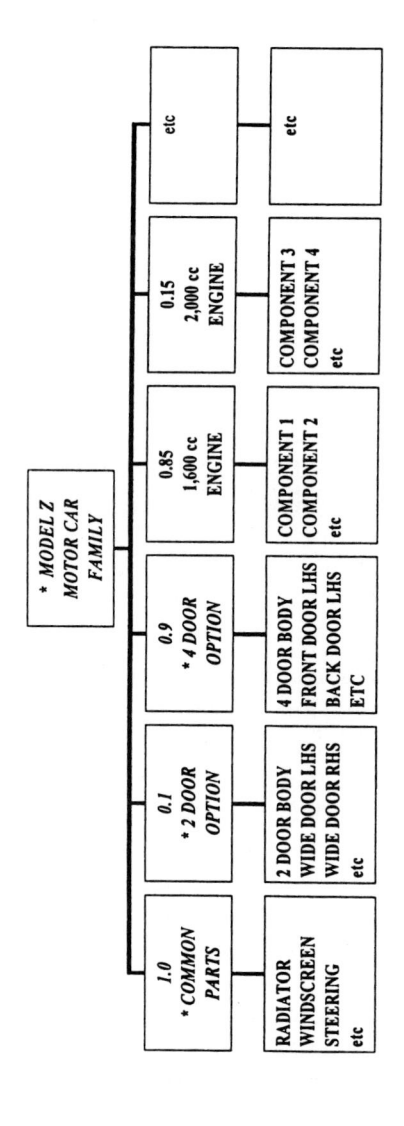

```
                           * MODEL Z
                           MOTOR CAR
                            FAMILY
      ┌──────────┬──────────┼──────────┬──────────┐
     1.0        0.1        0.9        0.85       0.15
   * COMMON   * 2 DOOR   * 4 DOOR   1,600 cc   2,000 cc
    PARTS     OPTION     OPTION    ENGINE      ENGINE
      │          │          │          │          │
  RADIATOR   2 DOOR BODY  4 DOOR BODY  COMPONENT 1  COMPONENT 3   etc
  WINDSCREEN WIDE DOOR LHS FRONT DOOR LHS COMPONENT 2 COMPONENT 4
  STEERING   WIDE DOOR RHS BACK DOOR LHS    etc          etc      etc
    etc         etc           ETC
```

Indicates Pseudo Part
Roman Characters indicate real parts
Quantities per for lowest items are all 1

7.1 Planning bill of materials for the Model Z motor car family.

printed labels and cartons, etc needed for final assembly would be obtained and the assembly carried out only after receipt of the customer's order. This can be an effective way of decreasing uncertainty and reducing the need for safety stock (see Chapter 6, Section 6.5), but it does assume that the printed components can be obtained within the time which the customer is prepared to wait for supply.

For many companies, this may require a rethink of their relations with their suppliers and the acceptance of arrangements such as sharing information, booking capacity in advance, accepting certificates of conformity and generally working with preferred suppliers, rather than maintaining the traditional adversarial relationship.

7.5 Nomenclature

Unfortunately, as with nomenclature in other areas of operations management, the bill of materials area suffers from a lack of agreed international definitions. The terms phantom bill, family bill, planning bill, pseudo-bill and modular bill are used in different ways by different authors. This author's personal preferred definitions are given below, but it would be presumptuous to claim that they are any better than alternative definitions in use.

7.5.1 Phantom bill

A phantom bill is a bill of materials for an item which can be made from its components and which can be stocked, but in normal circumstances is not so made or stocked. The MRP system ignores a phantom item and moves straight to the next level down in the bill of materials. If for special reasons there is a stock of a phantom item, MRP should use the stock before planning the requirements for components at the level below. Phantom items and bills are frequently used to simplify the bill of materials structure and to facilitate maintenance. A phantom part normally must be set up on the MRP data base with almost the same list of data items as a normal part.

As an example, consider a bicycle manufacturer. One way of working is to have a part number for a handlebar assembly, which has a bill of materials showing that it is made from a stem, a curved bar, two brake levers and two rubber hand grips. Manufacturing orders are required at intervals, to make handlebar assemblies and put them into stock. When an order to build bicycles is released, the appropriate number of handlebar assemblies are withdrawn from stock and incorporated into the bicycles.

Alternatively, the company may choose not to pre-assemble handlebars, but to issue the stem, bar, brake levers, and grips as part of the kit of items used to build a bicycle. The handlebar assemblies are then built as part of the manufacturing order for building the whole bicycle.

Maintenance of the bill of materials file is very much easier if there is a bill of materials for the handlebar assembly. Any changes to that bill, such as the use of a different hand grip, need only be made once. The new grip will then be incorporated in the bills for all bicycles using that assembly.

If the company wishes to assemble bicycles on a single order, but still wishes to enjoy the ease of maintenance provided by having a bill for the handlebar assembly, this can be done by defining the handlebar assembly as a phantom.

7.5.2 Family bill

A family bill is used to define a family relationship between items. The relationship can then be used to assist the production of summary reports or to break down a sales forecast at family level into individual forecasts for the members of the family. In this latter use it is identical to a planning bill.

7.5.3 Planning bill

A planning bill is for a family of items, usually used to break down a sales forecast at a family level into individual forecasts for the family members. A special case is the use of a planning bill in an Assemble to Order environment, to plan the component requirements for the final assembly operation for a product family with many options. It is very similar, if not identical, to a family bill.

7.5.4 Pseudo-bill

A pseudo-bill defines an artificial group of items which it is convenient to plan together, but which do not correspond to any real assembly and cannot be assembled. The MRP system treats pseudos like phantoms. They are not normally planned and MRP moves down to the level below.

7.5.5 Modular bill

Modular bill is a generic term describing a bill for a sub-assembly or group of items which can be used as a component on higher level bills of materials. The overall structure of the bills of materials is based on modules which are only defined once, but may be incorporated into other bills as often as is required.

There is considerable overlap between these definitions, but from the MRP point of view, there is a significant difference between phantom and pseudo-bills on the one hand and the remaining bill types on the other. The MRP system 'blows through' phantom and pseudo-bills, but the others are treated as normal bills by the MRP logic.

Exercises

7.1 A health care company manufactures and packs toothpaste. The paste is manufactured and then stored in intermediate bulk containers (IBCs). In order to carry out a manufacturing order for packing, the paste is pumped from the IBCs to the filling machine, which fills, seals and then cartons the nominally 100 g tubes in which the paste is sold. Filling, sealing and cartonning are effectively a single operation, i.e. packing.

In order to avoid potential prosecution for selling short weight tubes, the filler is set to fill 101 g into each tube. Although it achieves this on average, there is some random scatter. As a final precaution the tubes are check-weighed and any containing less than 100.5 g are rejected and destroyed. On average 3% are rejected.

The nominal manufacturing order quantity for packing is 100 000 tubes, after which all the equipment is cleaned and switched to another product. Typically 2% of the paste manufactured is left sticking to the walls of the IBCs and in the filling equipment.

The automatic cartonner is difficult to set up after a product change, and usually 500 cartons are crushed in setting up the cartonner. This is allowed for with a component shrinkage on the cartons. All other package component losses are allowed for in the parent shrinkage.

(a) How many tubes of saleable toothpaste would you expect to get into stock after each manufacturing order?
(b) What is the parent shrinkage on the filled 100 g tubes?
(c) What is the weight of paste required in IBCs for each packing campaign?
(d) If the bill of materials for packing shows the 'quantity per' for paste as 0.1 kg (i.e. 100 g per tube) what should the component shrinkage be on the paste?
(e) What is the component shrinkage on the cartons?

BILLS OF MATERIALS

(f) The company is asked to produce a similar but differently flavoured paste in an own label pack, for a customer who requires delivery of exactly 50 000 tubes.

What should the nominal packing order size be to provide 50 000 good quality tubes?

Will any of the shrinkage factors on the bill of materials be different from those on the standard product bill? If so, can you suggest and justify new values?

7.2 Managers wish to see a report of total sales forecast, actual sales, and actual production for the Superlem family expressed in litres of drink content. The planner proposes to use the family bill facility on the MRP system to aggregate the data. The family bill is agreed as follows:

FAM03	Superlem drinks family	(Unit = litres)
Code	Description	Quantity per
LEM01	Superlem 500 ml	–
LEM02	Superlem 1 litre	–
LEM03	Superlem 3 litre plastic	–

Add the appropriate quantities per.

(The quantity per in this case is the number of each pack which is equivalent to one unit of the family parent. In practice the value to be used may depend on the precise logic of the computer system used.)

7.3 Chopit, a successful domestic food processor, incorporating chopping, slicing, mixing and liquidising facilities, is sold in the UK, France (FR), Austria (AU), Switzerland (SZ), Pakistan (PK) and Thailand (TL). Monthly sales to individual markets are erratic but the total unit sales by market over the past 12 months are as follows:

UK	FR	AU	SZ	PK	TL
35 000	21 000	8 000	12 000	14 000	27 000

Each country requires a different electrical lead and specific labelling with hazard warnings in the local language. Internal circuitry automatically adjusts to the voltage of the local electricity supply. Two different self-adhesive labels are required for each unit in each language and the marketing department insists on having a specific carton for each market. The same multi-lingual instruction leaflet is put into each carton and all other components are common. The company has tried to operate a Make to Stock policy but with little success, because of the unreliable detailed sales forecasts. There always seems to be too much finished goods stock of the country variants which are not being ordered, and too little of the ones which are.

It has decided to operate an Assemble to Order policy. The cost of holding adequate safety stocks of self-adhesive labels and electrical leads is seen as acceptable.

Devise a suitable planning bill with the appropriate quantities per. Present the bill in a family tree structure as in Fig. 7.1.

8

Sales forecasting and Distribution Requirements Planning

Section 2.2.4 in Chapter 2 demonstrated how in order to drive by looking through the windscreen rather than the rear view mirror a view of the future incorporating sales forecasts or advance customer orders is needed. For special orders, for example large capital items such as turbines for power stations, armaments such as tanks and aircraft, and some government tenders, the customer is prepared to wait whilst all the raw materials and components are purchased and the product assembled, but for most companies this represents the exception rather than the rule. Consumer goods in particular are usually required off-the-shelf. In order to provide this sort of service, some advance forecast of sales is necessary. Figure 8.1, which is a copy of Fig. 1.3 shows how the need for sales forecasting depends on the type of service offered. Everything to the left of the point at which the customer's order is received and the customer's lead time commences needs to be initiated by some form of sales forecast.

Forecasting is a major topic, and no attempt will be made to cover it all here. This chapter will be confined to hints and principles which have proven to be of value in Make to Stock and Assemble to Order industries.

8.1 How are forecasts made?

All forecasting involves extrapolating the past to predict the future. Anything else is guessing. The extrapolation may be intuitive and may also be either direct or indirect. In direct sales forecasting a series of past sales data is extrapolated into the future, whilst for indirect extrapolation other parameters from which future sales can be calculated are extrapolated.

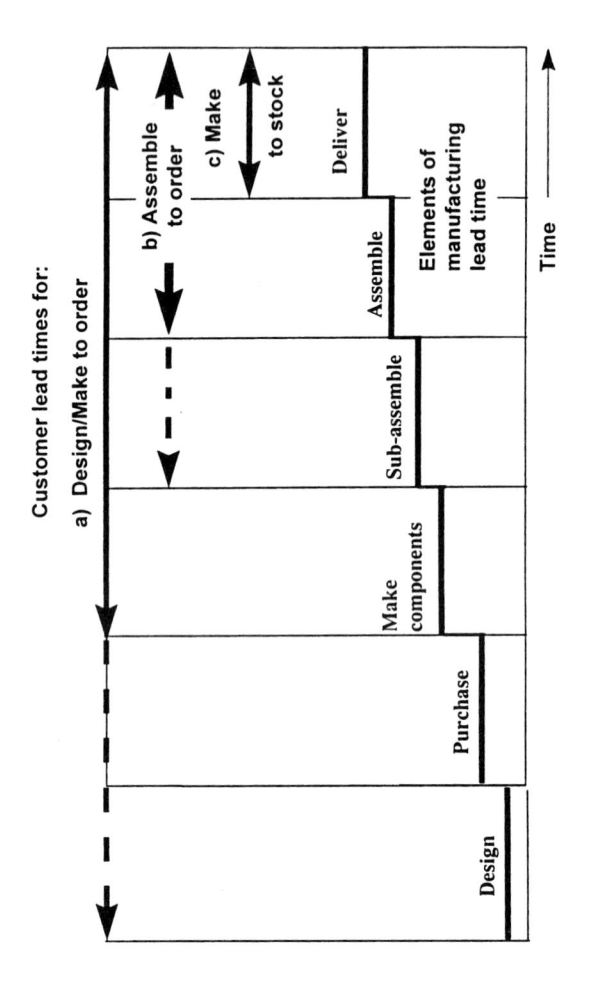

8.1 Relationship between customer and manufacturing lead times.

FORECASTING AND DISTRIBUTION REQUIREMENTS PLANNING 111

8.1.1 Indirect extrapolation

A sales forecast for a new medicine with no previous sales could be made by estimating the number of potential sufferers from the disease which the medicine treats, using the history of similar drugs to indicate the percentage of sufferers likely to be treated in the first quarter, second quarter and so on. Demand for a spare part for a household electrical appliance could be calculated from a knowledge of how many appliances had already been sold plus those expected to be sold and information about the distribution of service life before failure for the part.

Allowance must also be made for the distribution pipeline filling effect, as wholesalers and retailers build up stocks. Ex-factory sales will be greater than retail sales for a growing product. Again, past history from similar products can provide a guide.

8.1.2 Direct extrapolation

A simple but effective way of carrying out a direct extrapolation of past sales data is to plot the points on a graph, draw the curve of best fit by eye and extend the curve into the future, making use of market intelligence such as the imminent launch of a competitive product or a planned sales promotion. However, apart from having a low-tech image, manual extrapolation is not practical if there are large numbers of items to be forecast. Sophisticated computer packages are now available which test a dozen or more different mathematical algorithms by fitting each in turn to the actual sales data for the medium distant past (e.g. months -13 to -24) and predicting sales for the recent past (e.g. months -1 to -12), for which the actual sales information is known. The algorithm which is most successful is then used to calculate forecasts for the future. The operator can intervene if necessary to take account of special factors such as promotions, legislation or changes in the competition.

These systems have an excellent record of success in the right environment. One test showed that a student with a personal computer forecasting package outperformed a whole sales department which was forecasting by manual methods. A side benefit may be that the novelty and attractiveness encourages those in sales who regard forecasting as a painful imposition to take it seriously.

8.2 How far ahead should forecasts go?

The conventional answer to the question of how far ahead forecasts should go is as far ahead as the cumulative lead time, plus the planning time.

Thus, in a Make to Stock environment, the forecasts must cover the total production and purchasing lead time plus the time until the next set of forecasts has been collected and processed. This, however, ignores the need to predict the requirement for buildings and plant. A new factory may take three or four years to plan and build, and this does not allow for the time taken by senior management to believe the forecast. There is a natural tendency when faced with an important decision based on a forecast, to wait and see how the sales figures for the next month or year support the forecast. The implication that all forecasts should cover the next four or five years is however clearly suspect. Few companies will carry out long term planning for plant and buildings more than once per year, but forecasts controlling short term production need to be updated at least quarterly and preferably monthly or more frequently. Revising the long term forecasts monthly is a waste of effort.

One solution is to have two forecasting systems, a short term one to drive production, covering, typically, 12 months ahead with time periods of weeks or months, and a long term one with time periods of years. To provide useful financial as well as volume information, the long term system should include a forecast of an average selling price for each item for each year. Since detail is not required for long term planning, this system can operate at product family level, which makes the task of revising the forecasts very much easier.

However, such a solution is not without problems. The author remembers well how, having carefully developed a capacity plan based on the latest long term forecasts, he was explaining proudly to production management how they could accommodate the growth in output from the current forecast of two million units per year to 2.5 million in year two, only to be told that they had been operating at 2.6 million per year for the last six months. Further investigation showed that the short term forecasts, which were in volume units only, were completely out of step with the long term system, which covered volume and value and was used to set annual sales budgets as well as for capacity planning. Not surprisingly the salesmen liked to forecast conservatively in the long term so that they had achievable budgets, but high in the short term so that there was little danger of their products running out of stock. Needless to say, the production function, not the sales department, was accountable for stock levels in that company.

There is in principle no problem in having a sales forecasting system which operates at the detailed end-item level in the short term, and at an aggregated family level in the long term, with the first periods of the long term forecast being calculated by summing the short term forecasts for the

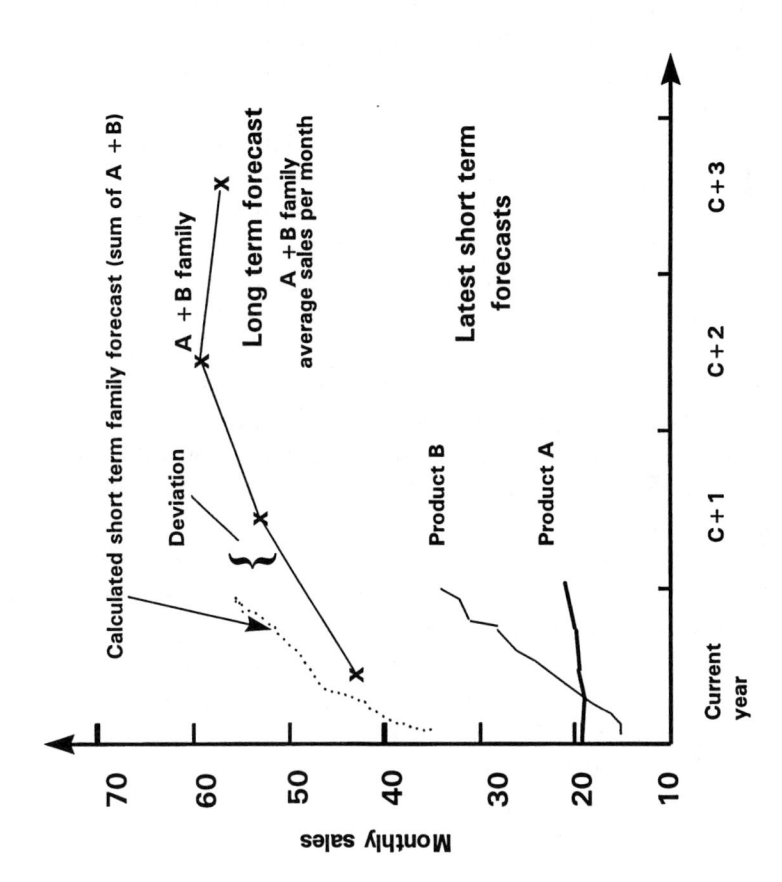

FORECASTING AND DISTRIBUTION REQUIREMENTS PLANNING 113

8.2 Forecast reconciliation.

items in the family. The short term forecast required for planning production can then be revised as often as necessary, and a warning generated if the calculated short term family forecast deviates by more than a specified percentage from the trend set previously by the long term figures. This situation is shown in Fig. 8.2 for a simplified family with only two members, product A and product B. However, until such systems are commonplace, there is little alternative to spending time and effort reconciling different systems serving different purposes.

8.3 Accuracy of forecasts

An oft-quoted expression is that the only thing that is certain about a forecast is that it will be wrong. Unfortunately this also is not always accurate, because just occasionally forecasts can be right. The accuracy to be expected from a forecast depends on the situation. A well established product selling regularly to many different customers in the home market is relatively easy to forecast, because reliable information is available and variations caused by individual customers tend to even out. Figures 8.3 and 8.4 show data from a real example of such a case. Product C, shown in Fig. 8.3 is an excellent example of a product and a market suitable for mathematical prediction. In general the fit between forecast and actual demand is very good. The worst fit is in January, during which demand was almost 40% below forecast, probably because the forecaster took insufficient account of post-Christmas stupor. If this phenomenon repeats each year, it is a prime case for manual intervention.

In contrast, a product sold to only one agent in a Third World country may be almost impossible to forecast, because even if the agent has an effective stock control system, he may only order infrequently and the timing of orders may depend more on the availability of foreign exchange than on demand for the product. (See Fig. 8.4 for Product D, an example of such a situation. Product D differs from Product C in Fig. 8.3 only in the labelling.)

It is almost a tradition for production planners to complain about the accuracy of sales departments' forecasts. Certainly forecasts should be as accurate as possible. There is no excuse for not trying or leaving a secretary to make the forecast, but the key requirement of a forecast is that it should be honest, the best available in the circumstances and not deliberately biased to influence targets or stock levels. The accuracy illustrated in Fig. 8.4 may be the best possible in the circumstances.

Several things can be done to improve forecast accuracy. Firstly, the person responsible for the forecast should have ready access to accurate

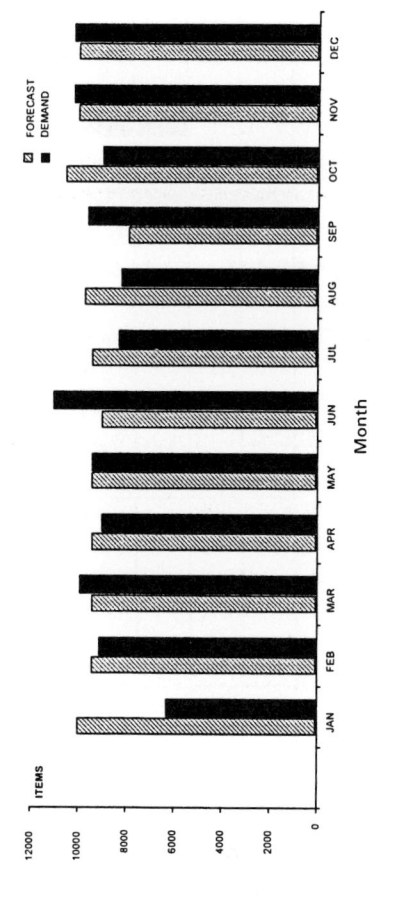

8.3 Demand versus forecast: UK market.

8.4 Demand versus forecast: Third World market.

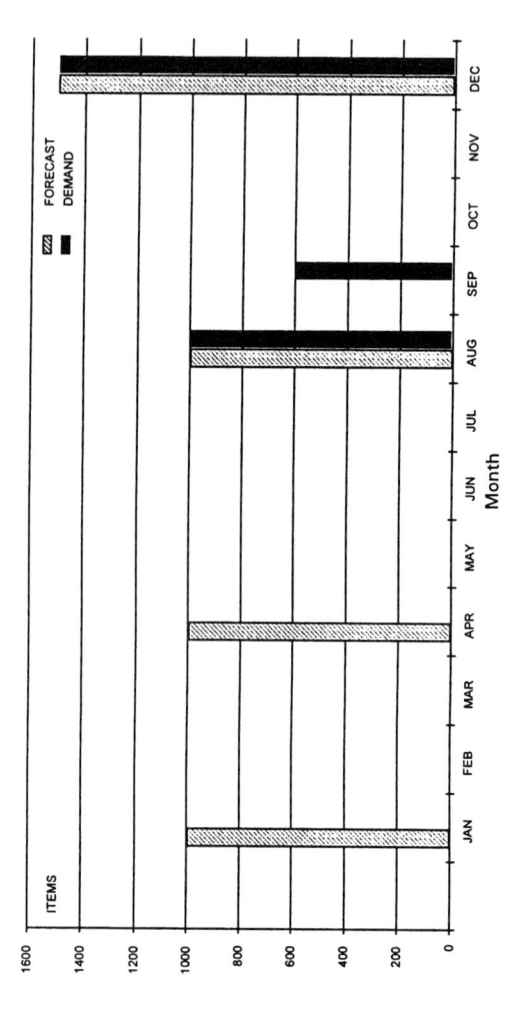

data on past demand. Demand is defined as orders received. This is a better basis for forecasting future demand than past sales from the accounting system, which usually will be invoiced sales and may be less than demand if the product has been in short supply, and normally will be dated considerably later than the date on which the customer's order was received.

In order to achieve maximum commitment to forecasting, the accuracy statistics must be displayed to senior management in summary form. In one case known to the author, publication of summary statistics by department brought about a significant improvement in accuracy. Any product for which sales over a three month period were within $\pm 20\%$ of forecast was defined as a 'hit'. The percentage 'hit rate' for each forecaster was displayed to the senior management team. The managers were not swamped with data. They only had to look at one figure per quarter for each forecaster, but the sales manager was so appalled by the figures that he offered a substantial prize, of the sort salesmen normally win by meeting sales targets, for the best improvement over six months. The results were spectacular.

In measuring forecast accuracy, it is important to compare actual sales with the forecast made an agreed lead time in advance. The proud boast that this month sales were within 1% of forecast is not very meaningful if the forecast is the revised figure made just before the sales figures were published.

Conventional wisdom suggests that a forecast should never be a single figure, but should always indicate a range within which the sales are expected to lie. Although one cannot disagree with this principle, in practice a manufacturing order must be for a specific quantity and it is very difficult to handle a range within an automated planning system. Experience suggests that the forecast should be the most probable figure, and uncertainty should be handled by discussion between the planner and the forecaster to agree whether safety stocks of finished goods will be held, components will be bought and capacity will be reserved, etc, or whether the risk of poor customer service is acceptable.

8.4 Making forecasting easier

There are several ways in which forecasting can be made easier and hence probably more accurate.

8.4.1 Lead time reductions

Forecasting is easier for the immediate future than it is for a long time ahead. Anyone who doubts this should look at success records for weather forecasting. Therefore the more manufacturing lead times can be shortened by continuously searching for improvements and moving towards Just-in-Time (JIT) manufacture, the easier forecasting becomes (see Chapter 11, Section 11.2). For some companies this may prove to be one of the major advantages of a JIT programme.

8.4.2 Forecast at family level

As seen in Section 8.2 above, forecasting for a product family takes less effort than forecasting each member of the family separately. Usually also the past actual sales for a family will exhibit a smoother trend than do the sales of individual members of the family. Hence extrapolation of the trend is likely to be more accurate at family level.

Consider a product family with 50 members, of which product D in Fig. 8.4 is one. Demand for some items like product D can be erratic and difficult to forecast. If, however, the past sales for all 50 items in the family are totalled, the situation will approach that shown in Fig. 8.5. The units may no longer be items. In the case of the soft drink family, they may well be litres. The demand curve is much smoother and relatively easy to extrapolate. Provided that there are enough members of the family this will always be the case.

Forecasting at this level will be much more accurate than forecasting individual items, but some information will be lost. The key question is how can such an aggregate forecast be used. If the final manufacturing operation, probably assembly or packing, can be accomplished relatively quickly, and if any items which are specific to the customer's order can be obtained quickly, then it may be possible to plan the manufacture of the generic or basic product against the family forecast and complete the required number of items to a particular specification when the customer's order is received, so that no sales forecast is needed for individual members of the family. The Assemble to Order planning of the Model Z motor car using a planning bill of materials, discussed in Chapter 7, is a case in point.

If finishing to order with an acceptably short lead time is not practicable for any reason, all is not lost. The family forecast can be used as an overall check on the individual pack forecasts, by summing the forecasts for the individual packs and comparing the result with the family

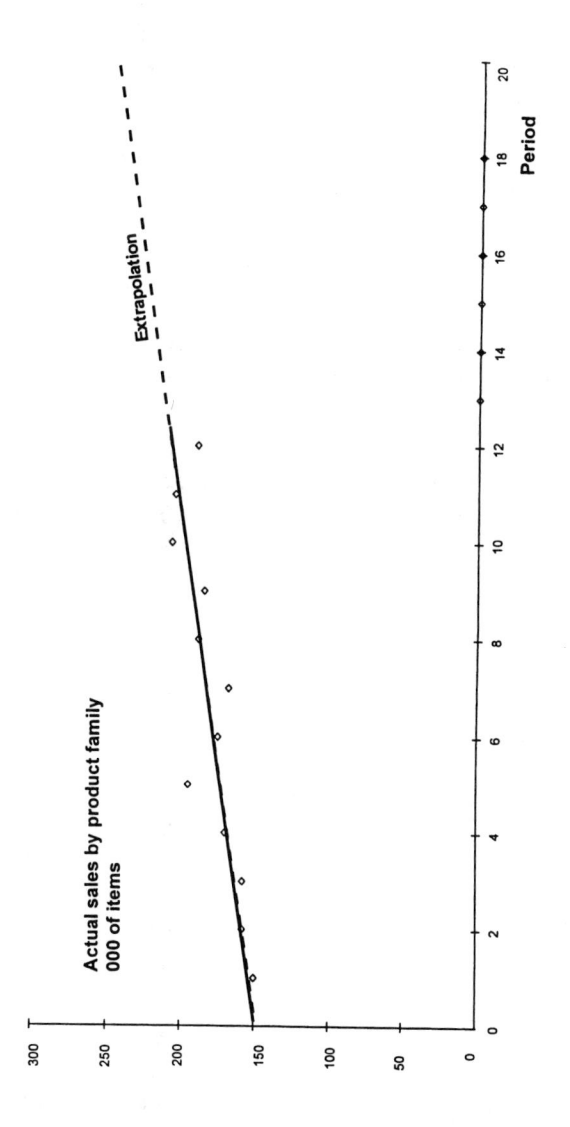

FORECASTING AND DISTRIBUTION REQUIREMENTS PLANNING 119

8.5 Manual extrapolation.

forecast, as illustrated in Fig. 8.2. Agreement does not of course ensure that the individual forecasts are correct. There may be compensating errors, but disagreement certainly means that it is worth re-examining the individual forecasts.

If the forecast is required to support the need for new facilities, a forecast at family level may be all that is required.

8.4.3 Pareto principle

An important step towards making forecasting easier is to take advantage of the Pareto principle, or the 80:20 rule. This is that 20% of the forecasts will cover 80% of the total demand, so care and attention should be focused on the forecasts for these items, with the other 80% being left to the computer.

8.5 Distribution Requirements Planning

A special case of making forecasting easier is a technique known as Distribution Requirements Planning, or in some cases Distribution Resource Planning, which also provides sufficient other advantages for it to be worthy of discussion in its own right.

Figure 8.3 illustrated how total sales to many customers will follow a smoother trend than sales to a single customer, because variations in requirements of individual customers tend to cancel each other. With many products the rate at which the end-users consume the product will be relatively smooth. Most men use roughly the same amount of shaving cream each day and housewives use approximately the same quantity of detergent for washing clothes each week, but the manufacturer can experience wide swings in demand as the various stock points in the distribution chain react to and magnify small changes in the rate of end use. By moving the forecasting point out towards the end-user, forecasting becomes easier because demand is smoother. Taking advantage of this requires visibility of stock levels at all points in the distribution chain. If a forecast of sales to the final users is available, and the stock replenishment policies used at each point in the chain are known, the demands on each stage including the demand on the factory can be calculated. This process is very similar to the MRP process used to calculate requirements on manufacturing stages. Instead of manufacturing orders it generates replenishment or movement orders. By analogy with MRP, the process is called Distribution Requirements Planning (DRP). In effect DRP turns the situation represented by Fig. 8.4 into that of Fig. 8.3. How successful

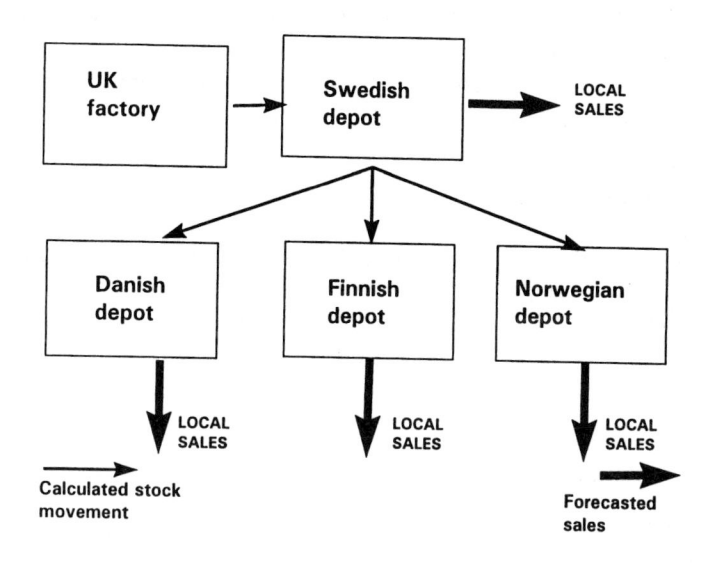

FORECASTING AND DISTRIBUTION REQUIREMENTS PLANNING 121

```
    ┌──────────┐      ┌──────────┐
    │    UK    │ ───▶ │ Swedish  │ ───▶  LOCAL
    │ factory  │      │  depot   │       SALES
    └──────────┘      └──────────┘
                    ↙      ↓      ↘
         ┌────────┐  ┌────────┐  ┌──────────┐
         │ Danish │  │Finnish │  │Norwegian │
         │ depot  │  │ depot  │  │  depot   │
         └────────┘  └────────┘  └──────────┘
              ↓          ↓            ↓
            LOCAL      LOCAL        LOCAL
            SALES      SALES        SALES
```

Calculated stock movement ⟶   Forecasted sales ⟶

8.6 International Distribution Requirements Planning.

this will be depends on the relationship between supplier and customer and the sophistication of systems available to the customer.

The situation illustrated in Fig. 8.6 is based on a real example. A UK factory supplies cosmetic and health care products to a major depot in Sweden, which in turn not only supplies the local market but also smaller depots in Denmark, Finland and Norway. Forecasting was originally aimed at predicting shipments from the UK to Sweden but demand for any one product tended to be lumpy and difficult to forecast. Changing to forecasting local sales in the four territories, and supplying stock figures for the four depots so that DRP logic could be used to calculate the demands on the factory gave significant improvements in control.

The calculations involved are illustrated in Fig. 8.7, which shows data for the hair restorer Hirsuto, which is sold in one pack with a common label in all four markets. The first step is to obtain local (ex-depot) sales forecasts and an opening stock figure for each of the outlying depots. Consider as an example the Danish depot in Fig. 8.7. The local sales forecast is 10 packs per week. Because of the importance of the product, the depot manager holds a safety stock of 20 packs equivalent to two weeks of sales. The stock at the beginning of week 1 is 55 packs. As

Hirsuto pack. Data for Danish depot

| Opening stock | 55 | Order quantity | 40 |
| Safety stock | 20 | Lead time | 1 week |

	Week		1	2	3	4	5	6	7	8	9	10
1	Sales forecast		10	10	10	10	10	10	10	10	10	10
2	Projected stock	55	45	35	25	55	45	35	25	55	45	35
3	Replenishment receipts					40				40		
4	Replenishment dispatches				40				40			

8.7 Distribution Requirements Planning: Danish depot.

shown in Fig. 8.7 this is projected to fall by ten each week until it reaches 15 in week 4. However this is below safety stock so a replenishment quantity must be received no later than the beginning of week 4. The shipping quantity is 40 packs which happens to be one pallet load and it takes one week for goods to be delivered from Sweden. Therefore a pallet of 40 packs must be dispatched from Sweden at the beginning of week 3. Continuing the stock projection shows that a further shipment of 40 packs must arrive by the beginning of week 8, which means that it must be dispatched no later than the beginning of week 7. Similar calculations can be made for shipments from Sweden to Finland and Norway, and from the factory to Sweden. These have been incorporated in Exercise 8.3 and the reader is recommended to do the exercise at this point.

The technique for the DRP calculations in Exercise 8.3 is almost identical with that for the MRP calculations in Chapter 2. The predicted shipments from the UK are far from smooth and would be very difficult to forecast directly from a past history of shipments to Sweden.

Some of the unevenness in demand results from the minimum order quantities of 40 and 80 which were specified. The smaller these quantities, the smoother the load on the central factory but the greater the transport and administration costs.

Modern telecommunications make DRP easy to operate technically, but considerable trust and mutual understanding are required to make it effective. The customer must be prepared to share the stock and sales forecast data with the supplier. A blanket order covering commercial data such as price, specification and terms of trade for, say, a year ahead, looks after the legal niceties, but the customer must be sufficiently trusting to leave timing and quantities of shipments to the supplier. Correspondingly the supplier must act responsibly. Shipping an unjustifiably large order just before the year-end to improve the factory's performance figures, without the agreement of the customer, would be a breach of trust and would erode the relationship needed for DRP. With today's technology, there is no technical reason why the customer should not have a computer terminal with access to the supplier's DRP plans, and proposed shipments can be discussed by telephone before being authorised.

From the forecasting point of view, DRP moves the forecasts down the distribution chain, nearer to the end-users, so that the off-take pattern becomes smoother and easier to forecast accurately than the lumpy ex-factory demand.

8.6 Summary

Forecasting is frequently difficult, and for this reason it is often neglected, but good forecasting can have more effect on customer service and working capital levels than any other single activity. In any organisation which attempts to supply customers from stock, forecasting must be happening somewhere in the organisation. Perhaps it is in effect being left to a junior stock clerk or scheduler, who buys or plans to make what he thinks the business needs, based on a mixture of past experience and intuition. Given the importance of forecasting to any Make to Stock or Assemble to Order business, this cannot be correct. Forecasting requires market intelligence and so must be the responsibility of the sales and marketing function. Senior commercial management must demonstrate that they see it as important by setting up and showing interest in performance reports. The Production Planning Department must also be involved, particularly in discussions about how to handle uncertainty.

The performance expected of forecasters must be related to the difficulty of the task and comparisons must only be made between like situations. In many cases, the absolute value of a performance measure is less important than the trend. It would be nonsensical to compare performance in the home market with performance in forecasting exports to Third World markets but current performance in each market can usefully be compared with previous performance. If improvement is not being demonstrated, questions should be asked.

Traditionally the production function is very scathing about the commercial function's ability to forecast but such attitudes are not

124 PLANNING AND CONTROL OF MANUFACTURING OPERATIONS

helpful. Getting a forecast wrong is not a crime. Not providing the best forecast possible, or manipulating forecasts to influence supply decisions, ought to be.

Exercises

8.1 During trials of a potential anti-cancer treatment, a pharmaceutical product, which was safe but ineffective, was found to have the side effect of promoting hair growth in balding men. Approval has been obtained to launch it as a hair restorer under the name Hirsuto. There have been no previously reliable treatments for baldness, so no direct comparison can be drawn.

You are asked to produce a forecast of ex-manufacturer sales in the UK, for the first year, by quarter.

Market research reveals that 15 million men in the UK suffer from baldness of which two-thirds are sufficiently concerned to be prepared to spend money to alleviate the condition. There is evidence that an effective product well advertised can achieve the following market penetration by quarter:

Quarter 1	Quarter 2	Quarter 3	Quarter 4	Quarter 5
0.1%	0.2%	0.4%	0.8%	1.2%

Once using the product, the patients must continue to do so and one pack lasts for three months.

Past experience suggests that pipeline stocking causes ex-manufacturer sales to be treble the retail sales in the first quarter and thereafter to run three months ahead of retail sales.

Make reasonable assumptions where necessary.

8.2 A new toothpaste, T1, sold in a 150 g tube with a novel cap fitting, was launched very successfully. After the first 12 months the ex-manufacturer sales by month were as follows:

Month	Sales (ex-manufacturer) in tubes 000s
1	9 000
2	11 000
3	10 000
4	14 000
5	13 000
6	22 000
7	21 000
8	31 000
9	29 000
10	34 000
11	34 000
12	43 000

Plot a graph of sales against time, suitable for extrapolating to month 18. Predict sales for month 18 by:

(a) fitting and extrapolating the best straight line by eye;
(b) fitting a freehand curve appropriate for a new product and extrapolating by eye.

8.3 The situations for the Hirsuto pack in the Norwegian and Finnish depots are shown below. Project the stocks forward in each case and determine when shipments must be dispatched from Sweden. Remember the convention that when a receipt is shown in a period it is intended to be available from the beginning of that period.

Hirsuto pack. Data for Norwegian depot

Opening stock	24	Order quantity	40
Safety stock	16	Lead time	1 week

	Week		1	2	3	4	5	6	7	8	9	10
1	Sales forecast		8	8	8	8	8	9	9	9	10	10
2	Projected stock	24										
3	Replenishment receipts											
4	Replenishment dispatches											

Hirsuto pack. Data for Finnish depot

Opening stock   21   Order quantity   40
Safety stock   20   Lead time   1 week

	Week		1	2	3	4	5	6	7	8	9	10
1	Sales forecast		11	11	10	10	10	9	9	10	12	12
2	Projected stock	21										
3	Replenishment receipts		40*									
4	Replenishment dispatches											

*In transit

The figure below shows part of the situation in the main depot in Sweden. The sales forecast for local Swedish sales is shown, as are the requirements for Denmark. Complete the entries for the requirements for Finland and Norway and calculate the total requirement on the Swedish depot from all areas. Use these figures to calculate the shipments required from the UK factory by projecting forward the Swedish stock. The order quantity preferred for shipping across the North Sea from the UK to Sweden is 80 packs (or two pallets). Policy is to keep a safety stock of 100 packs in Sweden.

Hirsuto pack. Data for Swedish depot

Opening stock   216   Order quantity   80
Safety stock   100   Lead time   2 weeks

Week		1	2	3	4	5	6	7	8	9	10
Dispatches to Denmark				40				40			
Dispatches to Norway											
Dispatches to Finland											
Local Swedish sales forecast		25	25	25	25	25	25	25	25	25	25
Total requirements											
Projected stock	216										
Replenishment receipts											
Replenishment dispatches											

8.4 Re-read this chapter and list eight points relating to improving the accuracy of sales forecasting. How many of them are in use in your company or in one which you know well?

9

Capacity planning and short term scheduling

Chapters 2 and 3 demonstrated how MRP is based on material needs, and how the automated parts of the calculation assume that production capacity is always available when required. It was also shown that plans must be realistic with respect to capacity if order due-dates are to be met reliably. This chapter will look at techniques available for planning capacity and show how they relate to production planning and scheduling. Finally, the relevance of lead times to capacity planning will be discussed.

In order to carry out a calculation of the load imposed on a particular resource by a manufacturing order, several key pieces of information are required. These are:

- *Which resource?* i.e. with which piece of equipment, group of machines, person or group of people is the calculation concerned?
- *How much resource is needed?* This has a variable element, the time required to process one unit of product (e.g. one part or one pack) and a fixed element, the set-up or change-over time.
- *When is the resource required?* How this is determined depends on the approach being adopted but it is normally related to the due-date of the manufacturing order utilising the resource.

The two most used forms of capacity planning are Capacity Requirements Planning (CRP) which looks at capacity in detail but because of computing time limitations has traditionally only been used typically to look up to six months ahead, and Rough Cut Capacity Planning (RCCP) which, as its name implies, is rather rough and ready but simple and quick to use. RCCP is typically used to look from a few months to several years ahead.

Each will be examined in turn.

Table 9.1 Routing for W1, paper clip wire   (units = kg)

Operation number	Work centre	Description	Change-over time (hours)	Run time (hours per unit)
10	HD01	Heavy draw	6	0.0012
20	FD07	Final draw	4	0.004
30	PLT02	Plating bath	4	0.0025

9.1 Capacity Requirements Planning

The data required for CRP are normally held in two places. The first is the **Work Centre File** which contains information about the resources which are to be planned. This information normally relates only to the resource, not to the product involved.

The second is the **Routing File**, which for a particular product specifies the operations and the associated resources required to make the product from the ingredients in its bill of materials.

CRP will be illustrated by reference to the manufacture of paper clip wire, item number W1 (a purchased item for the paper clip factory used as an example in Chapter 6). For the purposes of this chapter the manufacturing process for the bulk wire, W1, will be simplified and assumed to have only three significant stages. These are:

1 Heavy drawing, which takes place on the HD machines.
2 Final drawing, which takes place on the FD machines.
3 Plating, which takes place in the PLT02 bath.

The purchased starting material is steel rod of 18 mm diameter which is cold drawn down to a diameter of 8 mm in the first operation on the HD machines. In the second operation the 8 mm wire is drawn to 0.8 mm diameter on the FD machines. The third operation is chemical plating with a nickel alloy, which is achieved by passing the 0.8 mm wire through a chemical plating bath, identified as PLT02.

A routing for W1 is shown in Table 9.1. This assumes that the paper clip wire is made with a single manufacturing order, and that the bill of materials shows 18 mm steel rod as the only raw material required. It is convenient to number the operations 10, 20, 30, etc instead of 1, 2, 3 so that new operations can be inserted without renumbering.

Although the wire runs continuously through each machine, the capacity planning logic is exactly the same as if individual items were being machined, drilled, etc. The run time is expressed as hours per unit. The unit is kilograms in one case and items in the other.

Table 9.2 Work centre records

Resource units (hours)	HD01, heavy draw	FD07, final draw	PLT02, plating bath
Move time	4	4	4
Wait time	0	0	0
Average queue time	6	8	16
Productivity factor	0.9	0.9	0.9

Table 9.2 shows entries on the Work Centre File for the three work centres.

Resource units are the units in which the load and capacity on this work centre are specified – in this case hours. The move time is the typical time required to move an order to the next work centre or in the case of the final operation to the finished goods stores, and the wait time is the time for which a job must wait after the operation before being moved. In some industries this represents paint drying or cooling-off time but will be zero for all operations for wire W1. In a well laid out factory, move times should be negligible but for the purposes of illustration a move time of four hours will be assumed for every movement between work centres or into the stores. The average queue time specifies how much work on average should be queuing in front of the work centre. As will be seen later, this is one of the most important control parameters. A queue may be needed to even out work flow and to protect a heavily occupied machine from running short of work should delays occur at earlier stages but too long a queue increases lead times and increases work in progress unnecessarily.

The **productivity factor** specifies how much output measured in standard hours is achieved for each clock hour for which the resource is intended to work. Differences between the two may result from errors in the standard rates used for planning or from machine breakdowns, shortages of materials, shortage of labour, unauthorised extension to meal breaks, etc. Planned idle time, for which no work is planned because it is not required, is not counted as lost time.

The productivity factor can be split into two components, **efficiency** and **utilisation**.

Efficiency indicates how much output, measured in standard hours, is achieved for each hour for which the equipment actually runs:

Efficiency = standard hours earned/actual running hours

Efficiency will be less than 1.0 if the equipment runs more slowly than the standard rate or if there is more than the normal incidence of minor stoppages which are too short to record separately.

Utilisation indicates how many hours of running are actually achieved for each hour for which the resource is intended to run:

$$\text{Utilisation} = \text{actual running hours}/\text{clock hours elapsed}$$

$$\begin{aligned}\text{Productivity factor} &= \text{efficiency} \times \text{utilisation} \\ &= \frac{\text{standard hours earned} \times \text{actual running hours}}{\text{actual running hours} \times \text{clock hours elapsed}} \\ &= \frac{\text{standard hours earned}}{\text{clock hours elapsed}}\end{aligned}$$

Measuring efficiency and utilisation separately may be necessary for purposes of operations research and other performance improvement activities but this involves recording and analysing a considerable volume of data. For capacity planning purposes, utilisation and efficiency can be combined into their product – the productivity factor – which can be determined empirically by analysing past performance of standard hours achieved versus clock hours occupied.

The CRP system explodes each manufacturing order through its routing, rather like MRP did with its bill of materials. The run time per unit is multiplied by the order quantity to determine the total run time on each resource. These times are stored on a scheduled operations file. Scheduled operations can be attached to a firm planned manufacturing order in the same way as materials requirements. Operation details attached to a firm planned order can be changed manually and will not be changed back to the routing values by a subsequent run of CRP. For a planned order, scheduled operations are recalculated from the latest version of the routing each time CRP is run.

The key questions, *Which resource?* and *How much resource is needed?* have now been answered.

The third question, *When is the resource required?* is usually answered by a process known as back scheduling. This is illustrated in Fig. 9.1 which refers to a manufacturing order no 123 for 3000 kg of W1, the nickel coated steel wire described above. The calculation will also use data from Tables 9.1 and 9.2. The normal working day runs from 08.00 hours to 16.00 hours.

The starting point is the final order due-date. Assume that it is day 200 on the works calendar. If the wire is to be available for shipment during day 200, it must be delivered to the finished goods store before the end of

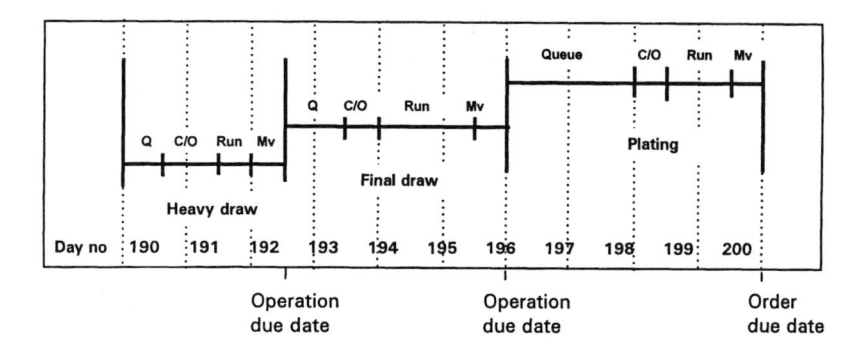

CAPACITY PLANNING AND SHORT TERM SCHEDULING   131

9.1 Schedule for manufacturing order no 123 for 3000 kg of wire, W1.

day 199. With zero wait time, but a move time of four hours, the latest time for finishing the plating operation is 12.00 noon on day 199.

Exploding the order through the routing shows that 3000 kg require 3000 × 0.0025 hours in plating. That is 7.5 standard hours. For simplicity, the productivity factor will be taken as 0.9 for all work centres.

Thus the standard hours available per day are 8 × 0.9 = 7.2, assuming single shift working. The 7.5 standard hours for plating can be rounded to one day, so the latest time to start plating is noon on day 198. Changeover, taking four hours, must be complete by this time, so the latest start time for change-over is the beginning of day 198. However, a 16 hour or two day queue has been specified. Thus the work should be available to plating two days before the latest start time for change-over, that is by the end of day 195, which becomes the operation due-date for final drawing. Provided that the final drawing operation achieves its due-date, the plating supervisor can choose to start the change-over any time on days 196 and 197 and still expect to meet his due-date.

The process can now be repeated for final drawing, working to the latest operation due-date of the end of day 195, and can be continued until earliest and latest start dates for heavy drawing have been calculated. The dates are stored in the scheduled operations file which, for this manufacturing order no 123, is illustrated in Table 9.3. In some systems, shop calendar dates are converted into Gregorian dates, with allowances for non-working days, before display.

In many companies, attempting to define operation dates to the nearest quarter of a day would be seen as attempting false precision, and it is normal to define dates only to the nearest day, as has been done in Table 9.3.

Table 9.3 Scheduled operations for manufacturing order no 123

Operation	Work centre	Description	Change-over (hours)	Run, (hours)	Earliest start	Latest start	Operation due
10	HD01	Heavy draw	6	3.6	190	190	192
20	FD07	Final draw	4	12	192	193	196
30	PLT02	Plating bath 2	4	7.5	196	198	200

When all the manufacturing orders have been exploded, the scheduled operations can be sorted by work centre and totalled to give the number of standard hours required each day or more probably each week, from each work centre. An assumption must be made about which start date is taken as the basis of the back scheduling calculations, but it does not matter whether it is earliest, latest, or a probable start date half way between earliest and latest, as long as the assumption is consistent for all operations. Aggregating the requirements in any planning period gives the total load in the period. The results can be conveniently plotted as a histogram, as in Fig. 9.2. The units are standard hours. The 100% figure is determined by multiplying the number of clock hours in the period by the productivity factor. In this example the work centre is overloaded initially but under-loaded from week 8 onwards.

The CRP system displays overloads to the planner. It can also display details of the individual orders making up the overload but it makes no direct contribution to resolving the problem. Because CRP plans an operation when it is needed, irrespective of capacity, it is sometimes called an Infinite Capacity Scheduling System, i.e. it schedules jobs as though capacity is infinite. Another way of putting this is that it takes no account of scheduling interference. CRP would show a week (five days) containing four jobs each of one day duration as 80% loaded even if all four jobs had to be completed on the Monday. The queuing allowance at each operation is the key to resolving such scheduling conflict. The flexibility which the queue provides permits the supervisor of a work centre to adjust the actual start dates to devise a workable schedule and still meet the operation due-dates.

If all the scheduled operations on file are sorted by supervisor (or foreman, depending on the terminology used), and operations due for completion in the next few days or weeks are printed daily, this provides each supervisor with a Work-To List, sometimes called a Dispatch List, from which a practicable schedule can be devised. This should aim to meet all operation due-dates and provided that the planner has resolved overload problems, and there is adequate queuing allowance, this should always be feasible.

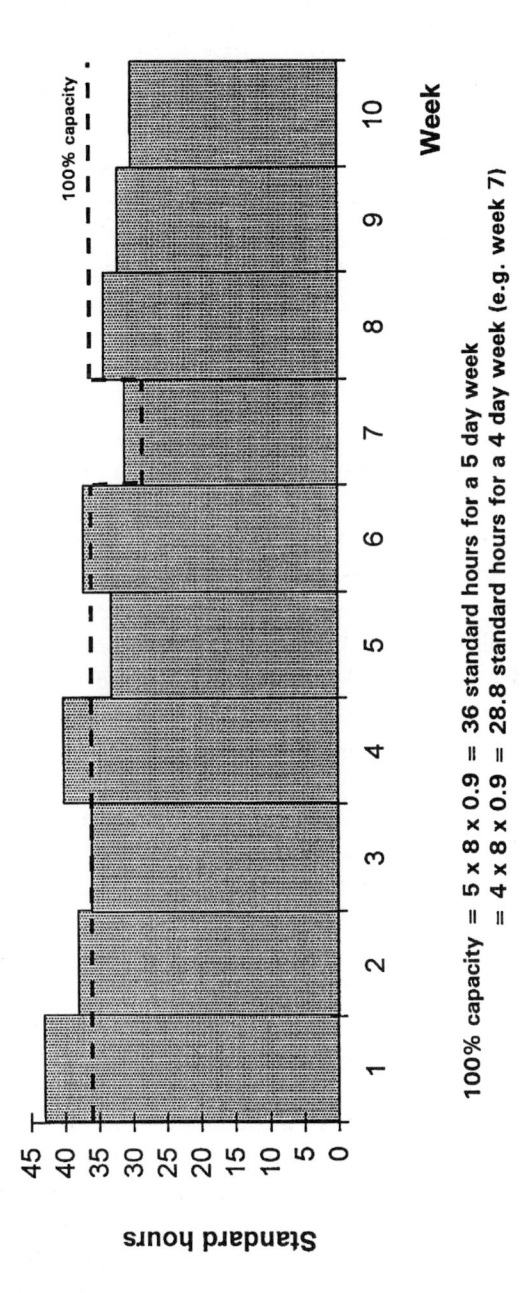

CAPACITY PLANNING AND SHORT TERM SCHEDULING 133

9.2 Load profile for work centre PLT02, plating bath no 2.

100% capacity = 5 × 8 × 0.9 = 36 standard hours for a 5 day week
= 4 × 8 × 0.9 = 28.8 standard hours for a 4 day week (e.g. week 7)

CRP and the associated shop floor control systems are very detailed. They cover every resource on the routings being considered and, provided that production achieved has been reported to the system, will allow for partially or fully completed operations on an order. The accuracy of CRP depends on a vast bank of detailed data being accurately maintained.

In the past, computer power limitations prevented CRP from being used for a horizon much longer than six months. A run with a 12 month horizon for a large company could take most of a weekend but with the power of currently available computers this is no longer a limitation and the effects of changes to a single order can be calculated on-line.

9.2 Rough Cut Capacity Planning

As we have seen, CRP is very detailed and time consuming and in many MRPII systems a major revision to the capacity plan requires a batch run on the computer, often run overnight. Master production schedulers need a quick way of assessing the feasibility of any proposed changes to the plan and RCCP was developed for this purpose. As its name implies it is rough and ready. Unlike CRP which must have data for every operation on the routing, RCCP considers critical resources only. If a resource is normally only 40% occupied it is unlikely to be over-occupied in the near future unless the pattern of demand changes significantly.

Rough Cut Capacity Planning answers the question *How much resource is needed?* by specifying the change-over time and run time per unit exactly as for CRP. However, the question *When is the resource required?* is answered by specifying an **off-set time** which indicates how long on average before the order due-date the resource is required, and a **spread time** to indicate over how many days the required amount of resource is spread. In some systems, the spread time is not adjustable and defaults to 1.

There is no requirement that the resource concerned should be on the real routing for the order. A simplified or **representative routing** is created to hold the necessary data. RCCP is usually applied only to MPS orders, but can cover any resource.

If, for example, the critical resources in the manufacture of wire W1, are the final drawing machines and the laboratory facilities used to analyse a sample from each batch of rod delivered from the steel supplier, a representative routing for W1 would be as in Table 9.4.

Table 9.4 Representative routing for W1, paper clip wire

Resource	Description	Change-over (hours)	Run/unit (hours)	Off-set (days)	Spread (days)
QC01	Test lab.	0	0.001	25	1
FD07	Final draw	2	0.05	10	3

Including the testing laboratory on the representative routing does not imply that the rod used on each manufacturing order is analysed as an entity. What the routing means is that on average each kilogram of plated wire is made from rod, received and analysed 25 days before plating, that 0.001 hours of analysis are required per kilogram and that the analytical work typically is spread over a single day. A manufacturing order for 1000 kg of wire should require $0.001 \times 1000 = 1$ hour of laboratory time.

Likewise final drawing takes place on average ten days before plating is complete and 1 kg of wire takes 0.05 hours of final drawing time.

If the company supplies the same size of wire with several different coatings, there would have to be separate manufacturing orders for each type of plated wire. Each order could cover the three operations of plating, final drawing and heavy drawing, as in the above example for W1. Each wire would have its own representative routing, which would be exactly the same as that for W1 since the operations on the critical resources are identical. The change-over time on the representative routing should be the normal average change-over time for a final drawing machine. However, the planners might choose to have separate orders for plating each wire type but a consolidated order for final drawn wire, producing sufficient 0.8 mm wire to cover the needs of several plating orders. RCCP would only be applied to the orders for finished coated wire. Their representative routings would cover the critical resources of final drawing and the testing laboratory as before, even though these are not operations on the real routings for the coated wires. In this case there will be one change-over on the final drawing machine for each wire drawing order, not for each plating order. The change-over time for a final drawing machine on each representative routing must be the fraction of the real change-over time allocated to each plating order. (Representative change-over time = actual change-over time × [normal plating order size/normal wire drawing order size])

Rough Cut Capacity Planning is accurately named, and many approximations have to be made in deriving representative routings. It is advisable to calibrate the data by calculating the resource required for past production and comparing it with the amount of resource actually

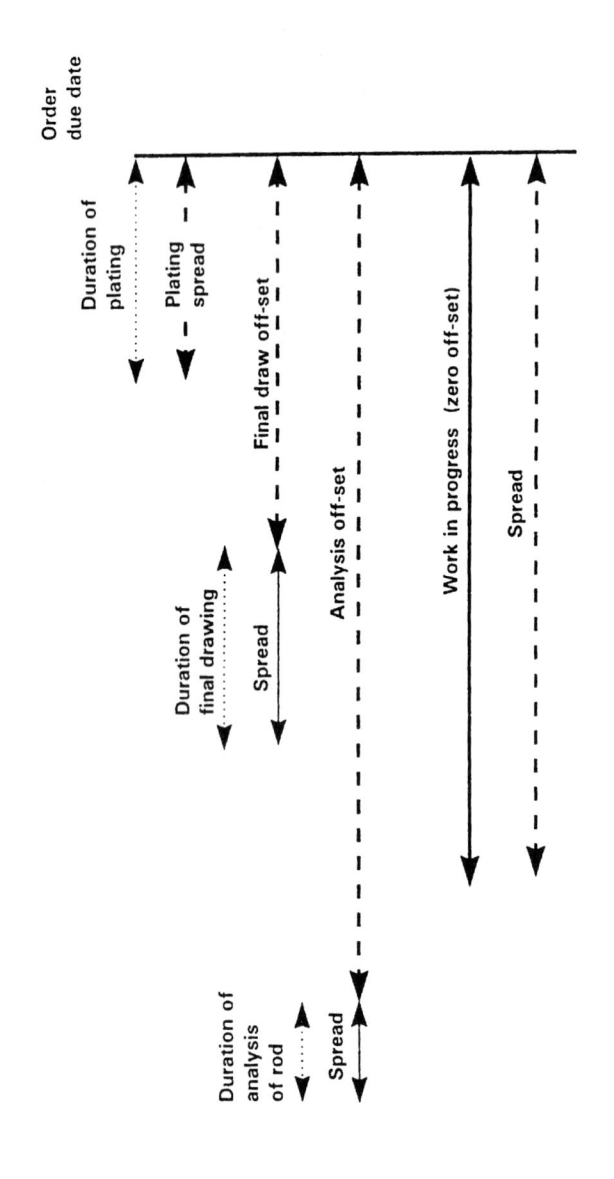

9.3 Examples of off-set and spread times.

used. Predictions will only make sense if averaged over relatively long time periods such as months, and since RCCP cannot take account of part completed orders, it does not give accurate predictions for the very short term. It is most useful for capacity planning over the medium and long term futures, for example from 3 to 36 months ahead.

By creating the appropriate representative routings, RCCP can be used to predict requirements for resources such as warehouse space or cost of work in progress. It is for such predictions that the spread factor is most useful. Figure 9.3 illustrates examples of the relationships between some typical off-set and spread times. For work in progress estimates in the wire drawing company, it would be necessary to estimate the spread as the average time between the issue of a particular batch of rod to heavy drawing and the emergence of that same batch as finished plated wire. Run time per unit would be the average standard cost of 1 kg of steel over the period from heavy draw to plating.

Although RCCP can require the acceptance of some wild assumptions, in many situations the roughness of RCCP is compensated for by flexibility and in practice it proves to be a useful tool, particularly if as is the case in many companies, the real choice is between RCCP or no capacity planning at all.

9.3 Short term scheduling

Section 9.2 explained how the scheduled operations file can be sorted to produce a Work-To List for each supervisor. There are two fundamentally different ways of operating with a Work-To List. These will be described under the titles 'Full Shop Floor Control' and 'Partial Shop Floor Control'.

9.3.1 Full Shop Floor Control

In the Full Shop Floor Control approach, back scheduling, as described in Section 9.1 is applied to all orders and operations. The operation due-date and earliest and latest start dates are calculated for each operation and kept up to date. The Work-To List shows both operations which have already arrived at the work centre and those that are planned to arrive within a specified time horizon, typically set at one to two weeks. Each order is tracked through each operation and the scheduled operations file is updated on-line or at least daily. The Work-To List does not specify the sequence in which the jobs should be tackled. This is left to the supervisor, whose primary objective is to meet as many operation due-dates as possible. Provided that this is achieved, the supervisor has freedom to adjust the sequence of jobs in order to meet secondary local objectives such as minimising total change-over time, or making best use of the individual skills of the operators.

Of course actual production rarely follows even the most carefully prepared schedule. Production rates may vary from standard, equipment may break down, purchased items may be late or manufactured items may not meet the quality specifications. Any of these events happening at a work centre can disrupt the schedule not only for that work centre but also for downstream work centres. In companies operating Full Shop Floor Control, it is common practice for supervisors and a representative of Production Control to meet early in the day, shortly after the updated Work-To Lists have been issued, to discuss any potential problems. In APICS terminology this is called a Dispatch Meeting. If the problems can be resolved by co-operation between supervisors without putting the final order due-date at risk, there is no need formally to report the problem to the production planners but if the delays cannot be recovered and the order due-date will not be met, the problem must be reported. In a small company, reporting can be informal. The planner concerned may be the same person as the production control representative attending the dispatch meeting, but in larger companies a formal document or e-mail message must be issued. This is usually called an Anticipated Delay Report or ADR. On receipt of the ADR, the planners do their best to solve the problem, for example by delaying a less important job, using an alternative resource, sub-contracting, etc. If all else fails, they must notify the sales department or the customer with a revised promise date. As in other areas of MRPII, the concept of 'silence means approval' applies to shop floor control. In the absence of an ADR, everyone else must be able to assume that orders will be completed by their due-dates.

Full Shop Floor Control can work extremely effectively but it is dependent on a large volume of data being adequately maintained and agreed procedures being followed. Plans must be kept realistic with respect to capacity and all planned operation due-dates and start dates must be kept valid, with no unstarted jobs scheduled to start in the past. If an order due-date is not going to be met, an ADR must be issued.

Working to these standards can be difficult, particularly if there are many products following diverse routes through many work centres. If several work centres are operating at or near full capacity, making a change to the dates on one order may cause overloads elsewhere. Resolving these can cause more problems and so on.

9.3.2 Partial Shop Floor Control

In a very large or complex company, the task of keeping the scheduled operations file up to date, and keeping all plans valid at a detailed operation level, can be beyond the capability of the available resources, particularly if such detailed control and anticipated delay reporting have not previously been part of the company culture. In such cases, Partial Shop Floor Control will be easier to introduce and operate than Full Shop Floor Control.

In a Partial Shop Floor Control environment, manufacturing orders are planned in the normal way. Although a routing must exist to define the operations needed to fulfil the order, no attempt is made to plan start dates or due-dates for individual operations, except possibly for capacity planning purposes. The key dates for each order are the order due-date and the order release date. The release date is calculated as in MRP by subtracting the planned lead time from the order due-date.

Orders are released on the planned date and progress through the plant is monitored by recording the completion of each operation. Provided that move times between operations are relatively short, this provides sufficient information to calculate which orders are at which work centre. If move times are significantly long, it becomes necessary to record both the completion of the operation at one work centre and the arrival of the job at the next. There is insufficient information in the planning system to show whether an order at a work centre is in the queue in front of the work centre or being worked on. Only those orders which are physically at a work centre appear on the Work-To List for that work centre. There are no planned operation due-dates, but a priority index is calculated for each order and the list is printed in priority order, usually with the priority index printed alongside each order. The priorities are re-calculated each time the list is displayed or printed. When the supervisor has to release a job to an operator, he releases the one at the top of the list, that is, the one with the highest priority index. When an operation is reported as complete, it is deleted from the Work-To List for that work centre, but appears on the list for the next work centre.

Partial Shop Floor Control requires some rule or formula for calculating priorities for each operation. Many suggestions have been tried and each has its adherents.

Examples of some of the most popular priority rules are:

- *Critical ratio:*

$$\text{Priority} = \frac{\text{Work to be done}}{\text{Time remaining}}$$

The work to be done includes change-over and run times for each remaining operation on the order. The time remaining is the time from now until the final order due-date. If the ratio is greater than 1, the order must be expected to be late, unless corrective action can be taken.
- *Maximum expected lateness.* The expected completion date for the order is calculated by forward scheduling from the present, taking account of all queuing, change-over, run, wait and move times which have not been reported as complete. The expected lateness for an order is the amount by which the expected completion date exceeds the order due-date. The latest order has highest priority.
- *Least slack per remaining operation.* The work to be done is subtracted from the time remaining (both defined as in critical ratio) and the difference (or slack) is divided by the number of operations still to be completed. The job with the least slack per remaining operation has the highest priority.

Unfortunately all rules do not give the same answer and there is no simple way of determining which rule is best in which situation.

In some Full Shop Floor Control systems, priority indices calculated according to one of these rules are used to print the Work-To List in decreasing priority order, with the index printed alongside each operation. It can be argued however that this negates one of the major advantages of the Full Shop Floor Control approach, where the emphasis should be on meeting operation due-dates, with the supervisor free to determine the schedule if there is good reason to do so, provided of course that operations are completed by the required dates. For example, the suggested sequence might be changed in order to meet some local objective such as reducing the total time spent on set-up, or to make best use of operators with special skills, objectives which are not considered by most mathematically based priority rules.

9.3.3 *Summary on Full and Partial Shop Floor Control*

Partial Shop Floor Control is much easier to operate than Full Shop Floor Control but a disadvantage is that it is difficult to see when an order part way through the system is running late, and opportunities for corrective action may be missed. Choosing between Full or Partial Shop Floor Control involves a trade-off between ease of operation and success in delivering orders on time. If both approaches are operated correctly, full control will undoubtedly yield the best on-time performance but it is notoriously difficult to operate well. Partial control operated correctly can

CAPACITY PLANNING AND SHORT TERM SCHEDULING   141

significantly out-perform full control operated badly. Even if the final objective is to operate Full Shop Floor Control, little is lost by implementing partial control first. It does not preclude moving on to full control at some later date, and meanwhile the experience gained will have increased the chance of implementing full control successfully.

9.4 Finite planning and scheduling systems

In Section 9.1, CRP was described as an infinite capacity planning system because it plans each job on the required date, even if insufficient capacity is available. A CRP system reports overloads but leaves the solution of the problem to the planner. Systems which take account of capacity and only schedule operations when the necessary resource is available are called **Finite Capacity Systems** or sometimes just **Finite Systems**.

The terms infinite capacity planning or infinite capacity scheduling are in common use but are in fact contradictions in terms. What is the value of a plan which cannot be carried out because the capacity requirements are unrealistic? An important part of operating CRP is the resolution of overload problems by the human planner. CRP software is correctly described as an infinite capacity planning system, but it is not designed to stand alone. The combination of CRP software and the competent human planner should definitely be a Finite Capacity System. However, for the remainder of this section common usage will be followed and the adjectives infinite and finite will be assumed to apply to the automated parts of the system. In this context, the Work-To List in a Partial Shop Floor Control system is best described as a finite scheduling system, since it specifies clearly the order in which jobs must be tackled and there is no scheduling interference. Calculation of planned operation due-dates is only a matter of arithmetic. No further decisions are required.

In contrast, the Work-To List in Full Shop Floor Control when first printed is not a full finite schedule, since the supervisor has some freedom to choose the preferred sequence but once the sequence has been determined, calculating operation due-dates is again only a matter of arithmetic.

9.5 Automated finite planning and scheduling

Manual finite planning and scheduling can be difficult and tedious operations, particularly if there is little spare capacity, and circumstances force changes onto the schedule almost before it is complete. Eliminating an overload in one area may well create one in another. Unfortunately in

Standard CRP - infinite

Backward pass

All orders on time

Potential overloads

↓

Finite capacity planning

Forward - simulation

No overloads

Some orders delayed

↓

MANUAL INTERVENTION

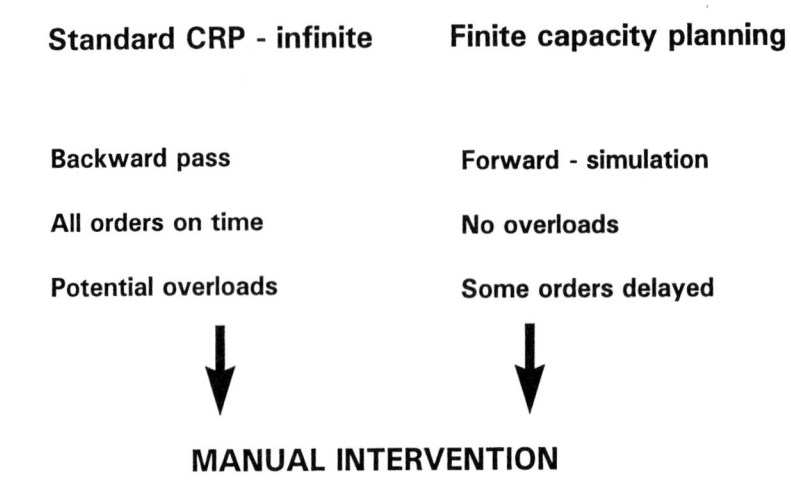

9.4 Finite versus infinite planning.

many companies the philosophy is that if an order is needed, plan it for its need date even if this causes a serious overload. Perhaps a miracle will happen and all the jobs will get done. Capacity planning and scheduling are either done badly or not at all. However, as demonstrated in Chapter 3, miracles rarely happen and this approach results in late deliveries and high levels of work in progress. The search for an easy solution to these problems has led to a growing interest in automated finite scheduling systems and many commercial packages are now available. Partial Shop Floor Control which, as described in Section 9.3, sequences jobs according to a calculated priority index, is one of the simpler techniques. Many other approaches are in use to allocate jobs to the appropriate resource and to determine a sequence for production. A common characteristic is that any potential overload is pushed out into the future, even if this means that due-dates are not met. If the scheduled dates are not acceptable, manual intervention is needed to solve the problems. This contrasts with CRP in which due-dates are met but manual intervention is needed to resolve overloads (see Fig. 9.4).

The more sophisticated finite capacity schedulers use a matrix of change-over times and products so that the change-over time can take account of both the preceding and current product.

9.6 Categorisation of finite capacity planning and scheduling systems

Figure 9.5 illustrates the range of approaches to finite capacity planning and scheduling. Most of the available systems are not designed to handle material and capacity planning simultaneously. A major distinction is between materials-led and capacity-led approaches, but there are a few relatively new systems adopting an integrated approach in which materials and capacity are planned simultaneously. The materials-led approaches are all based on MRP which first works out the materials requirements, followed by capacity planning if needed. Some form of 'post MRP' scheduling is then applied. This is the preferred approach in businesses with large numbers of parts or materials to be planned, particularly if some purchased items are on long lead times.

Each of the production control approaches shown in Fig. 9.5 will be considered in turn.

9.6.1 Materials-led categories

The **MRP plus expediting** approach is the simplest, but not very effective, approach to materials-led planning. The planners raise the orders recommended by MRP (with or without capacity planning) and release them to production a lead time ahead of the due-date. No attempt is made to monitor the progress of each order and production supervisors look at what is physically available at their work centres and usually apply their personal priority rules. If an order becomes urgent or overdue, an expediter searches the shop floor for the order, marks it with a red 'Urgent' label and uses his influence with the production supervisors to get the order treated as high priority. The system tends to break down when all the orders become urgent.

The **MRP plus Partial or Full Shop Floor Control** approaches have been described in Section 9.3. When applied in a disciplined way they can both be very effective but both approaches have their weaknesses. Partial Shop Floor Control depends on the effectiveness of the priority rule used to sequence the jobs on the Work-To List. No simple rule works well in all circumstances and if the suggested sequence is counter intuitive, i.e. it is very different from what the supervisor feels is best, it is likely that it will not be followed.

In a business with many different products and a large number of multipurpose work centres, the scheduling problems presented to the supervisors by Full Shop Floor Control may be too difficult for them to

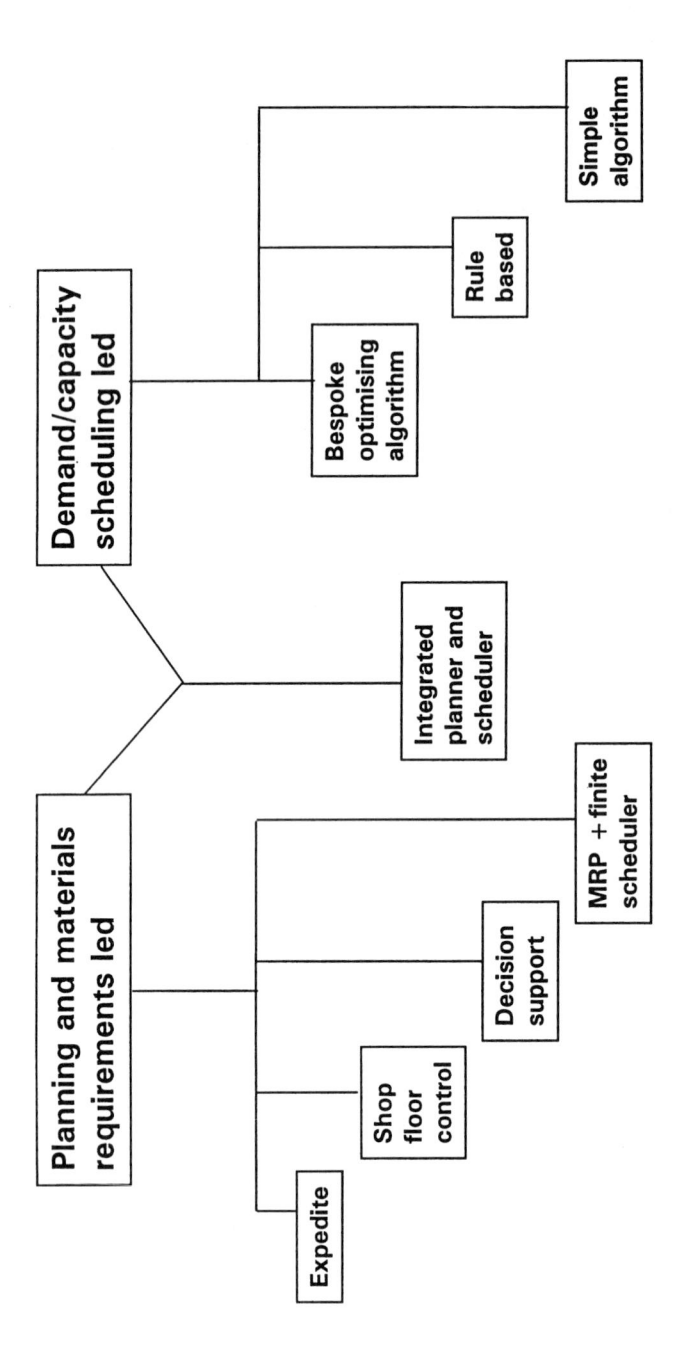

144   PLANNING AND CONTROL OF MANUFACTURING OPERATIONS

9.5 Classification of planning and scheduling systems.

solve unaided. One operation cannot be planned to start on a resource until the preceding one has finished. A proposed schedule must be checked to ensure that no operation is scheduled to start before the due-date of the previous stage and that no finish date is later than the planned operation due-date. Supervisors of some work centres will be able to do this checking in their heads or on the back of an envelope, others may need support from some kind of finite scheduling system.

In the **MRP plus decision support systems** approach, as much as possible of the information needed for scheduling the Work-To List is presented to the scheduler in an easy to understand way. The objective is to support both the manual decision-taking required to produce a schedule and the evaluation of provisional schedules produced. The support tools available range from the traditional manual planning board to its highly automated equivalents:

- *Manual planning boards:* The simplest form of planning board has a horizontal plastic channel for each resource to be scheduled. The channel is marked at intervals corresponding to one day, one shift or possibly one hour. Tickets are prepared for each job, with the length of the ticket corresponding to the expected duration of the job. The tickets are slotted into the channel in the specified sequence, so that the ends of the ticket indicate when the job should start and finish.

    Although such boards give an easy to understand indication of probable start and finish times, preparing the tickets can be time consuming and they do not indicate if jobs are scheduled to start before materials are available or to finish after the due-date. They also have limitations if more than one resource has to be scheduled for each operation.

    Consider, for example, the case of a group of packing lines manned by a group of multi-skilled operators but with insufficient labour to run all the lines simultaneously. The planning board has a channel for each line, and the ticket lengths are proportional to the line hours required for the jobs. The board gives a very good picture of line usage but in order to determine whether sufficient operators will be available at any time, the operator requirements for every line scheduled to be running at that point in time have to be totalled manually. There is no simple visual display of operator needs versus availability.

- *Electronic planning boards:* Some of the disadvantages of simple planning boards can be overcome by creating an equivalent display on the screen of a visual display unit which has access to the scheduled operations file. Jobs can be moved in time or between resources by using a keyboard or mouse and the system is designed to indicate if a job is scheduled too late and the due-date is missed, or too early before the planned completion date for the previous operation, or before all the required components or sub-assemblies are available. Several of the available commercial systems will display the requirements for more than one resource at a time. For example, the labour requirements for any group of equipment can be calculated and displayed to give warning if any change to plan requires labour in excess of that planned to be available.

Control systems based on electronic planning boards are particularly common in Germany where they are known as *Leitstand* which is best translated as 'control tower'. The most sophisticated systems which were pioneered in Germany are no longer decision support systems but automated post-MRP finite schedulers or in some cases fully automated finite planning systems in their own right, which can operate independently of MRP (see below). One of the key features of the *Leitstand* type system is that even when an initial finite schedule is produced automatically, the system facilitates manual amendments by providing a simple visual display of the schedule with warnings of potential problems.

The **MRP plus finite scheduler** approach can also be used. Because manual finite capacity planning and scheduling of MRP output can be difficult and is not always well done, most suppliers of MRPII software now offer a module which takes the orders generated by MRP and produces a finite capacity plan and schedule. These have had variable success. In the more sophisticated systems, the automatic calculation of new schedules can be designed to meet a chosen objective, such as maximum orders on time, minimum work in progress, minimum set-up time, or maximum output. The user can choose from a range of priority setting algorithms or priority rules.

In some cases, key operations can be firm planned, which means as in MRP that the system is not permitted to re-schedule them. Once a new sequence and any key dates have been specified, start and end dates for all operations can be automatically recalculated.

9.6.2 *Capacity-led categories*

In contrast to a company buying or making large numbers of components and assembling them in many different ways, a company operating a large piece of capital equipment such as a steel rolling mill may produce many differently sized products but from very few purchased input materials. The rolling mill may start with only three or four different types of steel bar but roll them into tens or even hundreds of products with different shapes, sizes and tensile strengths. The preferred schedule must make the best use of the expensive equipment, even if this means non-optimum use of labour or the holding of finished goods stock. Once the optimum sequence has been determined, the requirements for purchased materials can be identified. A combination of strategic stock holding, the small number of different input materials and the ability to buy with a short lead time means that the optimum schedule should be only rarely disrupted by material shortages.

Optimising algorithm systems normally apply to make to order companies and the purpose of the scheduling system is to sequence the customer orders which have been received but not supplied. Typically the user can specify one or more scheduling objectives, such as maximum number of orders on time, minimum total set-up time for a resource, best match of labour requirements with availability, maximum overall output, etc. The system then attempts to produce the schedule which best meets these objectives, using internal logic, which in some cases the supplier may attempt to keep confidential.

Once the preferred schedule has been set, the material requirements can be determined, using an MRP type calculation. If there are shortages which cannot be remedied, manual intervention in the schedule may be necessary. A potential difficulty with the optimising algorithm approach is that if the users cannot understand the internal logic, they may have little faith in the schedule and be only too ready to deviate from it, particularly if it appears to be counter-intuitive.

With **rule based** systems, the user specifies a series of scheduling rules appropriate for the business. For example, to minimise the effects of cross-contamination in a mixing operation, the rules might be: light colours before dark; dilute formulations before strong formulations. In the steel rolling mill discussed above, the overall objective is to minimise the effect of wear on the expensive rollers and suitable rules might be: wide products before narrow ones; soft bars before hard bars. The system must attempt to meet the delivery dates required by the customers, whilst observing as many of the rules as possible. Often no perfect solution will be found. The system, possibly aided by manual intervention, must look for the best compromise.

If the resource being scheduled is expensive, such as the steel mill, the planners should be prepared to spend two or three days each week working on optimising a schedule for the next one or two months because the penalty for using a less than ideal schedule may amount to tens of thousands of pounds. In contrast, a company supplying consumer goods to major supermarket chains may be expected to deliver today replacements for what was sold by the stores yesterday. Speed of response then becomes the most important requirement from the scheduling system. In this case, a workable but possibly non-ideal schedule produced in fifteen minutes is more valuable than an optimised schedule produced in three hours.

Integrated planners and schedulers are also available. A few systems, of which 'Optimised Production Technology', usually abbreviated to 'OPT', is the best known, plan materials and capacity simultaneously. OPT, which will be discussed in more detail in Chapter 10, was invented by Eli Goldratt, a nuclear physicist who turned his attention to manufacturing control problems. The initials OPT are a registered trade mark of Scheduling Technology Ltd but are widely used as a name for the technique. The OPT system simplifies the finite scheduling problem by concentrating on developing and refining the schedule for the bottleneck resource only. Schedules for non-bottleneck resources, which by definition have spare capacity, do not need to be as carefully refined as the bottleneck schedule.

At the date of writing, several integrated systems which will run on a moderately powerful personal computer are now available. The suppliers, understandably, are not keen to reveal their internal logic but there is no doubt that the best integrated systems, given accurate information about the plant, stocks, existing manufacturing orders and customer requirements, can quickly produce workable schedules even for complex environments.

9.6.3 Future developments in finite planning and scheduling

Although there are successful implementations of all types of finite planners and schedulers, the total number, at the time of writing, is a tiny fraction of the number of MRPII implementations. Since integrated finite systems avoid the need for manual capacity planning (a difficult area of MRPII which is rarely done well), it is surprising that they have not been more successful. One possible explanation is that although most of the data required by integrated planners and schedulers are available on a typical MRP data base, the interfaces provided to integrated planners and schedulers can be difficult to operate. As an example, consider the case of finished goods stock records and manufacturing order records. With an integrated on-line data base, a single transaction for an order receipt will increase the stock record of the item made and decrease the quantity

CAPACITY PLANNING AND SHORT TERM SCHEDULING   149

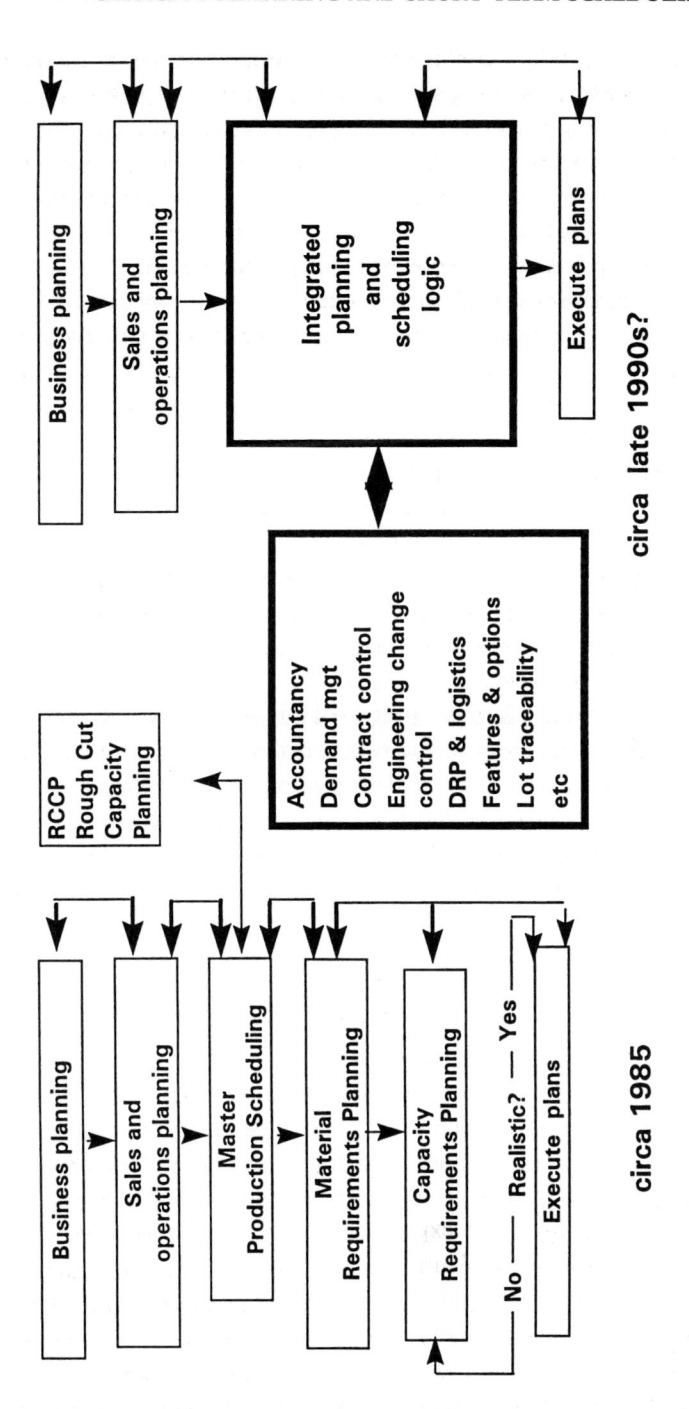

9.6 Development of MRPII systems?

circa late 1990s?

- Business planning
- Sales and operations planning
- Integrated planning and scheduling logic
- Execute plans

Accountancy
Demand mgt
Contract control
Engineering change control
DRP & logistics
Features & options
Lot traceability
etc

circa 1985

- Business planning
- Sales and operations planning
- Master Production Scheduling
- Material Requirements Planning
- Capacity Requirements Planning
- Realistic? — Yes → Execute plans
- No

RCCP Rough Cut Capacity Planning

expected from the order. The 'straightedge' between stock and orders is maintained. If batch transfers to the scheduler of stock records and manufacturing order records are made effectively simultaneously, whilst the data base is off-line, the straightedge should be preserved but in practice errors can be made and the straightedge lost. For example, if the transfer was made after the manufacturing order quantity was decreased, but before the stock record was increased, the information in the scheduler would indicate a false shortage. Similar problems are rare with MRPII because usually there is a common on-line data base covering most business functions such as stock recording, sales forecasting, sales order processing, manufacturing order progression, purchasing and accounts ledgers, etc.

It is highly probable that the next few years will see the launch of comprehensive business software in which much of the traditional MRP planning logic has been replaced by built-in finite planner/schedulers, or capacity-led scheduling systems (see Fig. 9.6). The persistent problem of the failure to produce plans which are feasible with respect to material supplies and capacity, either because it is too time consuming or too difficult, will at last be solved. It may be that in some businesses the plans and schedules produced automatically may not be as good as those prepared by the expert human planner, but this is almost beside the point. To be successful, automated finite planners and schedulers only need to outperform the typical overworked planner found in industry.

9.7 Queues and scheduling

As discussed in Chapter 6, the major element in a manufacturing lead time is usually queuing time. Materials can spend up to 90% of the time waiting between manufacturing stages, either waiting for the rest of the batch to be completed, or for the equipment for the next stage to become available. In order to minimise lead times, queues should be as short as possible but, as was demonstrated in Section 9.1, a queue of work in front of each work centre gives the supervisor some scheduling freedom either to resolve scheduling conflict or to make the best use of resources by minimising total change-over time, etc. (Readers are recommended to undertake Exercise 9.8 at this point.)

9.7.1 Setting planned queue lengths

Determining optimum queue lengths is one of the major problems of manufacturing control. Too little queuing disrupts production, too much

CAPACITY PLANNING AND SHORT TERM SCHEDULING 151

queuing limits responsiveness and increases work in progress and lead times.

In a typical jobbing shop in which production is largely non-repetitive, jobs arrive at a work centre with a high degree of randomness. Even if they are carefully planned to arrive at regular intervals, variations in production rates at earlier stages will introduce randomness. Sometimes jobs will arrive in bunches and the queue of work awaiting processing will increase. At other times, there will be long periods with no work arriving and the queue will decrease. It is sensible therefore to consider only average queue lengths, where the average is measured over a time which is long compared with the duration of an average job. Sometimes the actual queue will be greater than average, at other times lower. If work arrives faster than it is completed, the work centre is overloaded and the queue will grow and vice versa.

9.7.2 *The causes of queues*

Some insight into the characteristics of queues can be gained by considering that familiar phenomenon the supermarket. In the middle of a Saturday morning when the rest of the world appears to be shopping too, there will almost certainly be a queue at each check-out. However, at an unpopular time such as a Monday afternoon, queues will be much shorter, particularly if the same number of check-outs are operating as on Saturdays. Two general rules are obvious. Firstly, queues are not deliberately planned; they arise because of variations in the rate of arrivals. Secondly, the average length of queue is related to how heavily occupied the resource is. Queues can be eliminated almost entirely by providing sufficient resource, for example by manning all the check-outs on a Monday afternoon. This however costs money. The supermarket manager probably chooses not to employ enough staff to operate all his check-outs on a Monday because he judges that some queuing is acceptable to his Monday customers and so he chooses to save money on wages. Should he reduce staff too much, long queues will develop at the few check-outs which are operating and he will start to lose business as customers react to the reduced service and shop elsewhere.

Exactly the same compromise exists in manufacturing. All the benefits associated with short queues can be achieved by investment in sufficient spare capacity. Alternatively, a company can choose to minimise investment, operate with limited spare capacity and accept the costs of high in-process stocks and poor customer service.

The relationship between the average queue length at a work centre and the occupation of the work centre is illustrated by the curve in Fig. 9.7.

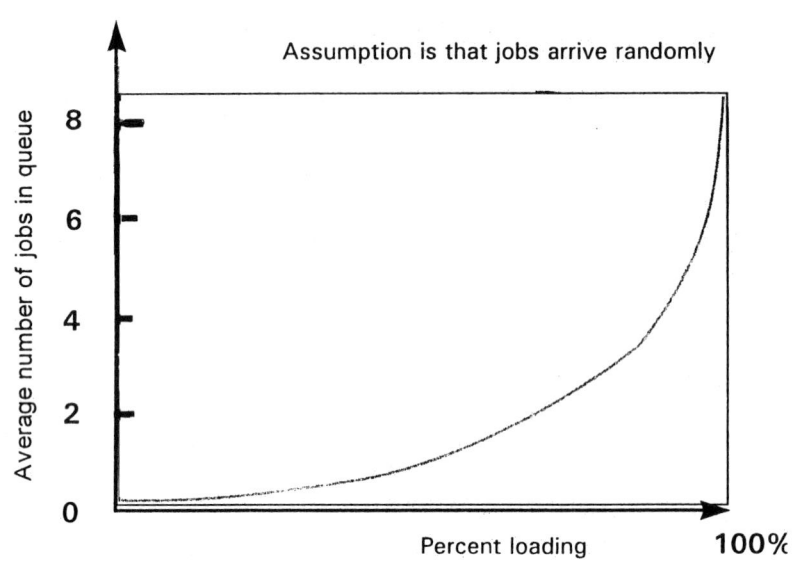

```
                    ↑
                    |  Assumption is that jobs arrive randomly
                  8 |─
Average number of jobs in queue
                  6 |─
                  4 |─
                  2 |─
                  0 |_____→
                       Percent loading              100%
```

9.7 Queue probability and loading.

The average queue length rises very steeply as the occupation rises towards 100%. Indeed if the occupation exceeds 100%, the equilibrium value of the queue will be infinity since work is arriving faster than it is being completed.

The exact shape of the curve can only be predicted mathematically when all jobs are of equal size and arrivals are truly random. Real life manufacture is somewhat more complicated but the curve will still be of the same general shape.

Examination of the curve casts doubt on the frequently held view that maximum efficiency is achieved by using resources as close to full occupation as possible. This may appear to make efficient use of fixed capital but makes poor use of working capital and leads to poor customer service. Some managers find this concept difficult to understand, perhaps because for years accounting systems have related overhead recovery to running time, even if there is no requirement for the product being made. The stock arising from the unnecessary running is rarely the responsibility of the production manager, and anyway is conventionally treated as an asset, so the accounts still look good. The inadequacy of this view can be demonstrated by using the fire brigade as an example. If an emergency call, reporting a fire, received the answer 'Sorry there is a queue, we will be with you tomorrow afternoon,' the caller would be rightly concerned. In order to avoid queues, the fire service operates its equipment at the extreme left hand end of the curve in Fig. 9.7, with low occupation and low queues. No one minds seeing a fire engine parked at the fire station in readiness should a fire occur, but even in industries for which good customer service is a prime objective, many managers become concerned if expensive equipment is idle, and are reluctant to sanction the purchase of additional equipment until the existing equipment is demonstrated conclusively to be fully or over occupied.

Of course it is unlikely to be economic to run manufacturing equipment at the same low levels of occupation as a fire appliance, but it is still necessary to examine carefully the balance between investment in working capital and in fixed capital. The problem is too complicated to analyse rigorously by mathematics, but the shape of the curve in Fig. 9.7 provides some clues. The curve starts to rise very steeply when the occupation exceeds 70–85% at which point the average queue is two to four jobs. Any further increase in occupation will cause a rapid rise in average queue length.

A reasonable rule of thumb is to aim not to run at greater than 70-80% occupation and indeed lower levels will be appropriate if the products are very expensive or customer service is particularly important. Conversely, higher occupations can be tolerated if the products are cheap, not bulky to store and service levels are not critical. Note that 100% occupation means the maximum practicable output, not the theoretical maximum based on equipment design specification.

As a working compromise, average planned queue lengths should be set to n times the average change-over and run time, where n is in the range of two to five depending on the occupation level of the work centre and the value and bulkiness of the products.

9.7.3 *Setting lead times*

Manufacturing lead times are made up of queue, change-over, run and move times for each operation. Change-over, run and move times can be measured directly so the only unknowns for the calculation of lead times are the average queue times for each work centre. These can be estimated using the rule of thumb developed above.

A practical approach is initially to allow a queuing time of three or four times the average change-over and run time, for a work centre which is 75–85% occupied, a larger allowance of five times for more heavily occupied equipment and a shorter one for lightly loaded machines. The lead times can then be calculated for each product and put into MRP. After a few months, when equilibrium has been achieved, the queuing element in the lead time can be experimentally reduced by, say, 20%. If no ill-effects occur, the reduction can be repeated until pain is felt in terms of missed

154   PLANNING AND CONTROL OF MANUFACTURING OPERATIONS

due-dates. A small increase in planned lead time should then restore efficient running.

Setting target queues is not a precise science. Some experimentation is essential but once an acceptable position has been found, actual queue lengths in front of each work centre should be monitored to highlight potential problems in advance, particularly if production volumes and hence equipment occupations are changing.

Exercises

9.1 (a) How much time (in standard hours) will be required on final draw machine FD07 and on heavy draw machine HD01 to produce an order for 2000 kg of paper clip wire W1. Use the data in Table 9.1, page 128. All equipment was previously producing a different product.
(b) If both work centres have productivity factors of 0.75, what percentage of a five day week at eight clock hours per day would the order occupy?
(c) If two identical final draw machines, type FD07, are used simultaneously with half of the wire going through each, how will the total machine hours for final drawing change?

9.2 The standard times for producing a manufacturing order for 4000 kg of piano wire, W2, on multipurpose equipment shared with many other products are:

	Change-over (hours)	Run (hours)
Heavy draw	3	18
Final draw	6	27
Plating	3	12

Completion of plating is required by day 115 of the shop calendar. Average queuing allowances and productivity factors are:

	Average queue (standard hours)	Productivity factor
Heavy draw	12.8	0.8
Final draw	5.6	0.7
Plating	11.2	0.7

The plant works for a nominal eight hour day. Wait and move times are negligible.

Back schedule this order to determine the earliest and latest planned

CAPACITY PLANNING AND SHORT TERM SCHEDULING   155

start dates for heavy drawing. When scheduling, round times to the nearest day. There is little point in scheduling too precisely, since when the order is in production the actual times taken will probably deviate from the averages used for planning and scheduling.

9.3 *Calibration of productivity factor.*
Over the past five weeks work centre 01 has achieved production which at standard rates should have taken 125 standard hours.

Normal working is eight hours per day for five days per week. Over the five weeks a total of ten hours overtime was worked, there was one day of national holiday when the factory closed, one day of planned maintenance on work centre 01 and two days when the work centre was planned to have no work. What is the achieved (or demonstrated) productivity factor over the five weeks?

9.4 Consider the following three manufacturing orders for cartons of pet food biscuits:

Order no	Product code	Description	Quantity	Due-date
M01	P20	Cat food – beef flavour	10 000	190
M02	P21	Cat food – chicken flavour	5 000	187
M03	P22	Cat food – salmon flavour	4 000	185

Dates are day numbers on the shop calendar, which leaves out non-working days.

The cooked bulk biscuits for all three flavours are prepared in blending room BR02. The bulk biscuits are quite stable and can be stored if necessary, before filling into 500 g cartons, which are sealed, labelled and over packed. Filling of the three packs can be carried out on any one of three lines, which use a common pool of operators. Critical resources are believed to be the filling operators and the blending room BR02 which are both, on occasions, overloaded.

The representative routings for the three products are:

	Resource	Change-over	Run time/pack	Off-set	Spread
P20	OP01 filling operators	20 000 (op hrs × 10^{-3})	4 (op hrs × 10^{-3})	0	4
	BR02 blending room 2	0	0.5 (hrs × 10^{-3})	20	1
P21	OP01 filling operators	20 000 (op hrs × 10^{-3})	5 (op hrs × 10^{-3})	0	2
	BR02 blending room 2	0	1.25 (hrs × 10^{-3})	20	1

P22	OP01 filling operators	20 000 (op hrs × 10^{-3})		6 (op hrs × 10^{-3})	0	2
	BR02 blending room	0		2.5 (hrs × 10^{-3})	20	1

Note that the units chosen to measure packing operator effort are milli-operator hours (i.e. op hrs × 10^{-3}), and for blending room usage, milli-hours (hrs × 10^{-3}). It is necessary to use these unusual units to avoid having too many decimal places in the run time per unit field which in this instance is run time per carton. This is a feature of the software being used by this company. The software was originally devised for the engineering industry, where orders may be for only a few items, and typical machining time could be minutes or hours per item. For process industries producing large numbers of small items, such as pharmaceutical or cosmetic manufacturers, it is convenient to be able to specify rates (i.e. packs per hour or kg per hour) rather than unit times but not all available software packages do this. It is usually advisable to adapt to the package if necessary rather than to modify it.

The company works to planning periods of 20 days' length. Period 1 is days 1–20 of the shop calendar, period 2 days 21–40, period 5 days 81–100 and period 10 days 181–200, etc. Calculate the work load in standard hours by period, arising from the three orders MO1, MO2, MO3 for filling operators and blending room BR02. Use an RCCP type calculation.

9.5 You are the supervisor of a single blending and milling facility which is making injection moulding powders by blending base polymers with anti-oxidants and pigments. Your Work-To List (see below) shows four operations. Each order will take two days to process and cleaning time between different products is one day.

MO number	Product	Qty, kg	Earliest start	Latest start	Operation due-date
122	Powder D	900	Started day 98		102
123	Powder A	900	101	106	108
124	Powder A1	900	102	107	109
125	Powder B	900	100	105	107

Powder A1 differs from Powder A only in that it has slightly less antioxidant. A small amount of cross contamination of A by A1 does not cause a problem.

Determine the order in which you would tackle this work and sketch a finite schedule as a bar chart starting immediately after the current production of order no 122 for product D which is due to finish at the end of day 99.

9.6 List the advantages of using planning boards to assist in creating short term schedules. Which disadvantages of simple manual planning boards can be overcome by the electronic equivalent linked to the planning data base?

9.7 (a) The three parts of the figure shown here are identical. Each shows the planned schedule for an order for which operation 1 is currently just starting. The diagrams show the time required to complete operation 1, and the planned queue, set-up and run times for the remaining two operations. Make a rough copy and annotate part (a) and add a formula to show how critical ratio is calculated, indicate the expected lateness on part (b) and show on part (c) how slack per remaining operation is calculated.

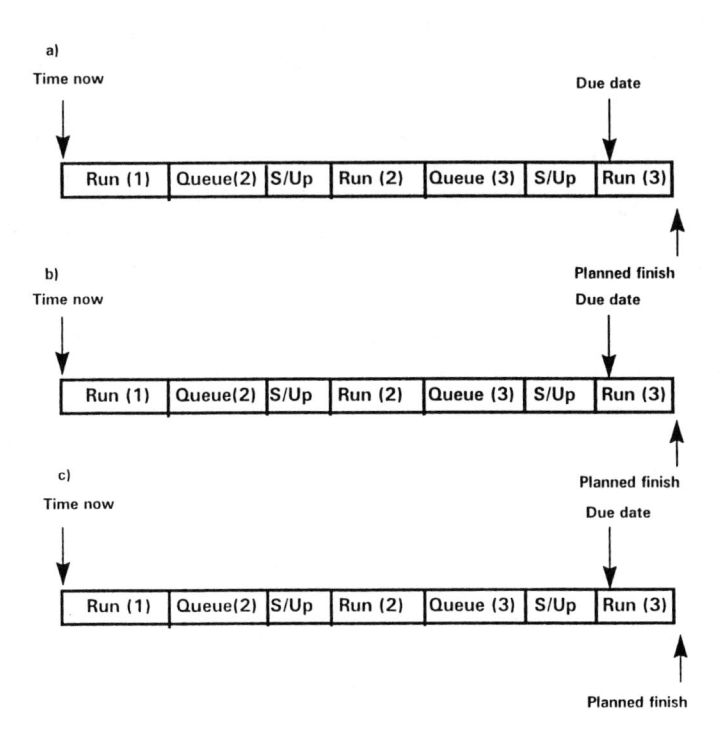

a)
Time now ↓   Due date ↓

| Run (1) | Queue(2) | S/Up | Run (2) | Queue (3) | S/Up | Run (3) |

↑ Planned finish

b)
Time now ↓   Due date ↓

| Run (1) | Queue(2) | S/Up | Run (2) | Queue (3) | S/Up | Run (3) |

↑ Planned finish

c)
Time now ↓   Due date ↓

| Run (1) | Queue(2) | S/Up | Run (2) | Queue (3) | S/Up | Run (3) |

↑ Planned finish

(b) Calculate priority indices based on critical ratio, maximum expected lateness and least slack per remaining operation for the two manufacturing orders, job A and job B, shown in the figure opposite. Time now is the beginning of day 1. Both are competing for the same blending equipment. Job A requires milling and packing after blending, job B only milling. Both orders are behind schedule.

9.8 Compile two lists, one of reasons why queues of work awaiting each work centre are a good idea, and one of reasons why queues are detrimental to effective performance.

9.9 A number of different steroidal creams and ointments, formulated in various pans according to product type, are all filled into 50 g tubes on a semi-automatic filling and packing line. All batches are of equal size.

The products are expensive, each batch costs £50 000, but have been very successful and output has increased to the point where the line is more than 90% occupied. There is concern about the value of working capital tied up in stock and a study shows that on average ten batches are awaiting packing. Records show that two years ago when sales were half of current volumes, on average only two batches were awaiting packing.

Prepare a case for buying a second line costing £100 000 to purchase, and £20 000 per year to operate including depreciation. (Borrowing capital costs 20% per annum. Assume that there will be no need to recruit additional operators to man the new line.)

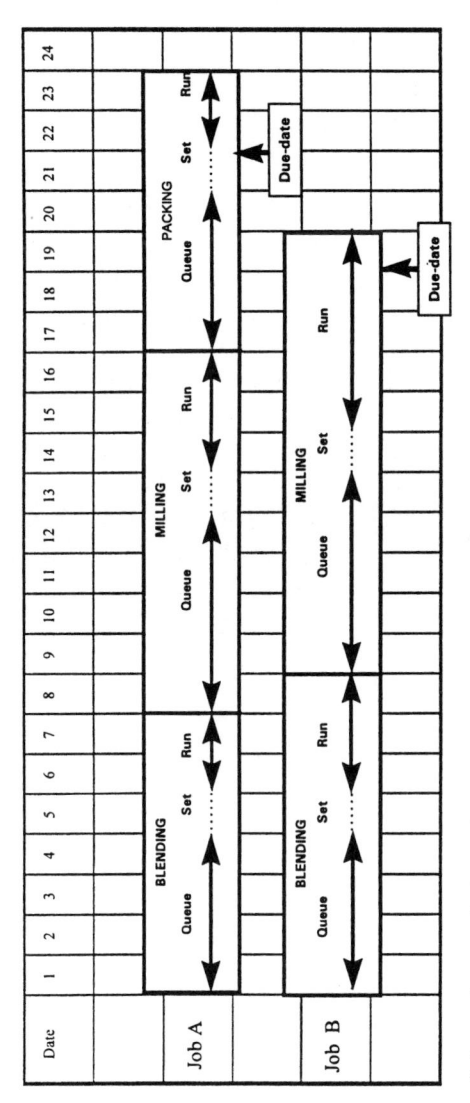

CAPACITY PLANNING AND SHORT TERM SCHEDULING 159

Date	1	2	3	4	5	6	7	8	9	10	11	12	13	14	15	16	17	18	19	20	21	22	23	24

Job A: BLENDING (Queue / Set / Run) → MILLING (Queue / Set / Run) → PACKING (Queue / Set / Run) ← Due-date

Job B: BLENDING (Queue / Set / Run) → MILLING (Queue / Set / Run) ← Due-date

Set = set-up or change-over

10

Optimised Production Technology

An Israeli physicist, Dr Eli Goldratt, who had been researching into random events in radioactive nuclei, turned his attention to the problems of production control and quickly realised that an effective control mechanism has to take into account random variations in performance. People and machines do not always produce at their average rate. In some periods they will exceed the average, in others they will fall behind. Based on his analysis, Goldratt developed Optimised Production Technology, known as OPT for short. This is both a philosophy and a software package to assist the application of the philosophy. The ideas involved are described in *The Goal* (E Goldratt and J Cox, Wildwood House, 1989). Although many of the OPT principles are not novel, they appear to have been forgotten or neglected by many contemporary managers, and this excellent and entertaining book is recommended reading for all interested in operations management.

The OPT software is in fact a highly developed finite scheduling system as described in Chapter 9, but before considering the software it is appropriate to examine the general principles of OPT, which are universally applicable to manufacturing operations and in many cases can be adopted without using the software.

10.1 Bottlenecks

In any multi-stage production facility, with a given product mix, it is highly probable that one stage will have less capacity than the others. This stage will restrict the overall output of the facility in exactly the same way that the narrow neck of a bottle restricts the rate at which water can be poured out, irrespective of the diameter of the bottle below the neck. If the bottleneck stage does not have adequate capacity to meet demands, the whole facility will not meet demands. Adding additional capacity at a non-bottleneck stage will not increase overall output.

It is clear therefore that any production time lost at the bottleneck is lost for good, since there is no spare capacity to catch up. Time lost at non-bottleneck stages may be recoverable by using some of the spare capacity. In order to maximise output, lost time on the bottleneck must be minimised. This can be done in three ways:

- A buffer of work can be held in front of the bottleneck so that it never runs out of work because of upstream delays. In effect this means that jobs must be scheduled to arrive at the bottleneck some specified time before they are required.
- The bottleneck should be given priority for maintenance should it break down. A fitter or operator should be prepared to leave a job on a non-bottleneck if required on the bottleneck. By definition the non-bottleneck has capacity to catch up with programme; the bottleneck does not.
- The bottleneck must never waste time working on inferior quality material which will eventually be rejected. It is desirable therefore that every reasonable quality control check should be carried out before, not after, the bottleneck operation so that unfit materials can be weeded out before they consume precious time on the bottleneck.

10.2 Effect of random variations in output

Consider the case of a manufacturing cell making electronic controllers, which has to carry out three operations, electronic assembly, mechanical assembly and testing. There is a separate work centre for each operation, and each has been designed with a capacity of 1000 units per day. The work centres are close together so that individual units can easily be passed to the next work centre. The cell has been carefully designed and balanced to meet a steady demand for 1000 units per day with maximum efficiency and minimum in-process stocks. Each stage has a capacity of 1000 units per day. The designers were aware that random variations in output from each stage were to be expected, as is the case in most manufacturing operations, but assumed that these would average to the design output of 1000 units per day.

In practice the situation is not so simple. Complications arise because each stage cannot be considered separately. Account must be taken of interaction between stages.

If electronic assembly, the first operation, has a good day and produces 1100 units but mechanical assembly, the second stage, has a bad day and only achieves 950 units, 150 units will accumulate between the stages.

Provided that storage space is available, this does not present a problem, other than the cost of holding stocks. Statistically, electronic assembly will be expected to have a bad day sometime and mechanical assembly a good one and the interstage stock will be consumed.

If, however, the first stage has a day of poor output, just as the output rate from stage two, mechanical assembly, is really beating the average, mechanical assembly will run out of electronic units and will be forced to stop. Since the work centre is not able to take advantage of all its good days, but will still suffer its statistical share of bad ones, the design output of 1000 units per day will not be achieved.

If there are random variations in output, the facility with carefully balanced and equal capacities at each stage will not achieve final output equal to the average capacity of each stage (1000 units per day). To achieve 1000 per day, provided that raw materials are always available, the first manufacturing stage can have an average capacity of 1000 per day, but an increasing amount of spare capacity is required at downstream stages to enable them to make up for production lost because of random variations upstream. The arrangement, in which the bottleneck is at the first stage and has a capacity equal to demand with capacity increasing progressively for downstream stages, is an ideal configuration. In-process stocks would be at a minimum, and would be self-regulating. Testing, for example, might have a capacity of 1500 per day but would be restricted by unit supply to the desired average of 1000 per day.

In practice, however, this ideal self-controlling situation with the bottleneck at the first stage rarely occurs. If Testing happened to be the bottleneck and there was spare capacity at upstream stages, demands would be met, provided that the bottleneck at Testing had adequate capacity. It would be essential, however, to control the input stage so that it worked on average no faster than the bottleneck, in spite of having capacity available to achieve more. If this was not done, the in-process stocks would increase alarmingly, since electronic assembly would inject say 1100 per day, whilst Testing only had the capacity to pass 1000 per day into sales stock.

10.3 Gateing the input stage

If a continuous build-up of in-process stocks is to be avoided, the input must be controlled to be no faster than the output. In effect the input stage must be 'gated' to allow materials in at a rate no faster than the output of the bottleneck stage which, wherever it is situated, will limit overall output.

This can be achieved in several ways:

- OPT software is designed specifically to do this.
- If the plant is producing the same or similar items continuously, a simple information link is adequate (the quantity allowed in each day is the quantity that the bottleneck produced the previous day). This only works well in repetitive environments. The Kanban technique discussed in Section 1.1 is an example of this form of control.
- MRP on average only demands from the previous stage sufficient materials to meet the plans for the stage, and so, provided that the MPS is both realistic and achievable (i.e. it does not exceed available capacity or call for materials which cannot be supplied), MRP will on average only call in material at the rate required by the bottleneck. This does, however, require that the planners are diligent in adjusting the plans to avoid overloads or shortages. Unlike OPT, MRP does not do this automatically, and if left to itself in an overload situation will call in materials faster than they can be used.

A consequence of gateing the input stage is that all stages other than the bottleneck will from time to time be restrained by lack of materials and will be idle. At first sight this appears inefficient, but if the stages were to operate all the time they would only be producing unwanted stock, which could not be processed by the bottleneck.

Spare capacity on equipment imposes no particular management problem, but partially-occupied people are a potential problem for managers. Ideally, manning levels should be adjusted so that people are just about to become the bottleneck. In practice this is not always possible, and as the understanding becomes more widespread that investment in spare capacity of plant and people is not only an alternative to investment in excessive stocks but also enhances flexibility and responsiveness, one of the increasing challenges for management will be how to occupy operators with frequent but random periods of spare time. Amongst the possibilities are training, housekeeping tasks or work improvement groups (sometimes called quality circles).

10.4 OPT software

Details of OPT software are confidential, but what is known is that it contains sophisticated finite scheduling logic which is applied only to the bottleneck. It is believed that the logic is as follows:

- Data for stocks, bills of materials and routings are required in a very similar fashion to MRP but are held in a different format. A conventional Capacity Requirements Planning type run is used to

determine the load on each resource. Overloads are then displayed to the operator who attempts to provide additional capacity by means of overtime, sub-contracting, etc. When no further capacity improvements are possible the most overloaded resource is the bottleneck.
- OPT then finite schedules the bottleneck stage. Jobs are loaded in priority order, each planned to start immediately after the preceding job has finished. If the stage is overloaded during a period, the planned completion dates of some jobs will be later than required, i.e. the overload has been accommodated by delaying work irrespective of need date.
- Once planned start and completion dates have been determined for all operations on the bottleneck, downstream operations are conventionally forward scheduled using logic similar to the back scheduling logic described in Section 9.1 and illustrated in Fig. 9.3.
- This enables planned order completion dates to be determined. Some of these may be later than the required dates. If so, the priorities at the bottleneck are adjusted, the completion dates recalculated and the comparison repeated. The bottleneck schedule which gives the best fit of order completion dates with required dates is then accepted. Upstream stages are then back scheduled from the bottleneck to determine planned start dates.
- OPT software will split orders into two at non-bottleneck stages if this enables the first part of the order to be progressed before the completion of the second part, in order to meet an immediate need. If it can be done without serious detriment to customer service, OPT will combine orders at the bottleneck in order to save change-over time.

Although the mechanics are very different, OPT may be thought of as MRPII with automated work smoothing and automated detailed scheduling. It automatically ensures that plans are feasible with respect to capacity, a process which in MRPII is left to the planner.

Undoubtedly OPT is more effective than poorly operated MRPII. Whether it can out perform a well run MRPII system depends both upon the skill of the MRPII planner and the complexity of the scheduling problem.

A weakness of OPT is that it assumes that the bottleneck is fixed and that solving an overload at one bottleneck does not create another. This is not always valid, but will be a reasonable assumption if there is adequate spare capacity at all stages except the bottleneck.

OPT software has been particularly successful in engineering companies with complex products such as aeroengine components, complex routings and many work centres, probably because the scheduling problems left to the planners by conventional MRP are sufficiently difficult to motivate management to look for alternative solutions. In simpler companies in which manual capacity planning and scheduling are effective, there is less incentive to look for alternatives. However the general principles about the identification and control of bottlenecks are just as applicable to simple control problems as they are to complex ones.

Exercises

10.1 A manufacturing cell dedicated to making a high performance fastener for the motor industry consists of three work centres. The first is cold forging with a single forge. The second consists of six identical milling machines and the third is a single pan polisher. The cell operates continuously for 24 hours per day for five days per week.

The average demonstrated output rate from each work centre is:

- *Cold forging:* one batch of 10 000 fasteners in four hours.
- *Milling:* each machine produces 600 fasteners per hour.
- *Polishing:* a polishing load of 4000 fasteners takes two hours.

Sales demand is for 250 000 fasteners per week. Will the cell meet this output? Which is the bottleneck stage?

10.2 In a dog food processing and packing facility, raw materials are brought in at a rate equivalent to 1.5 tonnes of output per day, but packing works only at the rate required to meet sales of 1 tonne per day. On the first of the month, total work in progress was equivalent to 5 tonnes of output. What will the total in-process stocks be after a further 10 days of operation?

10.3 Make a list of all the OPT principles which you can glean by re-reading sections 10.1–10.3. If you are in a position to do so, identify all those which are followed in your work environment (or in a company you know well), and also those which although apparently common sense are not.

10.4 Re-read Section 10.4 carefully and list the key differences between the logic of MRPII and the logic of OPT.

11

Just in Time and Continuous Improvement

11.1 What is Just in Time?

The concept of Just in Time manufacturing or JIT has received a lot of publicity since the mid-1980s, much of it based on some significant misunderstandings. Visitors to Japan in the early 1980s came back with stories of how suppliers to Toyota made deliveries several times a day and took parts directly to the production line such that they arrived just before they were needed. Just in Time delivery was seen as the key to the process. Investment in stock was minimised and only minimal storage space was taken up by components alongside the production line.

However, attempts to emulate the Japanese and implement Just in Time deliveries in the west all too often resulted in Just Too Late or JTL. In placing the emphasis on timeliness, the western observers had missed the point that Toyota had devoted a vast amount of effort to improving the quality, reliability and effectiveness of their products and processes so as to make Just in Time delivery of components feasible. Manufacturing does not become efficient and effective because deliveries are made Just in Time. Just in Time deliveries become possible when manufacturing becomes efficient, effective and reliable.

In companies which have not had a specific improvement programme, adopting a Just in Time approach would put production at risk of stoppage for many reasons. The most easily identified include equipment breakdown at the component manufacturing stage, transport delays if, as is possible, the supplier is several hundred miles away, quality problems, unreliable processes and inadequately co-ordinated design changes. Less obviously recognisable risks result from long lead times, long set-up times and large order sizes. The reasons why the last three parameters are incompatible with Just in Time will be discussed later in this chapter.

The process of eliminating inadequacies and weaknesses so as to move towards a Just in Time environment is best thought of as one of **Continuous Improvement**. Alternative and equally descriptive names are **Lean Manufacturing, Agile Manufacturing** and **Elimination of Waste,** where waste is anything which adds cost without adding value to the items involved. Thus storage is waste. Items are not normally worth any more than their original value after sitting in a warehouse for several weeks. Indeed if they are subject to deterioration such as rusting, obsolescence or pilferage they may be worth less than their value before storage. Similarly transport adds cost without adding value and this is true whether the transport is between factories and possibly between countries, or whether it is between work centres within the same factory. Inspections can be examples of waste, particularly goods inwards inspections which follow immediately after a pre-dispatch inspection by the supplier. With a suitable degree of trust between supplier and customer, a certificate of conformity can remove the need for the second inspection.

It could therefore be said that CI, LM, AM or EW would be more descriptive acronyms than JIT, but the latter is well established. Any attempt to introduce an alternative is unlikely to be successful but in the rest of this text the acronym JIT will be used instead of the potentially misleading full name. The alternative acronyms will be used only if needed by the context.

The JIT process may be illustrated by the so-called **River of Inventory** analogy. Figure 11.1(a) shows a cross section through a river. There are many rocks on the bed but provided that there is enough water in the river, the ships can navigate safely. The water level is analogous to the stock in a business, which helps cover up rocks such as poor quality, large order sizes, long change-over times, unreliable equipment, etc. If there is sufficient stock in the system, good service can be provided to customers in spite of late deliveries, production failures or quality problems. If a batch is rejected there are plenty of others available. If a packing line breaks down, there is plenty of packed stock available to supply the customer. This situation has been accepted as normal for so long that if the water level falls, revealing a rock (Fig. 11.1(b)), management's instinctive reaction is to increase the water level again, that is, to replenish stocks. The alternative approach, pioneered in Japan, is to remove the rock. If this is done successfully, the water level can then be lowered again to reveal the next rock, which can then be removed (see Fig. 11.1(c)) and so on until the ship can sail safely up the river with a very low water (or stock) level as in Fig. 11.1(d).

In Chapter 5, Fig. 5.1(a), it was shown that for an item with smooth continuous demand, the average stock level is equal to half the order size.

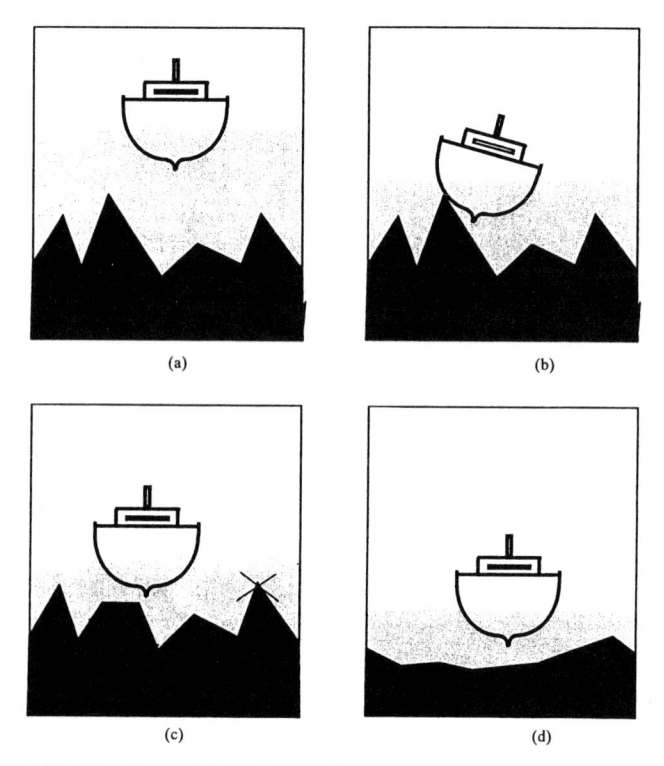

11.1 The River of Inventory analogy.

Even in situations in which the off-take is not smooth, the average stock level will increase with increasing order size. The funnel analogy illustrated in Fig. 6.2 showed how work in progress levels are proportional to average lead time. Effective ways of reducing stock levels either to save money or to reveal rocks are therefore to reduce lead times and to reduce order sizes.

11.2 Lead times, order sizes and JIT

Long manufacturing lead times not only increase work in progress but also add to uncertainty by increasing the period ahead over which sales must be forecast. Forecasts for the near future are easier to make and more likely to be accurate than are long term forecasts. Shortening lead times is therefore an important part of JIT or the continuous improvement process.

As was shown in Chapter 6, the major elements of a manufacturing lead time are:

JUST IN TIME AND CONTINUOUS IMPROVEMENT

- Queue time.
- Change-over time.
- Run time.
- Move time.
- Inspection time.

For many companies the simplest way to reduce actual lead times is to reduce planned lead times, which in effect means reducing queuing allowances. If ten weeks are allowed to meet a sales forecast requirement, it is unlikely to take less than ten weeks. It was also shown that if a planned lead time is reduced below the time actually taken plus the minimum queuing allowance appropriate for each resource, orders will on average be late. One empirical but effective approach to setting queuing allowances was to aim for a given number of orders in the queue (approximately three if 70–80% occupied). Smaller order sizes therefore mean a shorter queue.

Thus two elements of manufacturing lead time, queue time and run time are proportional to order size. The smaller the order size the shorter the run time and the shorter the queues (in hours) expected to form in front of the work centres. For a given level of occupation of the work centre there will on average be the same number of orders in the queue, but the smaller the order sizes, the less the corresponding working time represented by the queue.

From the JIT point of view, small orders are good news. They reduce sales stocks, they contribute to reducing lead times and work in progress, and it can be demonstrated by computer simulation exercises that work flows more smoothly with small orders because flow is not interrupted as a result of a critical resource being tied up for long periods by a large order for one product.

JIT philosophy claims that the ultimate order size is one unit, although it recognises that this may be a target to be striven for, rather than something to be implemented immediately. JIT philosophy was developed in the engineering industry and must be interpreted carefully in other industries, particularly in the process industries. Clearly an order size of one tablet or even 1000 tablets in a pharmaceutical factory turning out one million tablets a day is nonsense, as would be an order size of one carton of 6 × 60 g tubes of toothpaste in a plant filling 200 000 tubes per shift. There is, however, no reason why both businesses should not aim to make today what was sold yesterday if off-take is continuous, or if off-take is discrete to have a manufacturing order no bigger than each customer's order.

The principle that the economic order size involves a trade-off between stock holding costs and set-up costs remains valid, even if in practice the costs cannot be determined accurately. Smaller order sizes mean more change-overs. Very small order sizes only become feasible if change-over times can be eliminated or reduced and for this reason, reducing or eliminating change-over is often the first major step in a JIT programme.

11.3 Reducing change-over times

As industries have grown, the belief has developed that for equipment, faster means better. Unfortunately faster equipment usually takes longer to set-up or change-over between products. An automated liquid filling and packing line is much more complicated to change over than a number of jugs, funnels and a table. Changing and aligning the punches on a semi-automatic sheet metal punch takes much longer than a human operator takes to select a new hand punch, even though once set up the former may be a hundred times faster than the latter. In many industries during the 1970s and early 1980s, long change-over times tended to be accepted as a fact of life, or at least as the price to be paid for automation and higher running speeds. Allowances of two days to set up a large multi-axis milling machine, or half a day to clean a high speed paint filling line between colours and pack sizes were rarely questioned. When in the 1980s western companies started to recognise that long set-up times caused problems, the approach was often to increase automation by incorporating a higher level of computer control. With digitally controlled machine tools providing larger tool cassettes and enhanced degrees of tool movement, a wider range of products could be made without the need for human intervention for mechanical changes. Automated lines for making fibre board cases, used almost universally as outer packaging but frequently required in specific sizes, were equipped with computer controlled change-over systems which only required the operator to dial up the required size on a knob at the end of the machine or to select the next size on a VDU screen. Although often effective, this approach tends to be expensive. Whilst in the west these developments were seen as a way of reducing labour costs in order to compete with low cost producers in the east, the Japanese, as part of JIT, were adopting a very different approach. Japanese manufacturing industries had been so successful in capturing world wide market share that they were often able to minimise the need for change-overs by dedicating equipment to one product and size and using repetitive manufacturing techniques for items such as cameras which previously had been thought of as small batch items to be lovingly assembled by craftsmen.

Japanese managers realised that standard set-up or change-over times should not be accepted as inevitable. Even cursory examination often identified illogical and unnecessary practices.

At first many western managers dismissed as unbelievable reports that Japanese motor manufacturers had reduced the change-over times of the large presses which stamp out body panels from two days to less than ten minutes but investigation quickly verified the reports.

The teams responsible for the change-over time reduction projects found that much of the two days used to be spent in waiting time. The change-over would not start until the previous job was finished. The team of fitters responsible for carrying out the changes would not be pre-warned that a change-over was imminent and may have been enjoying a coffee break (or should it be tea break in Japan?) when the message was first passed that their services were required. Delays could then occur whilst the new change-parts were withdrawn from stores, and further delay whilst the fitters searched for the right tools which may have been left on the site of a previous job. These delays were easily and cheaply eliminated by providing the fitters with an up to date change-over schedule so that they could make preparations by, for example, assembling the change-parts before the previous job finished. The time spent searching for hand tools was eliminated by having a complete kit of tools in a locked cabinet alongside each press. Further savings were made by changing the equipment design so that change-parts could be assembled in advance and the new assembly slid into replace the old one. Bolt-on electrical and hydraulic connectors were replaced by snap-on varieties and so on. Planning and practising the change-over and continuous monitoring of the times achieved in both practice and live runs play a large part in maintaining the morale and commitment of the change-over teams. It is rumoured that in one leading example, the tool cabinet contains two pairs of training shoes which the fitters put on before the operation starts, because they have to climb on top of the press at one point, and wearing trainers to do this saves ten seconds per climb. Irrespective of whether this rumour is true, it illustrates the 'can do' approach which is necessary to break out of a mind set which accepts that long change-over times are an intractable problem. Readers may find it helpful to do Exercise 11.4 at this point.

11.3.1 Reducing change-over or set-up times: summary

The general principles for reducing set-up times are:

- Plan ahead. Do as much as possible before the previous job finishes.

- Monitor times taken and report to senior management regularly.
- Minor changes to the equipment can help at relatively low cost. For example:
  — reduce the number of bolts holding a change-part to the safe minimum;
  — shorten bolts so that only the safe minimum amount of thread must be engaged;
  — fit spring loaded clips or clamps in place of bolts where feasible.
- Fit graduated scales on adjustable items, so that preferred settings can be recorded and reproduced quickly.
- Where possible, have duplicate modules which are set up off line and wheeled into place as soon as the change-over starts. This can be particularly useful in the process industries, where cleaning of equipment either for hygiene reasons or to avoid cross-contamination may be a major part of a change-over.

In many cases the simple low cost steps described above will lead to reductions of more than 75% in total change-over time. Further reductions may require sophisticated equipment or expensive modifications to existing equipment, such as computer controlled units which automatically adjust to a new product sizes. However, such investment may not be justified. Maximum return for minimum effort can be achieved by exploiting Pareto's principle and identifying those changes which will give 80% of the benefits at 20% of the total cost.

In process industries, cleaning is probably the factor which most limits change-over reduction but even this limitation can be minimised by designing or choosing equipment which is easy to clean or duplicating items such as filling heads so that they can be cleaned off-line.

If equipment can be dedicated to a product, the need for change-over or set-up can be eliminated or very much reduced. Three relatively simple semi-automatic machines, each dedicated to a product, may be more effective than a single high speed machine which is used to produce all three products. If total dedication to a single product is not possible, an alternative may be to dedicate the equipment to a product family, of which the members require the same or similar settings on the equipment. For example, a piece of filling equipment for liquids or creams could be dedicated to one pack size, so that only the products have to be changed. Alternatively it may be possible to dedicate the equipment to a product or family of similar products and only carry out pack size changes.

An effective approach to change-over reduction is to set up a small team of people who are closely involved, e.g. fitters, operators first line supervisors and possibly, depending on the industry, a Quality Assurance representative, and to make them responsible for reducing change-over on a particular item of equipment. After initial training to make them aware of the techniques which have been successful elsewhere, a useful first step is to make a video recording of an actual change-over, so that it can be replayed and analysed at leisure. Wasteful activities will quickly become obvious. Such teams should have a reduction target, a budget under their control and the necessary managerial and technical support.

Reducing change-over times can if necessary be used to increase the time available for production, but a more effective approach is to use the reduction to accommodate an increased number of change-overs so that the average order size can be reduced.

11.4 Reducing movement or transport times

As described in Chapter 6, move times between operations are a component of total lead time. In the ideal arrangement, consecutive operations should be on work centres which are adjacent to each other so that move times can be as short as possible. How closely this ideal can be approached in real life depends on the production routing and the layout of the facilities available. It may be necessary for jobs to move between sites. In international companies it is possible that consecutive operations take place not in different factories but in different countries. This may happen for good manufacturing reasons. If an expensive resource in one country has spare capacity, it may make sense to send the work to the resource, rather than to invest in duplicate equipment. Alternatively the reasons for the cross border routing may have little to do with manufacturing efficiency. It may be, for example, that the company wishes to demonstrate support for a local economy by having manufacturing facilities in the country. The additional cost is in effect part of the publicity budget. There may be tax relief or subsidies available, which more than compensate for the increased manufacturing costs. It may be that import restrictions prevent the import of the finished product and the choice is to carry out at least the final manufacturing operation locally or to abandon the market.

With a high value, low volume product such as electronic instruments or a typical pharmaceutical, the actual transport costs are unlikely to be a significant fraction of the total cost, although this may not be the case with high volume, low value commodities or household products such as cleaners or polishes. The hidden costs of transport, however, lie in the additional complexity of control and the extended lead times, both of which hinder a flexible low stock JIT approach.

A JIT implementation should not ignore international move times. The original justification for moving part-complete orders from country A to country B may no longer be valid. The expensive under-occupied resource in country B may now be heavily occupied and the new equipment needed can be located in country A. Legislation may have changed or it may now be possible to carry out all the stages on the order in country B. Such investigations are rarely easy. Reasonable costing data may not be available, and in the absence of firm facts, many justifications may be based on emotions or gut feel. The view of the local sales managers that sales would fall by 30% if there was no local manufacture may or may not be correct, but it is extremely difficult to challenge.

These problems should not be taken as reasons for ignoring the international aspects of a JIT programme but they are probably excellent reasons for setting limited objectives initially and then proceeding cautiously.

Transport times within a factory can most easily be reduced by careful factory and process layout. On long-established sites, the layout has probably evolved with only limited planning, as plant has been installed or demolished over the years. One major chemical manufacturer with just such a site, discovered that the fork lift trucks on the site were driving 150 000 miles per year, a distance comparable to the separation of the earth and the moon. Investigation showed that merely by knocking doorways through two walls, the distance driven could be reduced by two-thirds.

Unfortunately major changes to layout are often difficult to make without disrupting production so it is important that careful attention is given to layout on those infrequent occasions when the opportunity arises.

11.4.1 Factory layout

The traditional approach to layout is to concentrate similar activities in the same area. In the example shown (Fig. 11.2), all the lathes are in one area, all the milling machines in another and so on. Each area has its own supervisor. This is generally described as a functional layout.

Such an arrangement makes effective use of equipment, because for example, a batch of part-finished items arriving at milling can be allocated to whichever general-purpose machine happens to be free. It does tend however to lead to high in-process stocks because the opportunity is taken to use the equipment at high utilisation and this causes queues to form. The mix of products and equipment in one area complicates scheduling

Gives good utilisation of equipment

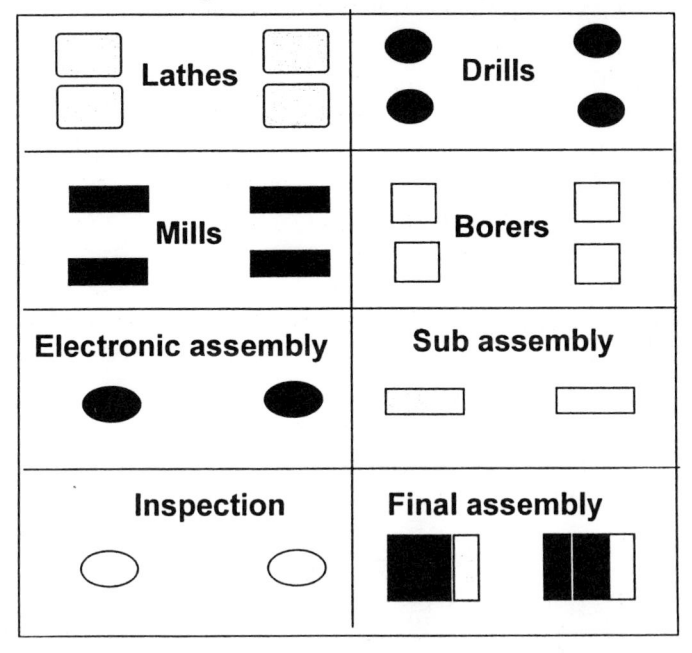

Lathes	Drills
Mills	Borers
Electronic assembly	Sub assembly
Inspection	Final assembly

11.2 Traditional or functional factory layout.

and often requires the use of some of the scheduling techniques described in Chapter 9. No one supervisor can be held responsible for delivering a particular product on time. Responsibility is either shared by all or accepted by no-one depending on your point of view.

An alternative approach to layout is shown in Fig. 11.3. Each product family has a dedicated area or production cell which contains all the facilities needed to make the products in the family, which by definition use similar equipment. A single supervisor has responsibility for the whole area and can be held accountable for supply of his or her products.

Cells of this nature reduce lead times and hence work in progress, reduce the need for change-over and improve responsiveness. They do not, however, make the best use of equipment since spare capacity in one cell cannot be used to meet a peak demand for a different family.

The operators within a cell become a tightly knit group which is good for morale and facilitates training them in multiple skills. It is easier, for example, to persuade a lathe operator to help pack the final product into cartons should the need arise if he feels part of the family, and if packing is physically close to his lathe, so that he can see that there is a real problem there.

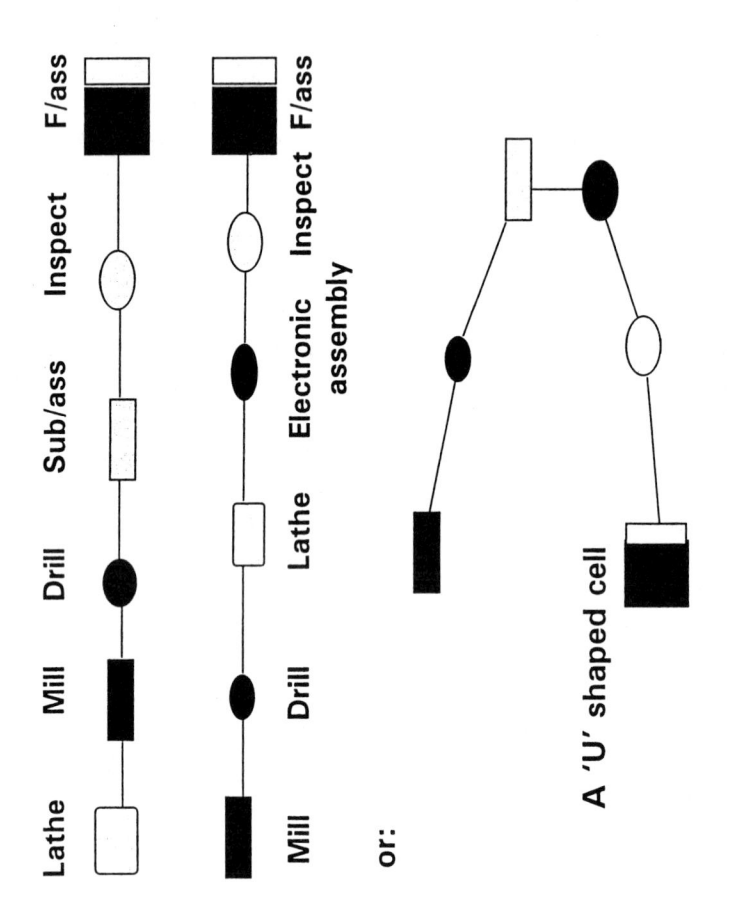

11.3 Cellular layout.

11.4.2 Kanban control

Scheduling a dedicated cell in which all jobs follow the same route through the cell is much simpler than scheduling a multi-product facility, and the control of inter-stage stocks is much easier. Reporting and recording of progress between stages can be dispensed with, and a simple visual control system such as Kanban can be used. In its simplest form an area called a Kanban square is marked out on the floor or bench between stages for each product. The square is just big enough to accommodate an agreed number of containers of the product. In the simplest case, between stages 1 and 2 there would be one square capable of holding one box of ten of the intermediate items produced by stage 1. When the box is taken by stage 2, the empty square is the signal for stage 1 to produce another box of ten. When the space is again occupied by a box of ten items, stage 1 stops producing that item.

Alternative signals to unoccupied space can be used. For example, as originally used in Japan a card can be the signal. Kanban is the Japanese for signal or card. In the above example there would be one or more cards for each item produced by stages 1 and 2. The card is a licence to produce. When a full box is produced by stage 1, the card is placed in the box which is then passed to stage 2. When the box is taken for use by stage 2, the card is returned to stage 1 and provides the authority for the production of another box of items. If a stage has no cards, it stops production (see Fig. 11.4).

Kanban works best in a repetitive environment. It is very simple to introduce and provides effective control. Production stops, however, only when all the Kanban cards are accompanying products; that is when all the authorised inter-stage stocks are at the permitted maxima. If product is sold or used intermittently, Kanban fills the line with components for the products which are not going to be needed for some time. Kanban is in fact nothing more than Order Point control using the two bin system (see Chapter 2). As with Order Point, it can be likened to trying to drive a car forwards whilst looking only backwards. This can be done if the road is straight. That is if the future can be safely assumed to be the same as the past, but is difficult if there are bends ahead.

Kanban can also be used outside a cellular environment if an item is used repetitively. For example, the supply of 5 litre containers to a packing line which is filling them with a variety of products could be put under Kanban control, with the package component warehouse supplying a further pallet whenever a Kanban signal is received. The 5 litre container would be taken off the kitting list for each separate filling order,

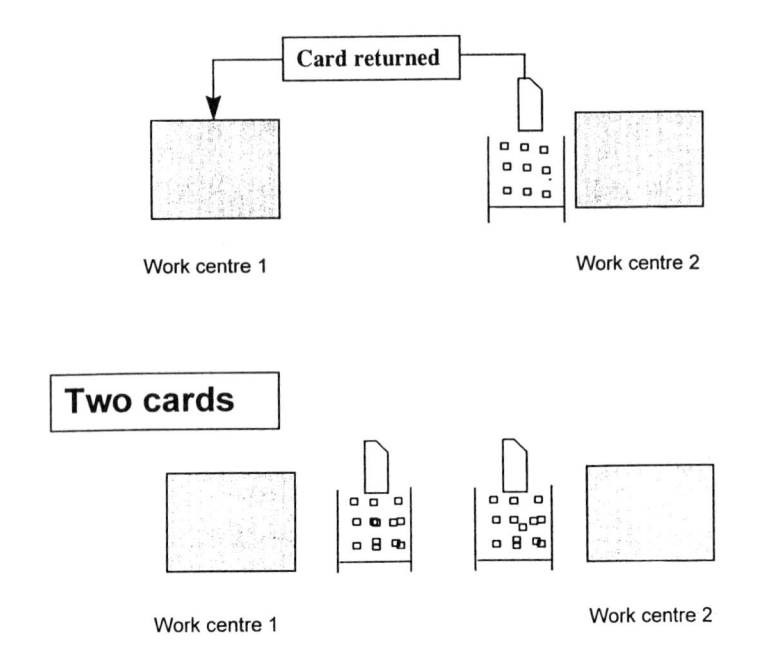

11.4 Kanban: A simple mechanical control system.

simplifying both paper work and handling and reducing the need for line-side storage space.

11.5 Reducing product complexity

An important aspect of a JIT or a Continuous Improvement programme is to review continuously the product range to see if it can be made easier to manufacture without reducing the appeal to the customer.

Product proliferation is often a problem. Products may have to be tailored for a market to satisfy safety legislation, to include instruction leaflets in the local language or to conform to electrical supply voltages and plugs. Variants for such reasons are difficult to avoid, but the justification for variants such as changing the colour of the case or putting a gold stripe on the front panel should be carefully investigated, and only authorised or retained if it can be demonstrated beyond reasonable doubt that they generate sufficient increase in sales to justify their true cost including the hidden costs of complexity. Agreement to add products to the range is usually much easier to achieve than agreement to remove them. In many long-established companies, variants will have been added slowly over the years, each one seeming to have a good case at the time, but the overall result is that the product range has a long tail of marginally profitable products, which add to the hidden complexity costs to a degree which cannot be justified by their contributions to operating margin.

A successful product and pack rationalisation exercise will require co-operation between Marketing and Production and it will usually be advisable to devote time to understanding each other's problems and objectives before attempting to review the product range. The exercise has a much greater chance of success if it is openly supported by the Managing Director and preferably by both the Sales and Production directors.

Standardisation of packaging also assists JIT. Use of fewer different container sizes not only assists purchasing and control but facilitates change-over reduction. Using the next standard size upwards and adding ullage to take up the excess space may well be cheaper than using a non-standard container, particularly when the savings from not having to place additional purchase orders or not carrying out extra set-ups are included in the equation.

In the pharmaceutical industry, tablets are frequently sold in blister packs. The tablets are each in a separate blister, moulded into a sheet of thermoformable plastic film. The blisters are sealed by laminating aluminium foil to the film. Adopting a standard blister tray size even if this means a spacious layout for small tablets, may be justified if savings in change-over costs on the blistering and cartonning machines are greater than the potential waste of foil, film and carton board by having larger packs than necessary for the smaller products.

11.6 Reducing process complexity

It is often possible to simplify the manufacturing process dramatically by redesigning the product. In a well documented example, by use of unconventional design, the number of parts required to make a gas hob was reduced by 85%, and assembling the new hob required only a screwdriver. No particular techniques were used to achieve this improvement other than encouraging lateral thinking by brainstorming sessions.

Such improvements may not be available in all cases but how many manufacturers accept unreliable processes as a fact of life and achieve acceptable quality by testing and rejecting sub-standard product? The correct solution must be to investigate the process and eliminate the cause of the problem. Perhaps tighter specification of a temperature or stirring rate or tighter control of a raw material specification is all that is required. Reliable and simple processes make planning easier, save money and are a step towards JIT.

Once again, however, in industries with strict codes of practice, such as defence, medical or pharmaceutical, rigorous procedures for controlling changes to specification can work against JIT. New products are rushed onto the market as quickly as possible in order to meet deadlines. Often non-robust processes are accepted and quality of the end-product achieved by inspection and selection. If major process changes are needed to overcome the problems, the costs of achieving approval of the changes may be prohibitive. This restriction emphasises the need to incorporate as many JIT principles as possible when the process is first designed.

11.7 Purchasing and JIT

The traditional approach to choosing suppliers has been to have several and play one off against the other. This can be an effective way of achieving minimum prices but since it forces suppliers to cut costs and possibly to compromise on quality, it is unlikely to be a minimum total cost approach. Inferior materials or components may lead to slower production rates on key equipment or even to rejection of the items produced. Purchasing policy must be to achieve the lowest overall costs for the business, which can be a very different objective from achieving minimum purchase costs. Although few would disagree with this objective, in many companies an important performance measure for the purchasing function is still 'average percentage reduction of purchase spend achieved' and an adversarial relationship with suppliers is seen as the best way to achieve this. However, the realisation is growing, that in return for a promise of all or a substantial share of a buyer's business, many suppliers are prepared to co-operate in agreeing specifications, to ensure that the specifications are met, to accept responsibility if not, to deliver on-time in full, to accept other JIT principles, to co-operate on design and specification of new products as well as to be flexible on prices.

The advantages of small order sizes in respect of improved material flow and lower stocks apply equally well to purchase orders as to manufacturing orders. A supplier with whom a good relationship has been established may well accept a blanket order for a year's supply with the price determined by the total quantity but with much smaller delivery quantities to be called-off when required. It may even be possible to use Kanban to control call-off. Testing requirements or analysis of each batch will impose a practical minimum on order size but the effects of this can be minimised by agreeing the testing specifications with suppliers, checking their capabilities and then accepting their certificate of analysis.

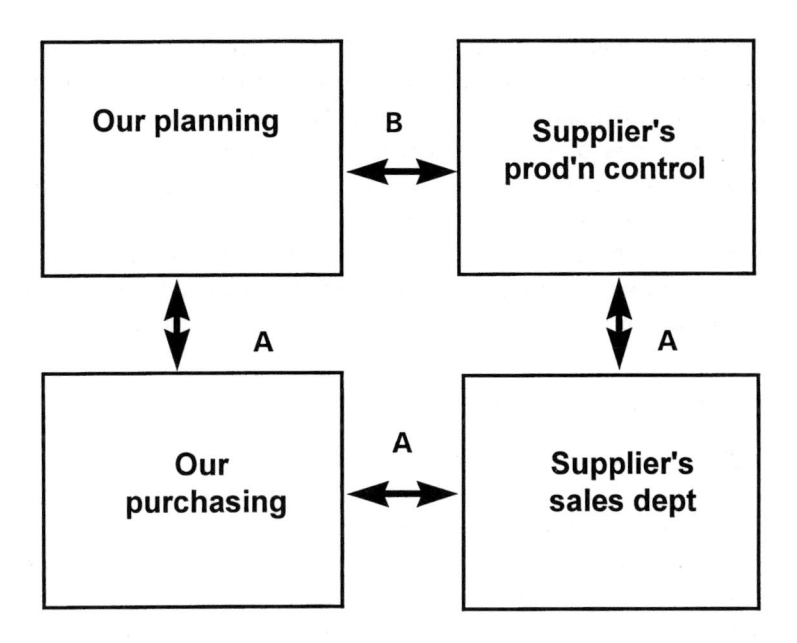

```
┌─────────────┐    B     ┌─────────────┐
│ Our planning│ ←─────→  │  Supplier's │
│             │          │ prod'n      │
│             │          │ control     │
└─────────────┘          └─────────────┘
      ↕ A                      ↕ A
┌─────────────┐    A     ┌─────────────┐
│    Our      │ ←─────→  │  Supplier's │
│ purchasing  │          │  sales dept │
└─────────────┘          └─────────────┘
```

11.5 Purchasing communications.

All too often communications with a supplier follow the path represented by links A in Fig. 11.5. The need for a purchase order or a change to a purchase order is normally recognised by our Production Planning Section which passes on the request to our Purchasing Group. Purchasing contacts the supplier's Sales Department which passes on requests to the supplier's Production Planners. If documents sit in an in-tray for two or three days at each stage, this process can be very time consuming. Any answer about the feasibility of bringing forward a delivery date, for example, comes back along the same tortuous route with plenty of opportunity for delay or distortion *en route*. Commercial negotiations about price and specifications must be the responsibility of the professional purchaser and the supplier's Sales Department, but how much simpler routine progressing of delivery dates would be if our planners spoke directly to the supplier's planners about such routine matters (link B in Fig. 11.5).

Suppliers will often, in good faith, quote lead times of weeks or even months for items which may only take hours of machine time to make. This is partly because the new order joins a queue with orders from other customers and partly because the supplier may have to order materials which in turn may have a long lead time. By sharing information with a supplier the effective lead time can often be reduced. Take, for example, printed cartons, and let us assume that the purchaser orders ten different prints in the same basic size. The supplier only needs to know the details of which print copy to use a few days or possibly hours before printing commences. If the buying company calculates forward requirements in terms of total cartons irrespective of print and shares this with the supplier, machine capacity can be booked in advance and a place reserved in the queue. The appropriate printed version can then be called off, according to the latest schedule, with a lead time of only a few days. If the long term predictions are incorrect, there may be some risk for the supplier. The buyer must be prepared to share this. If booked capacity is not used, the supplier must be compensated according to agreed terms. The long term contract must specify the maximum volume over the period of the order, the maximum rate of supply per day, week or month to which the supplier is committed, and the minimum rates of off-take below which the buyer will not fall without paying compensation.

For Purchasing, JIT means working with suppliers, rather than against them, sharing information, sharing targets, sharing risks and if any quantifiable benefits accrue, sharing these in an equitable way. The aim is to achieve co-operation rather than conflict. It would clearly be unwise to move directly from a traditional relationship with a supplier to a JIT relationship. This can only be achieved effectively by a slow process of building trust and sharing information. Often the first stage is a formal education programme run by Purchasing to which selected suppliers are invited. Many experienced purchasing managers feel concern about having only one supplier for each range of items. Even if they accept fully the supplier's competence and integrity, their concern covers events outside the supplier's direct control, such as fires, explosions, strikes, insolvency, serious machine breakdown or failure of the supplier's suppliers, etc.

Such concerns must not be dismissed lightly. Interestingly, there is often less concern about single sourcing for internally manufactured items, probably because of the feeling that it is under our own control and exceptional measures can be taken if necessary. If the relationship with the supplier has developed sufficiently, the supplier can be relied upon to take exceptional measures just as effectively as internal suppliers but this may not be an argument in favour of a single external supplier as much as an argument against a single internal source. As with other aspects of JIT, management judgement is required as to how far along the road towards the ultimate JIT objectives it is sensible to go at any time. JIT is a journey not a destination. It must be undertaken at a speed compatible with the travellers' capabilities.

The benefits of a JIT relationship can be great, but as in other aspects of JIT there is also a downside. The losses if a relationship fails can be crippling.

11.8 Summary

Value is added to a product when a transformation occurs to make it closer to the end-product which the customer requires. Value is not added when it is moved, stored or subjected to unnecessary testing. Cleaning and changing-over the machine do not add value to the product which is about to be made. If the definition of non-value adding activities as waste is accepted, then an alternative definition of JIT is the systematic **Elimination of Waste**, which in practice means much the same thing as the previous definition, **Continuous Improvement**.

JIT is unlikely to be achieved by dramatic changes. Progress is much more likely to be achieved in a series of small steps. An effective way of making improvements is to set up multi-disciplinary teams or Work Improvement Groups (WIGs), similar to the teams proposed for change-over reduction. A typical WIG might consist of a process operator, a storeman, a buyer, a planner, a scheduler, a maintenance engineer, a quality representative and a production supervisor. Experience suggests that the teams are more effective if given specific problems to solve. Figure 11.6, the **JIT Spiral**, illustrates this approach. The process usually starts with management action, for example, to reduce planned lead times, reduce order quantities or to reduce safety stocks. In terms of the River of Inventory analogy, shown in Fig. 11.1, the river level has been lowered. If this does not cause any pain (or reveal any rocks), stocks, order sizes or planned lead times must be reduced further until pain is felt (or a rock revealed). A WIG is then given the objective of alleviating the pain (or removing the rock). When that particular pain has been alleviated – management take a further initiative to reduce stocks, etc – a WIG is set up and the process continues.

For this process to be successful the team must first of all be educated and trained in JIT techniques. Management must receive suggestions sympathetically and constructively and be prepared to be supportive if initial results are disappointing. Ideas will not continue to flow if the initial suggestions are dismissed out of hand. The team will need technical support and above all will respond to positive feedback from management as ideas are successfully applied.

The JIT Spiral approach has been critically described as shooting oneself in the foot every time things are running smoothly and there is

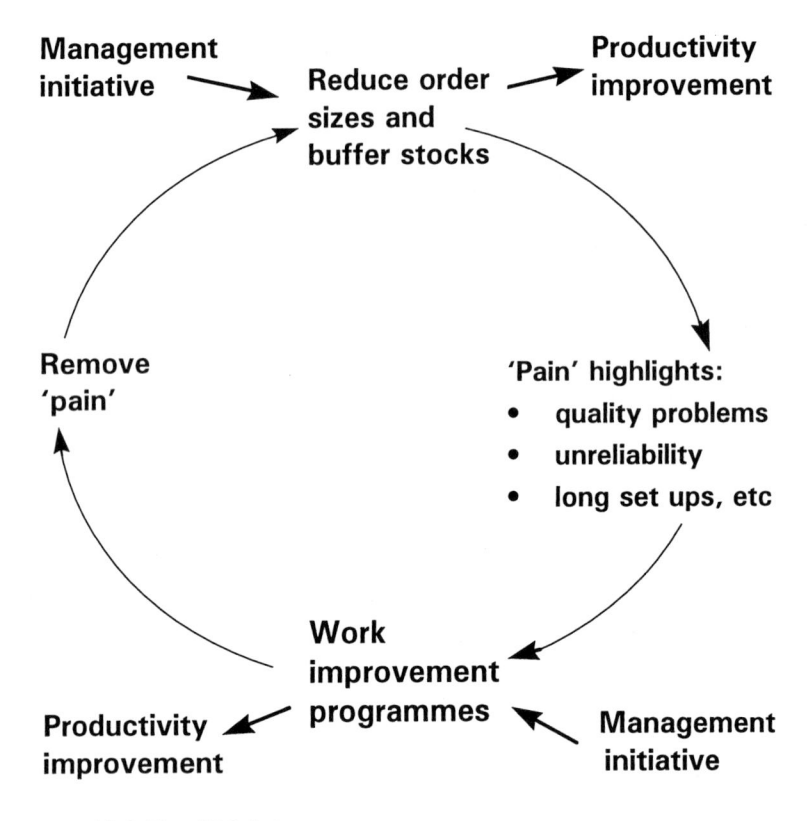

```
Management                          Productivity
initiative  ──►  Reduce order  ──►  improvement
                 sizes and
                 buffer stocks


Remove                              'Pain' highlights:
'pain'                              • quality problems
                                    • unreliability
                                    • long set ups, etc


                    Work
                    improvement
Productivity  ◄──   programmes  ◄──  Management
improvement                          initiative
```

11.6 The JIT Spiral.

some truth in this criticism. In terms of the River of Inventory analogy, using an echo-sounder to detect the rock and then removing it before lowering the water level is less painful than lowering the level until the rock is hit and then dealing with the problem. If problems can be identified and improvements made before pain is experienced, then this should be done. In many companies, however, the water will be too turbulent and murky for the echo-sounder. Even if potentially painful problems can be identified, it will be difficult to persuade busy people, all with their own pressing problems, to give high priority to something not yet causing widespread difficulty. The JIT Spiral approach provides a common focus and helps develop the motivation needed for improvement.

11.9 JIT and MRPII

Often JIT is presented as an alternative to MRPII. Certainly Kanban within a cell, for example, is an alternative to some of the more detailed scheduling activities of MRPII. However, if a JIT improvement project shortens a lead time, reduces an order size or reduces a change-over time, these must all be fed back to MRPII, which will then produce plans consistent with the improved performance. Even if Kanban is used within a manufacturing cell, MRPII is likely to still be needed to plan the overall load on the cell and schedule the raw material supplies. MRPII and JIT are entirely compatible.

Should a highly successful JIT programme simplify a business to the point where MRPII is no longer necessary and simple manual control systems suffice, then JIT is a true and desirable alternative to MRPII, which should then be discontinued. There is no point in using an expensive and complicated system if a cheap simple one gives equally good results.

11.10 Total Quality Management

During the first half of the twentieth century, western Europe was regarded as the source of high quality manufactured items. In the 1950s, 'Made in Japan' was synonymous with 'Cheap, unreliable and low quality' but in less than a decade there was a dramatic turnround. Japan followed by other Pacific Rim nations became recognised as the suppliers of the best quality available. Western companies were forced to improve the quality of the goods they sold in an attempt to remain competitive. This was initially done by inspection, with products which did not meet specification being identified and rejected or rectified before shipment to the customer. This inspection based approach, centred on the products, is usually called **Quality Control**.

Although traditional quality control had its successes in the west, the Japanese had recognised that preventing defects from occurring in the first place was much more effective and profitable than **inspecting them out** later. This became known as **Quality Management** rather than Quality Control. Quality should be the responsibility of everyone, not just of a professional Quality Control function. When defects are detected, the cause of the defect must be identified and changes made so that the defect will not recur. Quality Management is about developing realistic specifications for purchased items, manufactured intermediates and for finished products, developing detailed operating procedures for all manufacturing activities and then ensuring that the specifications are met and the procedures followed.

In the past, Quality Management tended to concentrate on product quality but in recent years interest has grown in improving the quality not only of products but of all aspects of the business. For example, the way telephones are answered or the standard of cleanliness of wash rooms are both indicators of the quality standards achieved by a company.

A quality business is not only committed to doing things right but also to doing the right things effectively at the right time. This approach is known as **Total Quality (TQ)**, **Total Quality Management (TQM)** or, less accurately, **Total Quality Control (TQC)**. A full discussion of TQ is beyond the scope of this chapter. It will only be discussed with respect to its relationship to JIT.

TQ is based on the premise that everyone is responsible for maintaining and improving quality. Quality is too important to be left to a specialised group of quality controllers. Production staff are responsible for product quality, just as they are for the effectiveness and efficiency of production. Operators check their own or each other's work against agreed standards, and it is their responsibility to pursue improvements in quality. It is usually helpful and in some industries a legal necessity to have a professional Quality Assurance Group, independent of Production, which does not test or approve products, but is responsible for checking and approving the techniques and procedures used by production to ensure quality, but the prime responsibility for all aspects of quality is shared by everyone.

11.10.1 Internal and external customers

It is generally recognised that a prime objective of all parts of the business is to satisfy the needs of external customers. If this is done better than the competition do it, the business will thrive. It is not so generally recognised, however, that within the business each function is both a customer and supplier. Purchasing supplies the warehouse, the warehouse supplies production, production supplies distribution and so on. It is a reasonable premise that if the quality of service supplied to the internal customers improves, the effectiveness of the business as a whole will improve. Most employees are conscientious in ensuring that they carry out their responsibilities to what they perceive as the correct standards but how often do they check that their internal customers share their concept of what is required?

A useful and interesting exercise is to get all managers in a business to identify their internal and external customers and then to prepare specifications for the services they need or provide. Comparison of the customers' and the suppliers' view of the same relationship should at the very least identify some problem areas.

11.10.2 Quality Circles

A technique for identifying opportunities for improvement in internal service levels is to assemble a multi-disciplinary team of representatives from a particular function and from its internal customers and suppliers. In Japan such groups are known as Quality Circles. The key members should be of similar status and be people who meet and interact to get things done on a day by day basis. They are well placed to identify deficiencies in internal service levels and to devise and implement improvement programmes. A Quality Circle may require support from technical experts such as engineers or systems analysts.

If this sounds familiar it is because Quality Circles bear a striking similarity to the WIGs discussed earlier in this chapter. An important difference is that Quality Circles, as originally conceived in Japan, identified their own problems and improvement targets but this does not appear to work well in a western culture. WIGs in contrast are usually set up to solve a particular problem or, in JIT Spiral jargon, to alleviate a particular pain. The concept of the internal customer, however, can provide a useful mechanism for identifying the underlying cause of a problem.

11.11 TQM and JIT

Not only are Quality Circles and WIGs effectively different names for very similar activities, further examination shows that TQ and JIT are very similar processes, which happen to have started from different ends of the same spectrum. JIT looks initially at equipment, processes and procedures to detect and eliminate waste and then moves to examine products. Inferior quality is a prime example of waste. TQ starts with product quality and then seeks a quality approach in other areas, not only in production but possibly covering activities such as new product development or contact with customers.

Both are processes without end. The quest for quality is continuous as is the search for improvement. Both techniques depend on the analytical skills and creativity of people. Both require management support if they are to be effective.

It is semantic to argue whether we have two different names for the same technique or two separate techniques with a large area of overlap. Both can be very successful in improving the effectiveness not only of manufacturing but also associated activities.

Exercises

11.1 List all those features of the control system and operations of a traditional western company, which would mean that the adoption of JIT deliveries of raw materials, components and sub-assemblies would be a high risk option.

11.2 Attempt to identify the two biggest 'rocks' preventing the reduction of stock in a business you know well, or if you do not have a direct connection with a particular manufacturing business, make an informed guess about the two largest rocks in un-reformed businesses in Europe and the USA. Write down a list of actions you could take to remove these rocks.

11.3 List all the objections that are likely to be raised against a project to halve the change-over times on high speed soft drink bottling equipment. Consider and write down possible ways of overcoming each of the objections.

11.4 Readers who find it difficult to accept that significant reductions in change-over times can, in most companies, be made cheaply and easily should find this exercise interesting.

Make estimates of the following times and costs:

1. You are driving home from work and suffer a puncture. You are competent with tools and look after your car well. How long, approximately, will it take to change the wheel?
2. You are competent with tools but because of other pressures you have not located where the jack is stored in your new car, and you do not know where the safe jacking points are. The handbook is not in the car. When you finally get it jacked up you find that the wheel nuts are too tight to be undone with the short brace provided. You have to telephone for assistance. How long, roughly, is this wheel change likely to take? How much would you have had to spend if you had made the necessary preparations so that you could have changed the wheel easily as in the case above?
3. On a different occasion you recognise the feeling of a flat tyre but are fortunate enough to be able to drive into a specialist tyre centre before your tyre deflates completely. How long will it take them to change a wheel? What equipment do they have and, very approximately, how much does it cost?
4. A Grand Prix racing car pulls into the pits for a wheel change during a race. Approximately how long does it take? Is the cost of all the special

equipment and preparation likely to be in hundreds, thousands or tens of thousands of pounds?

What lessons can be deduced from the four cases above?

11.5 List all the reasons why a change-over reduction exercise is often a first step in a JIT programme. Which reason do you consider to be the most important?

Draw up a proposal and justification for a change-over reduction exercise on a piece of equipment with which you are familiar. Outline the main steps you would expect to follow. (Your proposal should be no longer than one side of A4.)

11.6 Prepare a list of the advantages of manufacturing cells over more traditional functional organisations for production. List also the disadvantages. In what circumstances are cells most likely to be advantageous? Can you identify any opportunity for the introduction of cells into a business with which you are familiar? What difficulties would you face in trying to introduce cells and how might these be overcome?

11.7 What are the advantages of Kanban? List also the disadvantages. Why is Kanban unlikely to be appropriate as the main production control mechanism for an engineering job shop making largely one-off items?

11.8 What arguments might you use to justify:

- adding a new product to the sales range?
- deleting a product from the range?

Consider a high technology product, product A, which sells 1000 items per year at £100 per item, with the following cost and margin structure:

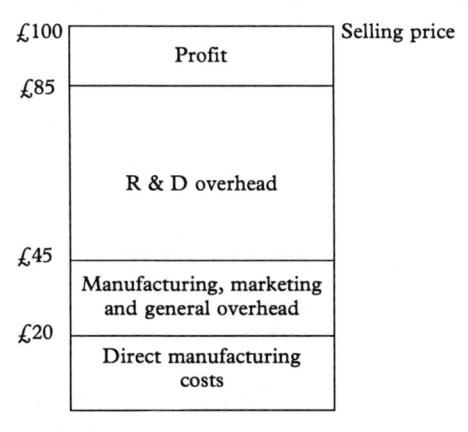

Price level	Component	
£100		Selling price
	Profit	
£85		
	R & D overhead	
£45		
	Manufacturing, marketing and general overhead	
£20		
	Direct manufacturing costs	

This company, probably in aerospace, defence, medical or pharmaceutical products carries a large research and development overhead.

If modifications to product A reduce manufacturing costs by 10% the saving would be £2 per item, or 1000 × £2 = £2000 per year.

If, however, this resulted in a 3% loss of sales because the redesigned product had less user appeal, sales would be reduced by 30 items per year with lost revenue of 30 × £100 = £3000 per year. The direct manufacturing cost of 30 items would be saved by not having to manufacture the lost sales, a saving of 30 × £20 = £600 per year. Marketing and research costs, however, would remain constant. The total saving would be £2000 + £600 = £2600 but this is outweighed by the reduction in sales income of £3000.

Even very large savings in manufacturing costs may not be beneficial if the change makes the product less attractive to the end-user and results in a significant reduction in sales volume.

Carry out a similar cost benefit calculation for a proposed redesign of product B, a domestic vacuum cleaner, which is intended to save 10% of the direct manufacturing cost, but unfortunately is also expected to lead to a loss of 3% of sales. This product also sells 1000 items per year at £100 per item. The cost structure of this product is:

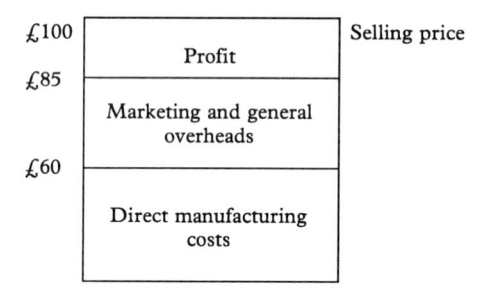

£100	Profit	Selling price
£85	Marketing and general overheads	
£60	Direct manufacturing costs	

11.9 Write a summary of all the improvements which could contribute to a broad-ranging JIT programme. What are the disadvantages and risks of such a programme?

11.10 List all the data items in an MRPII system which may require updating to reflect improvements arising from a JIT programme.

11.11 With respect to your job, identify your internal customers and suppliers. Prepare a draft description of the services which the two most important customers are likely to require from you. What parameters could you measure to quantify your success in providing the required services? How many of these parameters are currently measured? If you do not have a relevant job, do the exercise for a job which you know well, or failing that for a production manager responsible for final assembly in a Make to Order engineering company.

12

Implementing manufacturing control systems

A common feature of manufacturing control and improvement techniques such as MRPII, OPT, JIT and TQM is that they all require the adoption of new ways of working. Each requires the introduction of discipline, clarification of roles and responsibilities, and the fostering of a culture of co-operation rather than conflict. To be successful, the way people think and behave must be changed. Perspectives must be broadened, whilst still requiring attention to detail. All employees must become willing to contribute to the solution of a problem, even if they personally are not feeling any of the pain it causes. It is not surprising that successful implementation of all four techniques requires heavy investment in education and training in order to develop commitment and understanding at all levels in the organisation.

This chapter will consider how successful projects are initiated and organised, and will examine the factors critical to success. MRPII and OPT both involve large computer systems, but JIT and TQM do not. This clearly requires differences in the approach to implementation but the similarities are at least as significant as the differences.

12.1 Initiating the project

Almost invariably major improvements in manufacturing control are initiated by a Project Champion who typically will have been struggling with problems at a detailed level and will have become aware of the potential solutions offered by MRPII, JIT, etc.

After finding out more, his or her enthusiasm grows and support is slowly gathered until a sufficient number of senior managers become convinced of the benefits, and formal approval for a project is obtained. If the Project Champion happens to be the Managing Director, this can be a quick and easy process but if, as is more often the case, the initial drive

IMPLEMENTING MANUFACTURING CONTROL SYSTEMS

comes from middle or junior management, the task of gaining support and commitment from senior management can be slow and daunting. Some of the key steps in gaining support are discussed below.

12.1.1 Prepare a cost–benefit case

It is important to be able to demonstrate that the potential benefits of a proposal exceed the costs by a significant amount. A formal cost–benefit document should be prepared. Initially a number of rough estimates will be necessary but these can be refined as support grows.

For example, if customer service could be improved so that 99% of customer orders were supplied on time, how many extra sales would result? Usually no definitive answer will be possible but it is possible to calculate the additional margin (sales income minus variable materials and labour costs) for a range of potential increases in sales resulting from on-time delivery performance of 98% or better, e.g. 1%, 5%, 10% or 20%. It is not necessary to specify which at this stage. If the 1% figure yields an annual margin comparable with the project cost, the case is likely to be a strong one. Conversely, if increases in sales revenue of 20% or more are needed, the case looks less strong and more precise estimates are needed.

Readers or listeners can be asked for their best guess. The guess of the Sales Director is particularly valuable, especially if he or she has in the past complained about how much business is being lost because of poor customer service.

Benefits

Benefits can be expected from some or all of the following areas:

- Increased sales arising from improved customer service, shorter lead times, faster response to tenders, etc. The possible improvement depends on the starting point. Obviously a company already delivering 98% of orders on time cannot expect a 5% improvement but if no special attention has previously been given to improving customer service, a 10% increase is likely to be a conservative estimate for the benefits of a wide ranging improvement drive.
- A stock reduction. It is not unrealistic to expect 50% reduction. Savings will be the carrying cost of the value of the stock saved (at typically 25% per annum).
- Benefits of increased productivity. An increase in labour productivity of 5% is a reasonable target. For many companies direct labour is no

longer one of the major contributors to costs, so a 5% saving is unlikely to be a large sum. More significant will be the saving if it proves possible to delay expansion of the plant by making better use of existing buildings and equipment. With good control, equipment will spend less time awaiting materials and labour. Improvements in maintenance of equipment and improvements to the specifications of components should reduce the incidence of minor stoppages. Reducing the amount of work in progress will release storage space for other purposes.
- Savings on purchases. Developing a good relationship with suppliers, sharing information with them and using good information about future requirements as a basis for negotiations should facilitate agreement on more favourable prices. A saving (or increase avoided) of 3% is a realistic assumption.
- Unquantifiable benefits from improvements in job satisfaction and quality of life.

The benefits from successful and complete MRPII or OPT should include all of the above, but JIT or TQM programmes usually involve a number of separate exercises each focused on a specific area, so the expected benefits from each exercise will be more limited.

Costs

For MRPII and OPT the costs will include computer hardware, software, the cost of project team time and above all education and training costs. The last item must not be under-estimated. For MRPII and OPT a rule of thumb is that it will be at least as much as the software costs.

The major costs for JIT or TQM are likely to include training, education and the cost of the time of the WIGs, but if the group members can make time available without working overtime or neglecting other duties, the cost of their time is not a real additional cost. It is useful to define education as learning about the general principles of an improvement technique, whilst training is about how to operate a new way of working identified by the exercise. Education is normally required at the beginning or even before the formal start of a project. Training is usually needed towards the end.

The first draft of the cost/benefit case may contain some very approximate numbers. If the benefits greatly exceed the costs, or vice versa, there is no need to refine the estimates but if the case is not clear cut, further investigation and refinement will be needed.

12.2 Project organisation

Once formal approval has been given, a project team and the necessary organisation can be set up. A structure suitable for an MRPII or OPT project is shown in Fig. 12.1. For JIT or TQM the Steering Committee and the Project Manager are still required, but instead of the task forces, each responsible for an aspect of the overall project, there will be WIGs each with an objective to solve a specific problem or to bring about improvement in specific areas. The JIT or TQM Project Manager helps identify the problem areas to be tackled and sets up the WIGs, but unless invited to do so, takes no active part in their deliberations.

12.2.1 Steering Committee

The Steering Committee should consist of senior managers able to commit resources. For a minimum, the finance, marketing and production directors should serve, and the chairman should be someone to whom these three functions report, which usually means the Managing Director or equivalent. The Steering Committee typically meets at least monthly with the Project Manager to review progress and to provide advice and support as required.

12.2.2 Project Manager

Ideally the Project Manager for an MRPII or OPT project should be a full time appointment, but this is unrealistic in small and in some cases medium sized companies. If a company has only three senior managers, releasing one of them represents releasing 33% of the management team. Such companies may have no acceptable option other than to engage a temporary manager or consultant but it is essential that ownership of the project is retained, and is seen to be retained, by the full-time management team. The temporary manager's role is not to manage the project but to support the Project Manager so that he or she can operate effectively in the time that can be made available.

The work load is not quite so demanding for JIT and TQM projects but large companies will require a full-time manager even for the latter. Much of the Project Manager's time will be spent motivating the team or persuading fellow managers to agree to changes. The most essential qualification to have is good people skills. Experience of manufacturing control is desirable but not essential.

Appointing the Project Manager is one of the key decisions of the

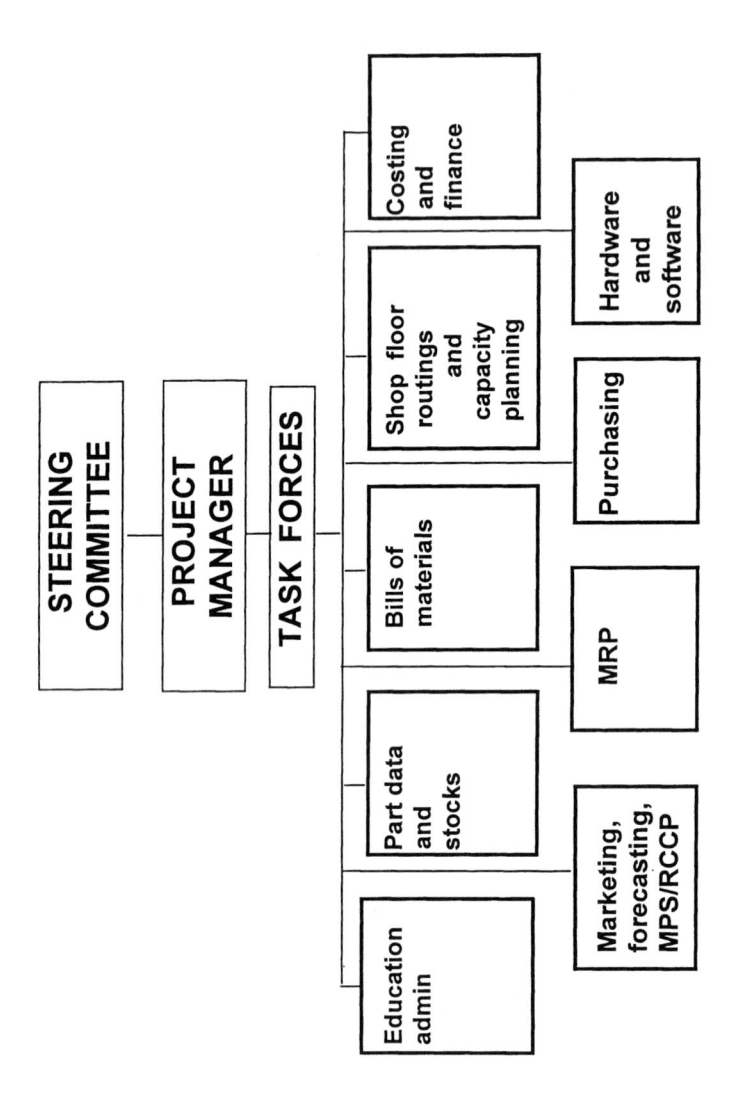

196 PLANNING AND CONTROL OF MANUFACTURING OPERATIONS

```
STEERING COMMITTEE
        │
PROJECT MANAGER
        │
    TASK FORCES
        ├── Education admin
        ├── Part data and stocks
        ├── Bills of materials
        ├── Shop floor routings and capacity planning
        └── Costing and finance
        ├── Marketing, forecasting, MPS/RCCP
        ├── MRP
        ├── Purchasing
        └── Hardware and software
```

12.1 Project structure for MRPII or OPT project.

project. It is important to select the best person, not the manager who can be most easily spared. A useful test of a provisional appointment is that the correct person is the one who can be released from his or her present job only with great difficulty.

Although both MRPII and OPT depend on computer systems, they are not computer projects. The software and hardware must work effectively but it is much easier to achieve this than it is to change entrenched behaviour and create a new culture. Appointing a Project Manager with an Information Systems or computing background sends the wrong signals about the nature of the project and unless the individual has exceptional interpersonal skills should be avoided. If employees believe that the computer is going to do all the work, they are unlikely to accept that the project needs any form of special effort or willingness to change from them.

12.2.3 Task Force

The Task Force responsible for organising education will be common to all four projects.

For MRPII or OPT, Task Forces are best led by senior managers from the appropriate functions, since they are more easily able to commit their functions to new ways of working. Almost the opposite is true for JIT or TQM where the groups will in general be tackling problems which require a detailed knowledge of how operations are carried out. Production supervisors or their equivalent are appropriate leaders for JIT or TQM Task Forces, and the members will be production operators, or staff primarily engaged in doing rather than managing. The presence of a senior manager is likely to inhibit suggestions from team members. Some Task Forces may need technical assistance from, for example, engineers. It is important that reasonable requests for such help are met if commitment to improvement is to remain high.

For MRPII or OPT the Task Forces may vary in size from a single part-time person to six persons or more, some of whom may be working for the project full time. Typically members should be knowledgeable representatives from the appropriate functions. In some instances it may also be necessary to include systems analysts and programmers.

12.3 The project plan and time scale

All projects should have a plan against which performance is regularly monitored. For JIT or TQM the overall plan need consist of little more than improvement targets and achievement dates for each task force, although the Task Forces themselves must prepare individual plans at an appropriate level of detail.

For MRPII and OPT a much more detailed plan is required to ensure that the activities of the various Task Forces are properly co-ordinated. A realistic time scale is unlikely to be less than 18 months, and many successful projects have taken three or more years, but for a variety of reasons it is desirable to complete the implementation in two years or less.

Figure 12.2 shows an MRPII implementation plan in outline. Note the activities which must occur before the project starts and note also that education is an ongoing activity to accommodate both refresher training of existing staff and the education of new starters.

A much more detailed plan than that in Fig. 12.2 is required if the project is to be managed successfully. Typically it will show several hundred separate activities, with a sub-plan for each Task Force or major group of tasks. For all but the smallest companies, the use of Critical Path Analysis (or Network Planning) software will be of great assistance in setting up and controlling the plan.

If careful analysis shows that a project duration of 24 months or less is not achievable with the available resources, it is advisable to break down the main project into consecutive sub-projects each with an identifiable outcome. For example, the first sub-project might be the recording of finished goods stock and the handling of customer orders, followed by MPS, and then MRP, but the details will obviously vary by company.

12.4 Educational activities

Education plays an important role in all projects and although the task is greater for MRPII and OPT than for JIT and TQM, the general principles of organisation are the same in all cases. For senior management pre-education, for the project manager and, in large companies, for the MRPII or OPT Task Force leaders, most companies will need to use external courses, or bespoke internal courses from a consultant.

An effective and inexpensive way of continuing the education process is for senior members of the project team who have attended professionally run courses to prepare courses on their specialised areas. These courses can be specially tailored to the requirements of the company and should use examples and case studies based on the company's products. Public courses may describe building bicycles or other engineering items which will be alien to attendees from the process industry, for example. The fact that the principles involved apply equally well to both product types may not be appreciated by the students at this stage. Examples based on

IMPLEMENTING MANUFACTURING CONTROL SYSTEMS   199

Months	-2 -1 0 1 2 3 4 5 6 7 8 9 10 11 12 13 14 15 16 17 18
Project champion prepares	
Educate senior managers	
Justification and approval	
Set up project structure	
Select consultant	
Educate project team	
Select & install software	
Learn about software	
General education	
Achieve data accuracy	
Load fixed data	
Develop policies & procedures	
Project team pilot(s)	(1)
Revise policies and procedures	
Specific training	
Conference room pilot	
Live pilot	
Load variable data (stocks, etc)	
Cut over to live running	(2)

12.2 Outline project plan.

familiar products will be received much more sympathetically than examples using unfamiliar products.

For MRPII and OPT, two courses are normally required for each area: an outline course for non-specialists and a detailed course for practitioners from the area. The requirements for JIT and TQM projects are not so demanding and a single course, if possible with examples tailored to the experience of the attendees, should suffice. In all cases, the Project Manager should prepare and deliver a brief general introduction suitable for all staff from senior managers to the shop floor operators. It enhances the credibility of the exercise if the Chairman of the Steering Committee is prepared to demonstrate his commitment by spending five minutes introducing this course each time it is delivered. A less satisfactory fall-back position is to prepare a video recording of this introduction.

In large companies it is advantageous to introduce an additional tier in the education process. Project team members present their courses to their management colleagues. Each manager, assisted by the project team, then prepares a course tailored to the needs of his or her staff. For example, the Purchasing Section Manager will cover MRP and Purchasing in great detail but will cover Sales Forecasting or Shop Floor Control in terms of general principles only. The Production Manager will cover Stock Recording, Manufacturing Orders and Shop Floor Control in detail but other areas in outline.

This cascade method of education via line management has two important advantages. Firstly, if managers are to teach they must first learn. Secondly, for those receiving it, the fact that it comes from their manager, and is relevant to their business, enhances the credibility of the message. A disadvantage is that, in large companies in particular, the message may become distorted as it is passed down. Involvement of the Project Manager in vetting course material can minimise this risk.

At a later stage, specific training will be required in the operation of the new procedures introduced by all types of improvement project. The best persons to deliver this training will vary according to each particular situation.

The role of the Education Task Force in MRPII or OPT is not to deliver the education but to organise it, to ensure that the correct people attend and to assist with the preparation of high quality teaching materials such as overheads and handouts. The Project Manager can undertake this role for JIT or TQM projects.

12.5 Project publicity

MRPII, OPT, JIT or TQM projects are largely about winning hearts and minds. Culture, attitudes and in some cases mind-set all need to be changed and experience has shown that some of the more reputable techniques of the public relations (PR) and advertising industries can be effectively employed to build commitment to the project.

A competition to choose an appropriately brief but meaningful project name or to design a project logo provides useful publicity. Other examples are using the logo on all educational material or rewarding attendance at courses with a small gift such as drinks coasters for the desk printed with the project logo or suitable slogan. Distribution of calendars or pens printed with the project name can help to spread awareness. If an atmosphere can be developed in which attendance at a course is seen as a privilege, it may be possible to hold courses out of normal hours or over lunch. Provision of a free pie and a pint or an attractive sandwich lunch increases acceptability, and the cost of such measures is a small fraction of total project costs.

Traditionally reserved UK managers tend to decry such overtly publicity seeking activities, but there is good evidence that they are as effective in the UK as in any other country. If the choice of soap powder can be influenced by PR and advertising, why should an employee's support for business improvements be different?

12.6 Technical activities

In addition to education, some project team members have technical roles. For JIT and TQM these are self-explanatory and relate to the problem areas being tackled. For example, a set-up time reduction project may require simple mechanical modifications such as shortening bolts, replacing bolts with spring clips or fitting graduated scales to adjustments. A Kanban implementation may require modifications to storage racking. It is obviously important that such changes are approved and carried out by suitably qualified persons, who if not already members of the WIG may have to be co-opted.

MRPII or OPT projects will all require computer expertise in some form and suitable people must be in the project team from the beginning. The rest of this section will consider only MRPII projects. An OPT implementation will be very similar. Choice of the key software is not part of an OPT project, because it comes as standard, but programming expertise will be essential for the development of interfaces to other business systems.

12.6.1 Choice of software

Often the choice of software will be dictated by a decision taken at group level and a need for standardisation. If this is not the case the choice can be bewildering, with a multitude of suppliers describing their products in glowing terms, sometimes with unrealistic claims. Almost all managers believe that their business has special requirements but in many cases these result from traditional ways of working for which there is no real current reason.

Recording and challenging all existing business processes is an important part of an MRPII project. Systems which have developed in an *ad hoc* way over many years will contain illogical and unnecessary activities, which are often associated with traditional organisational boundaries. When the company-wide systems are described on paper using one of the available charting techniques, illogicalities and duplications will often become obvious. Clearly these should not be replicated in the new systems and procedures and an important part of the project is to devise and get agreement to new operating procedures which not only eliminate illogicalities but also take advantage of the common data base, real time recording and report writing features of a modern computer system.

Once the proposed new operating procedures are documented and agreed and any special features identified, the next step is to prepare an Invitation to Tender (or ITT) which can then be sent to a number of likely suppliers of MRPII systems.

If adequate systems analysis expertise and a knowledge of what computers can and cannot do well are not available in the project team, it is wise to seek help from someone who has done it before. This person may be a manager with experience from a previous company, an employee of a different division of the company who can be seconded to the project team or an external consultant.

Defence or pharmaceuticals are the industry sectors most likely to require features which may not be available on all the leading packages. Some examples are:

- **Stock recording** with location, lot and possibly container detail.
- **A range of QC statuses** for each serial number or lot and for each container within the lot, for purchased items, intermediates or sub-assemblies and finished goods.
- **Appropriate units of measure** and an adequate number of decimal places on material quantities. As an extreme example, consider material which is normally stocked and used in kilograms but used in milligram

quantities on other products. 10 mg = 0.00001 kg so a satisfactory system must have either multiple units of measure for each item, with automatic conversion between units, or an adequate number of decimal places in all quantity records (e.g. stocks, quantities per on bills of materials, order and requirement quantities, etc).

- **Quarantine.** In some industries, goods received must be held in quarantine until they have been tested and approved. The simplest way of achieving this is to have a secure storage area into which all newly received items and materials are placed with an 'On test' status. The system should not permit the issue of items with status 'On test' or 'Rejected' except for rework orders, return to supplier or disposal.
- **Electronic quarantine.** An alternative to physical quarantine is electronic quarantine, which saves double handling of materials. Materials are stored in normal locations but not only will the system not permit issue transactions for On-test or Rejected status items, it will not even display their existence on the normal transaction screens.
- **Lot traceability.** In some industries, complete records must be kept to show which lots (or serial numbers) of materials or components were used to make each lot or serial number of product, so that if a component or material is found to be faulty, all products containing components from the same lot can be identified and recalled if necessary.
- **Potency recording.** In the food and pharmaceutical industries the active strength of materials such as tomato purée or antibiotics can vary from lot to lot. The system must be capable of recording the potency of each lot and adjusting the quantities issued to an order accordingly.
- **Production rates** in traditional engineering are normally specified as time per item. For high speed packing lines, producing thousands of items per hour, the time per item in hours can be too short to record with the available number of decimal places. Items per hour is a much more convenient unit.

12.6.2 Getting to know the software

Once the software is chosen, each team member must become familiar with all of it in broad terms and in detail for the modules particularly relevant. This is best achieved by using it in test situations and checking that the outputs achieved make sense.

Once they are familiar with the software, the groups can decide whether it fits in detail the proposed new operating procedures for the business. If the fit in any area is inadequate, it is almost always advisable to change the operating procedures rather than to modify the software.

12.6.3 Producing Standard Operating Procedures

Once a Task Force has decided how the business should be changed to support MRPII, it is necessary to agree the proposals with other task forces and then with the future users. This process requires writing proposals, followed by discussion and negotiation but should eventually lead to approved and signed-off Standard Operating Procedures for all aspects of operations. The long term aim must be to incorporate MRPII principles into any existing operating procedure documents written, for example, to comply with quality standards such as BS 5750 or ISO 9000, but initially it may be appropriate to have separate MRPII documents.

12.6.4 Testing proposed procedures and Project Team Pilots

An effective method of testing proposed procedures is to set up a model of a small business on a test version of the MRPII software. The model should have only two or three finished products, three or four components or raw materials, and two or three production work centres. The objective is to run the model as a simulation of the real business, in accelerated time.

The project team assembles in a conference room equipped with two or three computer screens and preferably a VDU projection system. Each section then takes its turn at optimising its plan on the model, explaining each action. When the plan is correct, the system date is moved on by a week and all the planning programs are run. Each task force responds to its output such as exception messages. An umpire can specify events such as purchase orders received, or manufacture completed, and the appropriate transactions such as raising new orders are then made on the system, in accordance with the proposed operating procedures. The date is then again moved on by a week and the process repeated until all the proposed operating procedures have been tested. This process in which the project team simulate operation of the business in accelerated time is called a Project Team Pilot.

If two or three runs per day can be achieved, the pilot will run 10 or 15 times faster than real time. Inevitably errors and inadequacies will be found in the proposed operating procedures. The pilot is not the forum for resolving these. Problems should be logged on a flip chart until the end of the exercise, when each is allocated to a task force charged with the responsibility for solving the problem and gaining agreement on revised operating procedures.

The Project Team Pilot is both a valuable learning experience and a test of procedures. It is useful to have two such exercises: one early in the project as a learning experience and one later as a test of the proposed Standard Operating Procedures.

12.6.5 Data preparation

MRPII and OPT involve a vast amount of data, all of which must be assembled, checked and entered onto the system. Procedures must be devised for its maintenance. Every item must have a designated owner who is held accountable for its accuracy. Relatively static data such as material codes, bills of materials or routings can be assembled over a convenient period of time, but volatile data such as stock records or details of manufacturing and purchase orders must be entered immediately before going live. This is most easily done during a weekend or annual holiday period, when the factory is not operating and the data is not changing as fast as it is input.

12.6.6 The Conference Room Pilot

When the project is almost complete, and user staff have been educated and trained, an invaluable final check of the procedures and training is to hold a Conference Room or User Pilot. This is exactly the same exercise as the Project Team Pilot except that the participants are the people who will operate the system when it is live. For a large company it may be necessary to hold more than one exercise in order to involve all staff. Contrary to the implication of the name, it is preferable not to have all the functions in a single conference room since this makes inter-departmental communication artificially easy. Ideally the functions should each have their own terminal in separate but adjacent rooms. Communications not involving the computer must then be by normal means such as notes, phone calls, personal visits, etc.

12.7 Cutting over to the new system

Providing that the Conference Room Pilot indicates that staff are adequately trained, the new system is ready to go live. The simplest way of doing this is to load up the variable data over a weekend, discontinue the old and start using the new from the Monday morning. This, however, is a high risk approach.

Should the new system fail, the old system will be difficult or impossible to reinstate, and serious problems will be faced. Running the old and new systems in parallel not only requires duplication of resources just when all effort should be concentrated on making the new system work, but will also become logically impossible as the plans created by the two systems diverge.

A much safer approach is to hold a Live Pilot. A small area of the factory which is as self-contained as possible is switched over to the new system and operated for a month or so. The rest of the factory remains on the old system. The live pilot is not a simulation like the Project Team and Conference Room Pilots. The new planning systems are live and operating in real time, albeit for a small section of the business, so that in the unlikely event of the new system failing, reinstating the old for a small part of the business is a manageable task. Once the new system is proven in the pilot area, the rest of the business may be safely switched over.

12.8 Operating MRPII

An MRPII system is unlikely to operate perfectly immediately. There will be a period of slow improvement whilst everyone involved becomes familiar with their new responsibilities. These include taking a broader view and being prepared to accept new ways of working in order to solve problems which impinge only on others. Everyone must be committed to maintaining accurate data, keeping plans realistic and above all to achieving due-dates. The rule must be **silence is approval**. Anyone saying nothing must mean that his or her contributions to the overall plan will be delivered on time. As soon as it is clear or probable that any planned due-date will not be achieved, this must be reported to the planners, who can then attempt to take remedial action. If this proves impossible, and delivery promises to customers cannot be met, the customer must be informed, even if the customer will not like the message and may threaten to 'shoot the messenger'. The customer's displeasure will be even more firmly expressed if the due-date is missed without prior notification. It must be remembered, however, that one of the prime objectives of MRPII is to improve customer service to the point where most – certainly more than 95% – customer orders are delivered on time in full.

12.9 Performance measures

Many traditional business performance measures are inappropriate for an MRPII environment. A volume or value target for output per month usually leads to a frantic scramble to achieve target in the last few days of the month. Everyone then pauses to recover and sort out the mess, only to find themselves already behind target for the following month-end.

An alternative, more rational approach under MRPII, is first of all to assess the plan to see if it meets targets for sales, stock levels and equipment occupation, etc. If it does and the plan is successfully followed, all the associated operations and sales targets will automatically be achieved.

Key monitors of business performance therefore are the percentages of manufacturing and purchasing order due-dates achieved, since these indicate how well the plans are being followed.

In addition it is desirable to monitor:

- Percentage of customer order promise dates met.
- Levels of outstanding customer orders (in Make to Order businesses).
- Sales versus forecast (in Make to Stock businesses).
- Production versus plan in suitable volume units (e.g. operator hours).
- Stock levels versus plan in value, volume (if a sensible unit of measure is available), and in weeks' cover.
- Percentage of operation due-dates met.

The initial aim should be to meet more than 95% of all due-dates. It is difficult to set general targets for other measures, since these will depend on the nature of the business. For many performance measures, achieving continued improvement is at least as important as the absolute value attained.

Since the success of MRPII depends on the way in which it is operated, it is also important that in addition to the business performance measures discussed above, senior management is also provided with measures of MRPII performance and how well a continuous improvement philosophy has been incorporated into MRPII, such as:

- Data accuracy for stock, bills of material and routing records.
- Stability of the MPS.
- Number of exception messages. Are these increasing or decreasing?
- Realism of plans with respect to materials supply. Percentage of imbalance. Messages unresolved by next MRP run.
- Realism of plans with respect to capacity. Number of unresolved overloads.
- Percentage improvements achieved over last 12 months in planned lead times, order quantities, safety stocks, set-up times, etc.

Successful MRPII will achieve control of the business, improve customer service, reduce stocks and reduce shortages of raw materials and intermediates. Significant extra benefits will be achieved, however, when MRPII is combined with a continuous improvement process such as JIT or TQM. The shorter change-overs, reduced order sizes, smaller safety stocks, simplified routings, shorter lead times, simplified bills of materials, etc, resulting from JIT or TQM can all be incorporated in the MRPII data, leading to a dramatic increase in overall performance.

12.10 Postscript

Operations Management is undoubtedly a demanding discipline, partly because of the complexity and uncertainty of many business environments but also because previous generations of managers have not understood the role of the planning and control functions. Production Control was all too frequently seen as a convenient home for a production operator who could no longer work on the shopfloor because of an injured back or similar physical problem.

The Second World War provided a catalyst for change but improvements came only slowly. Operations Research based on mathematical analysis, computer systems and reorganisation and simplification of the business all had their champions. With hindsight it is clear that two vital concepts were missing. These were:

- The preferred approach depends on the nature of the business and its trading environment. The type of product is less important than the complexity, diversity, degree of repetitiveness and customer service requirements (Make to Order, Make to Stock, etc) of the business.
- The effectiveness of an operations management approach depends more on the people who operate it than on the system used. Hearts and minds must be won and retained. Education, training and motivation are continuing requirements, not just significant parts in the original implementation.

As these concepts have been understood over the last 10–15 years, dramatic progress has been made. In the best companies, Operations Management is now highly professional and it is recognised that simplification and effective planning and control are key contributors to achieving a competitive edge and profitable operation. Unfortunately, the majority of companies still lag a long way behind the best, but an encouraging feature is that most managers now recognise that they have a problem, even if they are not sure exactly what it is or how to solve it. Some of the author's objectives will be achieved if this book not only helps managers identify what needs to be done but also contributes to the generation of informed support and commitment to change from their colleagues. Effective Operations Management requires contributions from everyone in the organisation, not just from a few specialists.

Exercises

12.1 Prepare a cost–benefit case for an MRPII or JIT project for the following company which has not been subject to a formal improvement programme during its 50 year history. It is a Make to Stock manufacturer of small domestic appliances. Make reasonable assumptions where necessary.

	£(000)
Annual sales	10 000
Annual materials purchases	3 000
Direct labour costs	2 000
General overhead	3 000
Annual profit	2 000
Work in progress	3 000
Sales stock	2 500

The business has been growing steadily at 5% per annum. A critical machining centre is approaching an 80% average occupation, which means that it can be overloaded during periods of peak demand. A proposal has been prepared for the purchase of an additional machine at a cost of £1 million, but sanction has not yet been given.

Other performance figures are:

Sales orders dispatched on time	70%
Manufacturing orders completed on time	55%
Productivity factor for manufacturing operators	80%

The sales director is unhappy about customer service levels and has complained at a board meeting that last year he lost business worth £3 million because stock shortages caused customers to go elsewhere.

12.2 Why do you think that an MRPII project becomes more difficult if it extends beyond 24 months? List as many reasons as possible.

12.3 Why is education such an important part of any of the projects we are discussing? What are the advantages of the Cascade method of providing project education? What are the potential disadvantages?

12.4 Produce a list of the possible disadvantages of making modifications to the purchased MRPII software.

12.5 If only a single measure of MRPII performance is to be circulated to management regularly, which should it be and why?

Answers to exercises

Chapter 1

1.1 A manufacturing strategy should cover at least:

- Manufacture or buy.
- Customer service objectives.
- Make to Stock, Make to Order or Assemble to Order.
- Quality policy.
- Health, safety and environment policy.

Answers will be to some extent personal. Additional items are not necessarily wrong.

1.2 Advantage of Make to Stock policy:

- We can supply the customer off the shelf. With Make to Order the customer must wait for new manufacture.

Disadvantages of Make to Stock:

- We need to anticipate the customer's requirements.
- This is difficult and errors lead to either high stocks or lost business.

1.3 It is not a wise decision. Since the 20 000 valves sent out do not represent a full work load for one operator, it is unlikely that the machine shop can operate with one fewer operators and its wage bill will not be reduced. Neither overall local nor general overheads will be significantly reduced by the decision. Thus the £8600 paid out will be an increase in real cost.

If all the machine shop operators were not fully loaded, sending out the 15 mm work could permit the number of direct operators to be reduced by one. This represents a saving of 33p per valve. However, this would be the only saving since the machine shop overheads would not reduce significantly. Each saving of 33p would be bought at a cost of 68p.

This exercise demonstrates that care is always needed in interpreting standard costs. Make in/send out decisions must be justified by savings in total factory expenditure, not merely in standard cost.

1.4 Stock holding costs include:

- Interest on money involved.
- Cost of providing and maintaining storage space and handling.
- Cost of losses due to spoilage and obsolescence.
- Insurance costs.

Change-over costs include:

- Operator costs for cleaning.
- Engineering costs.
- Costs of paper work.
- Quality Assurance costs.

If the equipment is fully occupied, the change-over cost must include any additional cost of doing elsewhere, possibly on less suitable and more expensive equipment, work which could have been accommodated if the change-over had not been necessary. (This exercise is examined in more detail in Chapter 5.)

Chapter 2

2.1 Average usage = 104 000/52 = 2000 per week
Usage over the four week lead time is 8000
Safety stock = 5000
Order Point is:

Usage over lead time plus safety stock = 13 000 since no material is on order

An order should be placed immediately after any transaction which reduces the stock below 13 000. It would be perfectly legitimate to find only 12 000 in stores and not to place an order, provided that an order had been already placed, e.g. with 20 000 on order the order point is 8000 + 5000 - 20 000 = -7000 and a stock of 12 000 is above order point.

2.2 With a two week lead time and four week review period nothing should be on order at review time. The order placed after the previous review, i.e. four weeks ago, should have been received after two weeks, leaving nothing on order.

Average usage is 1 200 000/48 = 25 000 per week

Maximum stock = safety stock + demand over lead time + demand over review period
= 50 000 + 50 000 + 100 000
= 200 000

Order quantity = maximum stock − current stock
= 200 000 − 80 000 = 120 000

The order will arrive in two weeks when the stock will have dropped from 80 000 to 30 000 (note this is below safety stock so usage in the previous month was higher than average). Immediately after the delivery the stock will be 150 000. This will fall to 50 000 over the four weeks before the next delivery, provided that usage returns to the average rate.

2.3 The completed planning grid for LEM03 is:

LEM03, Superlem drink 3 litre plastic container

Opening stock   85   Order quantity   80
Safety stock   50   Lead time   1 week

	Period	1	2	3	4	5	6	7	8	9	10
1	Sales forecast	5	0	20	0	40	20	70	0	70	10
2	Customer orders	20	40	10	10	30	0	10	0	0	0
3	Total requirements	25	40	30	10	70	20	80	0	70	10
4	Projected stock 85	60	100	70	60	70	50	50	50	60	50
5	Manufacturing order receipts		80			80		80		80	
6	Manufacturing order releases	80			80		80		80		

Planned releases of orders for filling 80 packs are required in periods 1, 4,

6 and 8. Each pack contains 2 litres, so ignoring losses 160 litres of bulk drink are required for each order.

2.4 (a) The total requirement of MD 200 is found by adding the unconsumed sales forecast, the customer orders which only appear in week 1 and the requirements for internal use.

Total requirements for MD 200

Opening stock　　18　　　　Order quantity　　30

Safety stock　　　5　　　　Lead time　　　1 week

	Period	1	2	3	4	5	6	7	8	9	10
1	Sales forecast	2	6	7	8	8	9	9	10	10	10
2	Customer orders	4									
3	For internal use	4	4	4	4	4	4	4	4	4	4
4	Total requirement	10	10	11	12	12	13	13	14	14	14
5											
6											

The manufacturing orders needed are then calculated in the normal manner, observing the safety stock level.

Plans for MD 200

Opening stock   18   Order quantity   30
Safety stock   5   Lead time   1 week

An open manufacturing order for 30 is due in week 2

	Period	1	2	3	4	5	6	7	8	9	10
1	Sales forecast	10	10	11	12	12	13	13	14	14	14
2	Projected stock 18	8	28	17	5	23	10	27	13	29	15
3	Manufacturing order receipts		(o) 30			30		30		30	
4	Manufacturing order releases				30		30		30		

(o) indicates open order

An order release may be required in period 10. This depends on the requirements for period 11. Provided that we are looking sufficiently far ahead we can ignore uncertainty in the last few periods. Alternatively we can extrapolate the forecast. A forecast for 14 or 15 in period 11 would require no manufacture in period 11 and hence no release in period 10.

(b) The total requirement for the MD 500 drive consists of the unconsumed sales forecast, customer orders (week 1 only) and the requirements for internal use. The external component of this demand is obtained by adding together the sales forecasts and customer orders lines of the table on page 40. The internal demand depends on the assembly plans for all computers using the MD 500 as shown below. There is one MD 500 per computer, so the internal requirements for MD 500 correspond to the planned releases of computer-assembly orders, which are calculated in the normal way by backing off from the order receipt date by the assembly lead time, as shown here.

Computer assembly plan for use in calculation of internal requirements for the MD 500 disk drive

Assembly plan for all computers containing the drive

Assembly lead time = 1 week

	Period	1	2	3	4	5	6	7	8	9	10
1	Manufacturing order receipts	(o) 10	(o) 12	12	12	16	16	20	20	20	20
3	Manufacturing order releases		12	12	16	16	20	20	20	20	20
3	Internal requirement for MD 500	0	12	12	16	16	20	20	20	20	20
4											

The calculated total demand for MD 500 is:

Total demand for MD 500

Opening stock	20	Order quantity	40
Safety stock	10	Lead time	1 week

	Period	1	2	3	4	5	6	7	8	9	10
1	Sales forecast	8	10	10	10	10	10	10	10	10	10
2	Customer orders	2									
3	For internal use	0	12	12	16	16	20	20	20	20	–
4	Total requirements	10	22	22	26	26	30	30	30	30	10

The manufacturing plans needed to meet these requirements for the MD 500 are:

Plans for MD 500

Opening stock   20   Order quantity   40
Safety stock   10   Lead time   1 week

An open manufacturing order for 40 is due in week 2

Period		1	2	3	4	5	6	7	8	9	10
1	Total requirements	10	22	22	26	26	30	30	30	30	10
2	Projected stock 20	10	28	46	20	34	44	14	24	34	24
3	Manufacturing order receipts		(o) 40	40		40	40		40	40	
4	Manufacturing order releases	40		40	40		40	40			

(o) indicates open order

No releases are shown in period 1 because the manufacturing order receipt of 40 in period 2 is open, i.e. already released and its component requirements satisfied. No receipt is shown in period 10, but this may be incorrect. The total requirement includes no requirement for internal use, because this would depend on manufacturing receipts for period 11, which is beyond the planning horizon for this exercise.

(c) The calculations involved are shown overleaf.

A purchase order for 80 must be released immediately, and followed by similar order releases in periods 2, 3 and 4. Two orders for a total of 160 must be released in period 5.

The cumulative lead time between receiving a finished computer into stock and placing a purchase order for bearings is five weeks. This is made up of one week for computer assembly, one week for hard disk assembly and three weeks for bearing purchase. Thus an order release for the purchase of bearings in week 6 would depend on an order release for disk assembly in week 9, which in turn would depend on a computer assembly order to be released in week 10 and received in week 11. The computer assembly plan and the forecasts for external sales of MD 200 and MD 500

Purchase plan for vibration free bearing VFB10

Opening stock   90   Order quantity   80

Safety stock   0   Lead time   3 weeks

An open purchase order for 80 is due in week 3

	Period	1	2	3	4	5	6	7	8	9	10
1	Requirements from MD 200				60		60		60		
2	Requirements from MD 500		80		80	80		80	80		
3	Total requirements		80		140	80	60	80	140	?	?
4	Projected stock	90	90	10	90	30	30	50	50	70	70	70
5	Purchase order receipts	0	0	80 (o)	80	80	80	80	160	0	0
6	Purchase order releases	80	80	80	80	160	0	0	0	0	0

only have a ten week horizon. If it is necessary to predict purchase order releases for week 6 and beyond, it is necessary to extrapolate the external demands for the hard disks and the computer assembly plans to week 11 and beyond. There is little point in striving for great precision in these extrapolations. Educated guesses based on the data in, say, weeks 8, 9 and 10 are probably adequate.

This exercise provides a good illustration of how the effective planning horizon shortens by the lead time for each stage as MRP moves down through the levels in the bills of materials.

2.5 Simple mechanistic MRP does not provide good manufacturing control for the following reasons:

- Sales forecasts can be volatile and sales orders received may differ from forecast. These changes can be amplified by the MRP calculation and

can result in an unmanageable degree of change for manufacturing and purchasing.
- Without capacity planning facilities it is often not possible to demonstrate that the plans could be achieved with the available resources. Unrealistic plans lead to poor customer service and high stocks.
- No feedback or plan modification procedures if actual production failed to meet plan. Hence plans could become unrealistic.
- Poor data accuracy for stock records and bills of materials.
- Inadequate commitment from all concerned, often caused by inadequate education and involvement.

Chapter 3

3.1 (a) The latest situation is shown below:

Grapefruit drink 500 ml

Opening stock 79 Lead time 2 periods
Safety stock   40 Firm planned fence 6 periods
Order quantity 50

	Period		1	2	3	4	5	6	7	8	9	10
1	Sales forecast		7	10	17	23	23	24	24	24	29	30
2	Customer orders		15	10	5							
3	Total requirements		22	20	22	23	23	24	24	24	29	30
4	Projected stock	79	57	37	65	92	69	45	71	47	68	88
5	MPS order receipts				(FP) 50	(FP) 50		(P) 50		(P) 50	(P) 50
6	MPS order releases		50	50			50		50	50		

(FP) indicates firm planned order, i.e. under human control.
(P) indicates planned order, i.e. under computer control.

Exception messages

- The projected stock in period 2 is below safety stock. Therefore a message to reschedule-in the firm planned order in period 3 will be produced.
- Without the production from the order in period 4, the projected stock would be 42 which is above safety stock. Therefore the order is not required until period 5 and there would be a reschedule-out message attached to it.

There would also be an action message, reminding the planner to open the firm planned order due in period 3.

In practice, messages would normally be referenced to an order via an order number.

Planned orders

The planned order for period 8 which is outside the firm planned fence, would be brought forward to period 7. New planned orders would be created for periods 9 and 10.

Judgement

1. The planner would have to check whether bulk drink, bottles, caps labels, etc, and filling capacity are available to permit the order in period 3 to be brought forward by a period. If this is the case he then would use his knowledge of the plant and product to decide whether it is wise to bring the order forward. If his own decision is in favour of a change, he should seek the agreement of the appropriate managers. (As should be specified in the company operating procedures for authorising changes to the MPS.)
2. There will be no material constraints on delaying or scheduling out the order in period 4 but it may create a capacity overload in period 5 depending on the other work on the filling line.

    If the planning periods are weeks or less there may be a case for ignoring both messages and running the two orders consecutively to save a change-over. However, it must be remembered that the convention in use is that an order shown in a period is due at the beginning of the period. Thus, delaying the order in period 3 to the end of the period could result in safety stock being further penetrated.

It is not normally good practice to delay orders to avoid change-overs.

No action is required from the planner concerning the planned orders in periods 7 to 10.

(b) With an opening stock of 72 the messages for periods 3 and 4 would remain unchanged but the stock at the end of period 6 would be 38 and below safety stock. There would therefore be a reschedule-in message on the planned order in period 7. The system would not automatically create an order inside the firm planned fence.

3.2 The jobs are presented in priority order and for this exercise there is no need to know how priorities are determined. (Amongst the possibilities are 'order of receipt', a calculated index such as 'Critical Ratio' (see Chapter 9, Section 9.3), or manually determined by discussion between the master production scheduler and the sales and marketing function, taking into account any component shortages or special situations.)

The jobs must be loaded onto the critical resource in sequence and the operator hours accumulated by week until the maximum load of 40 operator hours is reached. All the jobs completed in the week are given a promise date of that week. The remaining load from any partly completed job is carried into the next week. Orders are promised for the week in which they are planned to finish. The table below illustrates this process.

Order	Quantity	Hours/item	Total hours	Cumulative hours per week	Promise week
101	10	2	20	20	1
102	3	5	15	35	1
103	6	1	6	41	1
104	5	2	10	10	2
105	9	1	9	19	2
106	5	3	15	34	2
107	1	5	5	39	2
106	5	3	15	15	3
107	1	5	5	20	3
108	17	1	17	37	3
			Carried forward	−3	
109	5	2	10	7	4
110	6	2	12	19	4
111	10	2	20	39	4
			Carried forward	−1	
112	10	1	10	9	5
113	10	1	10	19	5
114	6	3	18	37	5

The revised Available to Promise chart is shown below:

Order slotting exercise

Low voltage transformer family

	Period	1	2	3	4	5	6	7	8	9	10
1	Manufacturing capacity per period	40	40	40	40	40	40	40	40	40	40
2	Customer orders	41	39	37	39	37					
3	Spare capacity available to promise			3	1	3	40	40	40	40	40
4											

It is important not to confuse precision with accuracy when calculating total loads. The 'Hours per unit' figures are at best averages of past performance and at worst little better than best guesses. The actual time taken by a particular order may deviate significantly from the average. Thus the cumulative hours of 41 and 39 for weeks 1 and 2 are acceptable. Making fine adjustments of one hour in 40 (2.5%), as has been done for week 4 is tidy but does not significantly improve the accuracy of the prediction. Carrying forward 3 hours (7.5%), at the end of week 3 is probably significant and worth doing. An urgent but small job of less than three operator hours could be promised for week 3.

3.3 The average output achieved in the past six months is 91 000 packs per month, even though the lines were striving for maximum output over that period. Unless therefore something has clearly changed, such as new equipment or longer working hours, it would be unwise to depend on achieving an output greater than the demonstrated capacity of 91 000 packs in any future month.

In fact the average output required over the next six months is 90 500 packs per month which should be achievable. The timing of the requirements presents a problem.

The following options should be considered:

- Investigating whether materials can be made available to permit scheduling the work at 91 000 packs per month and accept some temporary increase in finished packed stock.
- Planning to use sub-contract assistance in months 5 and 6.
- Using a combination of the above approaches.

It would be unwise to accept the packing line manager's belief that he could achieve 115 000 packs per month unless he had in mind some specific actions to increase output. One of the skills required of a master production scheduler is the ability to deliver unwelcome messages tactfully.

3.4 Amongst the possible costs of making a change in the production schedule are:

- Planner time.
- Additional change-over.
- Overtime or sub-contract working.
- Express freight charges to obtain components.
- Bad will with suppliers.
- Delays in other work resulting from the change.
- Reduced customer service of items delayed.
- Pressure and confusion resulting from too many changes, resulting in errors and omissions elsewhere.
- Redundant or out-of-life materials.
- Reduced morale and uncertainty amongst production personnel.
- Too many changes can cause the complete collapse of the control system.

Amongst the possible costs of not making a change to the production schedule are:

- Poor customer service resulting in ill will and lost business.
- Excessive finished product stocks produced, leading possibly to out-of-life materials.
- Scarce components being used for non-essential production leading to shortages.

Although the costs can be identified it is much more difficult to quantify them. Assessing the justification for change remains a largely subjective exercise. Experience suggests that in general the hidden costs of change are under-assessed and too many changes are undertaken too readily.

3.5

MX01   Mixed fruit drink 500 ml bottle

Opening stock   18   Order quantity   30
Safety stock   0

	Period		1	2	3	4	5	6	7	8	9	10
1	Sales forecast		6	10	10	10	10	10	10	10	10	10
2	Customer orders		(n) 4					(a) 9				
3	Total requirements		10	10	10	10	10	19	10	10	10	10
4	Projected stock	18	8	28	18	8	28	9	−1	19	9	−1
5	MPS order receipts			30			30			30		
6	MPS order releases											
7	Available to promise		14	30			21			30		

A message recommending the rescheduling of the MPS order in period 8 to period 7 would be expected. If this can be done the MPS will be back in balance until period 10, when a new receipt of 30 is required.

The negative projected stock means that if all the forecasts in periods 1 to 7 lead to customer orders, it will not be possible to accept one of them in full unless the MPS can be changed. The decision to accept the abnormal order for nine in period 6 gave preference to this order over a future order which may or may not arise in line with forecast. The plan is still realistic. It is acceptable to have a negative projected stock driven negative by a sales forecast. It is not acceptable to have a negative Available to Promise which would indicate that a firm order had been accepted to supply material not expected to be available.

3.6 The order is part of the forecast and is normal. Both the forecast and Available to Promise must be consumed. Nothing else changes.

MX01   Mixed fruit drink 500 ml bottle

Opening stock 18   Order quantity 30
Safety stock 0

	Period		1	2	3	4	5	6	7	8	9	10
1	Sales forecast		6	2 ~~10~~	10	10	10	10	10	10	10	10
2	Customer orders		(n) 4	(n) 8				(a) 9				
3	Total requirements		10	10	10	10	10	19	10	10	10	10
4	Projected stock	18	8	28	18	8	28	9	−1	19	9	−1
5	MPS order receipts			30			30			30		
6	MPS order releases											
7	Available to promise		14	22 ~~30~~			~~21~~			~~30~~		

The order for period 2 will be supplied from the receipt in period 2 leaving the 14 available in period 1 for alternative customer orders.

3.7

Safety stock	100	Order quantity 250
Opening stock	225	

Requirement	Qty	Date	Mfg order receipts	Qty	Stock balance
		31/12			225
Sales forecast	100	1/1			125
		7/1	MO123	250	375
P9 customer order	150	9/1			225
		27/1	MO124	250	475
Sales forecast	200	1/2			275
		25/2	MO124	250	525
Sales forecast	200	1/3			325
Sales forecast	200	1/4			125
		30/4	MO 125	250	375
Sales forecast	200	1/5			175
		31/5	MO 126	250	425
Sales forecast	200	1/6			225

The sales forecast for 200 items on 1 May drives the stock below the safety stock level of 100. Therefore, according to the convention previously adopted, a manufacturing order should be planned for receipt at the beginning of 1 May. Continuing the stock projection shows that the second new order is required to be received at the beginning of 1 June.

However, with daily time buckets and a vertical display, many people find it easier to understand the alternative convention that a receipt shown on a day must be received before the end of the day. The due dates for the two orders would then be 30 April and 31 May as shown in the table above.

A manufacturing order size of 250 when sales are forecast at 200 per month leads to increasingly high month end stocks, until the accumulated stock exceeds 200 and a month's requirements can be supplied without manufacturing. A manufacturing order size of 200 would lead to lower in-process stocks, but there may be technical reasons why an order size of 200 is not possible. (For example in a batch liquid mixing process there must be sufficient liquid in the pan to cover the stirrer, irrespective of any economic order quantity considerations.)

Chapter 4

4.1 Twenty working days represents four working weeks. Using the convention that when an order is shown as due in a period it should be available at the beginning of the period, the order must start four weeks before the first moment of Friday 28 February, which is by the beginning of Friday 31 January. The ready for release date will be two days earlier on Wednesday 29 January.

Using the alternative date convention, often preferred in systems with daily time buckets, that a receipt is due before the end of the period in which it is shown, gives the answer that the order must be released before the **end** of Friday 31 January. However, attempting to specify times so precisely is pointless, since the quoted lead time is based on past average performance and is unlikely to be accurate to a day.

4.2 (a) The requirements are obtained by multiplying each quantity per on the bill of materials by the order quantity, 10 000 in this case.

M19	Argento polish bulk (L)	1 000
C09	Bottle 100 ml printed	10 000
C21	Cap – child resistant	10 000
C29	Carton – printed	10 000
C32	Outer	1 000

(b) There are ten packs in each outer, since nominally the bill of materials shows 0.1 of an outer for each pack.

Chapter 5

5.1

(a) With no modifiers:

Week		1	2	3	4	5	6	7	8	9	10
Total requirements		7	13	9	5	4	3	12	18	7	6
Projected stock	21	14	1	5	0	3	0	18	0	6	0
Order receipts				13		7		30		13	

(b) With safety stock equal to 6 and a minimum order quantity of 10:

Week		1	2	3	4	5	6	7	8	9	10
Total requirements		7	13	9	5	4	3	12	18	7	6
Projected stock	21	14	15	6	11	7	18	6	13	6	10
Order receipts			14		10		14		25		10?

Remember that in the period in which a receipt is required, the net requirement is the quantity required to rebuild safety stock after the total requirement for the period is satisfied.

Projecting the stock predicts a level of 1 in week 2 after the total requirement of 13 has been satisfied. This is below safety stock so an order needs to be received. The quantity is 5 to rebuild the safety stock of 6 plus the 9 required in week 3, that is 14.

The receipt calculated for week 4 is 5 + 4 = 9, but this must be increased to 10 to satisfy the minimum requirement. Safety stock is again breached in period 10 but the receipt required cannot be calculated until requirements for period 11 are available.

5.2

Opening stock 7   Order policy Lot for lot
Safety stock 5

Week		1	2	3	4	5	6	7	8	9	10
Total requirements		8	0	4	11	6	5	7	2	9	10
Projected stock	7	5	5	5	5	5	5	5	5	5	5
Order receipts		6	0	4	11	6	5	7	2	9	10

The planned receipt quantity is the same as the total requirement in every period except the first, in which it is reduced by two to reduce the opening stock to safety stock.

5.3

$$EOQ = \sqrt{\frac{2RS}{Ci}}$$

Annual requirement R = 2 000 000 packs per year
Set-up cost S = 4 × 20 + 6 × 25 = £230
Cost per item C = £0.5
Cost of stock holding i = 0.25

$$EOQ = \sqrt{\frac{2 \times 2\,000\,000 \times 230}{0.5 \times 0.25}}$$

$$= \sqrt{7360 \times 10^6}$$

$$= 85\,790 \text{ bottles}$$

5.4

(a) Since the line is fully occupied every additional hour of set-up means an additional hour of work at the contractor. Thus there is an additional cost for a six hour set-up of £300 giving a total including operator and fitter time of £530 per set-up.

Thus

$$EOQ = \sqrt{\frac{2 \times 2\,000\,000 \times 530}{0.5 \times 0.25}}$$

$$= \sqrt{16\,960 \times 10^6}$$

$$= 130\,230 \text{ bottles}$$

(b) There is no longer the option of sending more work to the contractor. The alternatives are to buy new equipment or to run with larger order sizes to reduce the number of set-ups and increase capacity. Every hour of set-up reduces total capacity by one hour, so it is necessary to build into the set-up cost some allowance per filling line hour which covers the cost of having the line there.

Assume that £1 million is borrowed for the new line. This costs £150 000 per annum in interest charges at 15% per annum. (Alternatively if £1 million cash is available, spending it on a filling line loses the option of investing it and earning £150 000 per annum.) At the end of ten years the line will be worn out. The loan must be repaid over the ten years, which costs £100 000 per annum. (Alternatively if the money was not borrowed, depreciation must be set aside each year to ensure that after ten years money is available to buy new equipment.)

Whichever view is taken of the finances, it will cost £100 000 plus £150 000 per year just to have a new line standing there. With single shift five day week working and a two week shutdown, there are 250 × 8 available hours per year. The cost per hour is:

$$\frac{(100\,000 + 150\,000)}{250 \times 8} = £125 \text{ per hour}$$

If extra set-ups are likely to result in the purchase of a new filling line, an extra £6 × 125 = £750 must be included in the cost of a six hour set-up if the option of increasing order sizes rather than increasing capacity is to be correctly evaluated.

In practice the situation may be more complex. Can the set-up time be reduced? At what cost? Will the new line permit the bringing back of work from the contractor? Is shift working possible? Is sufficient warehouse space available to accommodate extra stock? Is space available to accommodate new equipment?

There is no single correct answer to this problem. The EOQ formula merely provides one of the clues.

If, however, the best calculations using the EOQ formula show an evenly balanced situation, the new filling line would be the preferred option, because of the belief that the EOQ underestimates the benefits of smaller order sizes in terms of flow, responsiveness and effectiveness of scheduling. To accommodate the extra set-ups, the new line is needed.

Of course the design of the new line should ensure that it is as easy and quick to set up as possible. With two lines it may be possible to dedicate each to a small range of products thus minimising the need for set-ups.

Chapter 6

6.1 The average lead time is eight weeks. If the eight million clips in process move through in sequence at a rate of one million per week it will take eight weeks for the most recently entered batch of wire to emerge as finished clips.

6.2 Arranging for samples to arrive 15 days before clearance is needed instead of five, will introduce a further ten days' worth into the queue. It will do nothing to the rate of output or to the arrears. The only solution to this problem is to increase capacity until the arrears have been eliminated, for example by:

- overtime or weekend working;

- engaging temporary staff;
- buying new equipment;
- improving effectiveness;
- using sub-contract analysts.

6.3 The first step is to calculate the deviation of sales from forecast for each month and then to square each value (which makes the + or - sign irrelevant). The sum of the squares divided by the number of months (12 in this case) gives the average square. The square root of this figure gives the 'root mean square' or σ.

Month	Forecast	Actual sales	Deviation	(Deviation)^2
1	100	85	15	225
2	100	105	−5	25
3	100	110	−10	100
4	110	115	−5	25
5	110	105	5	25
6	110	112	−2	4
7	120	110	10	100
8	120	128	−8	64
9	120	121	−1	1
10	130	125	5	25
11	130	125	5	25
12	130	139	−9	81

Total (deviation)^2 = 700
Average over 12 months = 58.33
Square root of average (σ) = 7.64

From the table under Fig. 6.4, the value of Z corresponding to a probability of 0.977 of no stock out in a month is 2.0. With the data in the table this is the closest available figure to a Z of 0.98 (or 98%).

Because the lead time covers two forecasting periods m in the formula is 2.

$$\text{Required safety stock} = Z\sigma(m)^{1/2}$$
$$= 2 \times 7.64 \times (2)^{1/2}$$
$$= 21.61 \text{ (or 22 items)}$$

Because the value of Z available was slightly lower than required for 98% service, this figure should be rounded up to 22 items. In this case the necessary safety stock represents approximately one week of sales.

Chapter 7

7.1

(a) Order quantity = 100 000 tubes
3% of tubes are rejected
Expected quantity into stock = $\dfrac{100\,000 \times (100 - 3)}{100}$
= $100\,000 \times 0.97$
= 97 000 tubes

(b) Parent shrinkage = 0.03

(c) Average fill weight = 0.101 kg

100 000 tubes require 10 100 kg of paste but 2% of the original quantity is lost.

Therefore original quantity required = $\dfrac{10\,100 \text{ kg}}{(1 - 0.02)}$
= $\dfrac{10\,100 \text{ kg}}{0.98}$
= 10 306 kg

(d) Quantity required per nominal tube = 0.10306
Quantity required with shrinkages = $\dfrac{\text{Quantity per}}{(1 - s)}$

$(1 - s) = \dfrac{100}{103.06}$
= 0.9703

Component shrinkage on paste = $(1 - 0.9703)$
= 0.0297 (i.e. 0.03)

Which to the accuracy to which we are working is the sum of the 1% over-fill and the 2% loss.

(e) 500 cartons are lost in set-up. Therefore starting quantity in order to fill 100 000 is 100 500.

$100\,500 (1 - s) = 100\,000$
$(1 - s) = \dfrac{100\,000}{100\,500}$
= 0.995

Carton shrinkage = $(1 - 0.995) = 0.005$

(f) Parent shrinkage = 0.03
Expected quantity = Order quantity $(1 - s)$

For an expected quantity of 50 000
Order quantity = $\dfrac{50\,000}{0.97}$
= 51 546

Therefore we set out to make 51 550 (say).

500 cartons will still be lost on set-up. Therefore we start with 52 050 in order to fill 51 550.

Shrinkage = $1 - \dfrac{51\,550}{52\,050}$
= $1 - 0.990$

Carton component shrinkage = 1%
(i.e. twice that required on the standard bill of materials)

We will lose the same percentage of paste on the IBC walls, since for the half size order we will use fewer IBCs. We will, however, lose the same fixed quantity in the filler. The percentage loss will increase compared to the standard 100 000 order. We do not have the information to calculate an exact figure. In practice, because toothpaste is relatively cheap compared to package components and the customer insists on exactly 50 000 tubes, we might play safe and double the component shrinkage on the paste.

If your answers were slightly different from those above you may have been applying the yield factor to the final quantity rather than the initial quantity. For example, if we wish to make 100 000 packs with a 97% yield we have to start out to make a quantity of which 97% equals 100 000.

Starting quantity $\times$ 0.97 = 100 000
Starting quantity = $\dfrac{100\,000}{0.97}$
= 103 092

This is not very different from the value of 103 000 which we could obtain by assuming that we lose 3% of the final quantity. Although not strictly correct, this simpler approach is usually acceptable in practice.

ANSWERS TO EXERCISES   235

7.2

FAM03 Superlem drinks family (Unit = litres)

Code	Description	Quantity per
LEM01	Superlem 500 ml	2
LEM02	Superlem 1 litre	1
LEM03	Superlem 3 litre plastic	0.333

The unit of the parent family is litres. Two of the 500 ml packs are needed to contain one litre, one of the 1 litre pack and 0.333 of the 3 litre pack.

7.3

	UK	FR	AU	SZ	PK	TL
Sales in previous 12 months	35 000	21 000	8 000	12 000	14 000	27 000
Total sales = 117 000						
Proportion of total	0.299	0.179	0.068	0.103	0.120	0.231

Planning Bill of Materials
For the Chopit Family of Food Processors

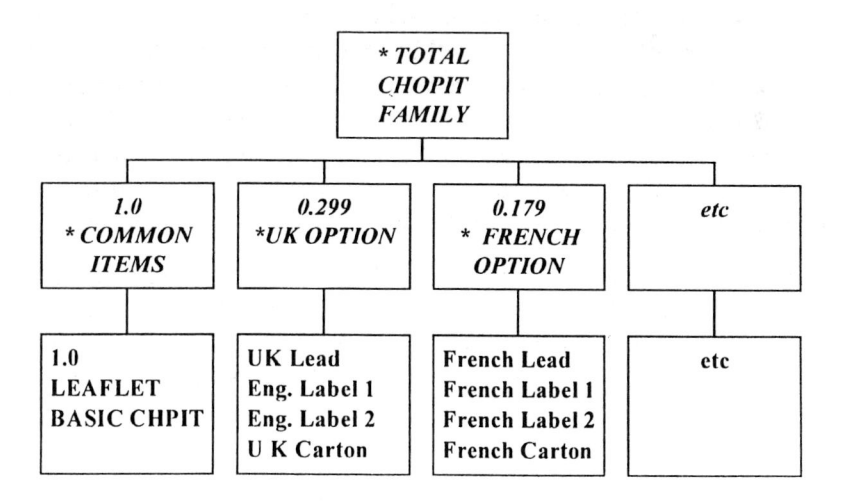

```
                    ┌─────────────┐
                    │  * TOTAL    │
                    │  CHOPIT     │
                    │  FAMILY     │
                    └──────┬──────┘
        ┌────────────┬─────┴──────┬────────────┐
   ┌────┴─────┐  ┌───┴────┐  ┌────┴─────┐  ┌───┴───┐
   │  1.0     │  │ 0.299  │  │  0.179   │  │  etc  │
   │ * COMMON │  │*UK OPT │  │ * FRENCH │  │       │
   │  ITEMS   │  │ ION    │  │  OPTION  │  │       │
   └────┬─────┘  └───┬────┘  └────┬─────┘  └───┬───┘
   ┌────┴─────┐ ┌────┴─────┐ ┌────┴──────┐  ┌──┴──┐
   │ 1.0      │ │UK Lead   │ │French Lead│  │ etc │
   │ LEAFLET  │ │Eng.Label1│ │French Lab1│  │     │
   │BASIC CHPIT│ │Eng.Label2│ │French Lab2│  │     │
   │          │ │U K Carton│ │French Cart│  │     │
   └──────────┘ └──────────┘ └───────────┘  └─────┘
```

The bill of materials for total Chopits is specified in terms of the pseudo items, **common items** and a **country option** for each market. Each pseudo item then has its individual bill of materials. **Common items** includes the basic Chopit and the multi-lingual leaflet. Each **country option** is made up of the electrical lead, labels and carton required for that market. This simplifies maintenance as the proportional split between markets changes. Using such a bill, MRP would predict a requirement for each printed component for each forecasting period. These could be used to buy components in advance of requirement as is normal MRP practice. Alternatively if a short lead time agreement has been negotiated with the printer, they could be ignored except that the total requirement for each label and carton type gives an indication of the amount of capacity to book at the printers.

In this mode of operation, actual purchase orders for specific language items would be confirmed only after receipt of a sales order from the market (see Chapter 7, Section 7.4).

Chapter 8

8.1 Since forecasting is an imprecise exercise there is no correct answer, but the following calculation illustrates the principles of indirect extrapolation.

Of the 15 million sufferers, two-thirds or 10 million are potential purchasers of Hirsuto. With the suggested degree of penetration of the potential market the anticipated retail sales at one pack per patient per quarter are:

	Q1	Q2	Q3	Q4	Q5
% penetration	0.1	0.2	0.4	0.8	1.3
Retail sales (packs)	10 000	20 000	40 000	80 000	120 000
	×3				
Ex manufacturer sales forecast	30 000	40 000	80 000	120 000	?

If the product manager is uncertain about his forecast, he may also request an initial safety stock equivalent perhaps to eight weeks' sales.

The data used above were designed for ease of calculation and would not necessarily be sensible for a real product.

8.2 The answer depends on judgement but possible solutions are shown on the graph.

Sales projection for toothpaste, T1 (150 g pack)

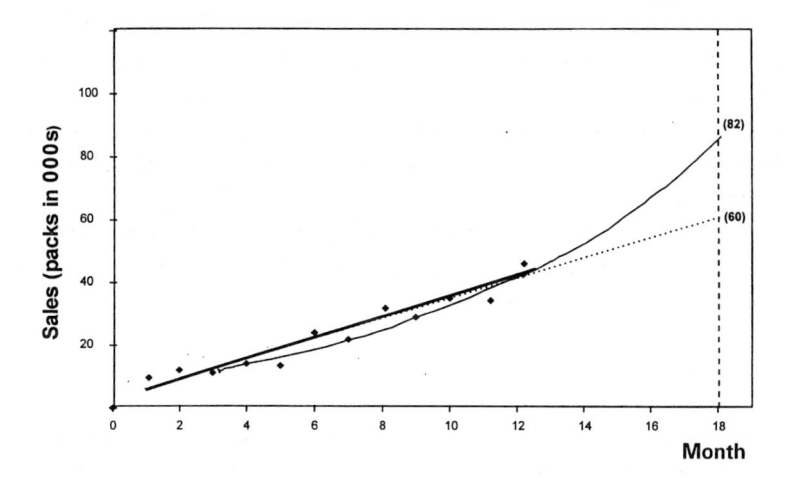

[Graph showing sales data points from month 0 to 12, with a linear extrapolation reaching (60) at month 18 and a freehand curve reaching (82) at month 18. Y-axis: Sales (packs in 000s), 0 to 100. X-axis: Month, 0 to 18.]

The freehand curve assumes that the growth rate will be faster than linear (that is, there is some exponential character). Forecasts of between 65 and 85 for month 18 appear reasonable with a probable value close to 82.

For the linear extrapolation an answer in the range 55 to 65 is reasonable with the most probable result close to 60.

If your answers are different from these, they are not necessarily wrong, but you should be able to understand how any differences relate qualitatively to different weightings you may have given to sales in particular months.

The answers are not very precise. It is possible that a more reliable forecast could be obtained by using sophisticated mathematical projections, but with the data available this is not very likely. The imprecision of the exercise shows the difficulty of forecasting new or rapidly growing products. In such situations it is essential to have a strategy for handling the uncertainty.

8.3

Hirsuto pack. Data for Norwegian depot

Opening stock   24   Order quantity   40
Safety stock   16   Lead time   1 week

	Week		1	2	3	4	5	6	7	8	9	10
1	Sales forecast		8	8	8	8	8	9	9	9	10	10
2	Projected stock	24	16	48	40	32	24	55	46	37	27	17
3	Replenishment receipts			40				40				
4	Replenishment dispatches		40			40						

Hirsuto pack. Data for Finnish depot

Opening stock   21   Order quantity   40
Safety stock   18   Lead time   1 week

	Week		1	2	3	4	5	6	7	8	9	10
1	Sales forecast		11	11	10	10	10	9	9	10	12	12
2	Projected stock	21	50	39	29	19	49	40	31	21	49	37
3	Replenishment receipts		40*				40				40	
4	Replenishment dispatches					40				40		

*In transit

Hirsuto pack. Data for Swedish depot

Opening stock   216   Order quantity   80
Safety stock   100   Lead time   2 weeks

Week		1	2	3	4	5	6	7	8	9	10
Dispatches to Denmark			40					40			
Dispatches to Norway		40				40					
Dispatches to Finland				40					40		
Local Swedish sales forecast		25	25	25	25	25	25	25	25	25	25
Total requirements		65	25	65	65	65	25	65	65	25	25
Projected stock	216	151	126	141	156	171	146	161	176	151	126
Replenishment receipts				80	80	80		80	80		
Replenishment dispatches		80	80	80		80	80	80			

The 40 packs in transit to Finland do not show in the requirements on Sweden, because stock had been allocated and dispatched before reporting the Swedish opening stock figure of 216.

8.4 Answers should include the following points. If others were found they are not necessarily wrong.

- Reduce manufacturing lead times by continuously striving towards JIT principles.
- Recognise that honesty in a forecast is at least as important as accuracy.
- Measure the accuracy of forecasts and feed back to the forecaster. Also provide summary statistics for senior management.
- Forecast at the highest level of aggregation which provides adequate detail for manufacturing.
- Move the forecasting base as close to the end-user as is practicable. Use DRP if appropriate.
- If possible have a consistent set of numbers covering the short, medium and long term future.
- Handle uncertainty by dialogue between the forecaster and planner.
- Exploit Pareto's principle. Concentrate human effort and intelligence on improving the forecasts for the really important items. Leave the rest to the computer.

Chapter 9

9.1

(a) **Final draw machine FD07**

Run time	$= 0.004 \times 2000$ hours
	$= 8$ hours
Change-over	$= 4$ hours
Total time required	$= 12$ standard hours

Heavy draw machine HD01

Run time	$= 0.0012 \times 2000$ hours
	$= 2.4$ hours
Change-over	$= 6$ hours
Total time required	$= 8.4$ standard hours

(b) 5 days at 8 hours per day $= 40$ clock hours per week
At 0.75 productivity, standard hours available per week
standard hours
$$= 40 \times 0.75 = 30$$

FD07 is occupied $\dfrac{12}{30} \times 100\% = 40\%$

HD01 is occupied $\dfrac{8.4}{30} \times 100\% = 28\%$

(c) With two final draw machines, the run time per machine will halve, but the total machine hours will remain constant. Both machines will have to be changed over initially so there will be an extra four hours of change-over. Total standard hours will be 16. However the elapsed time for drawing the 2000 kg of wire will fall to 8 hours.

9.2 Standard hours available per day are:

Heavy draw	$8 \times 0.8 = 6.4$
Final draw	$8 \times 0.7 = 5.6$
Plating	$8 \times 0.7 = 5.6$

A breakdown of times taken in standard hours and days is:

	Queue	Change-over	Run	Units
Heavy draw	12.8	3	18	Standard hours
	2	0.47(=0)	2.8(=3)	Days at 6.4 hrs/day
Final draw	5.6	6	27	Standard hours
	1	0.71(=1)	4.8(=5)	Days at 5.6 hrs/day
Plating	11.2	3	12	Standard hours
	2	0.53(=1)	2.1(=2)	Days at 5.6 hrs/day

Back scheduling can now be carried out from the order due-date of day 115 as follows:

Back scheduling

	Heavy draw			Final draw			Plating		
	Queue	C/O	Run	Queue	C/O	Run	Queue	C/O	Run
Duration (days)	2	0	3	1	1	5	2	1	2
Calendar date	98	100	100	103	104	105	110	112	113 115

Thus the earliest planned start for heavy drawing is day 98 and the steel rod for drawing should be available on this day. However the supervisor could still meet his operation due-date if he did not start the change-over until day 100.

The process of rounding times to the nearest day may seem haphazard but in practice the process is defining a range of possible start times for each operation. Also, although the productivity factor may be fairly accurate over a long period of, say, a month, it cannot be expected to predict accurately the average amount of stoppage over a short period of a day or less. Thus calculation of planned start and finish dates can only be approximate. The queuing allowance at each stage provides the flexibility necessary to permit due-dates to be achieved in practice.

9.3 During the five weeks there was a total of four days when there were no plans to use work centre 01 (i.e. one holiday, one maintenance and two of no demand).

Working time is therefore $(25 - 4) \times 8$ clock hours plus 10 hours overtime

$$= 178 \text{ clock hours}$$

Work achieved is equivalent to 125 standard hours.

$$\text{Productivity factor} = \frac{\text{standard hours}}{\text{clock hours}} = \frac{125}{178} = 0.7$$

9.4 To determine how much resource is required, the order quantity is multiplied by the run time per unit and any change-over time is added. To determine when the resource is required the off-set and spread values are applied to the due-date of the MPS order (i.e. the packing order).

OP01 Filling operators

MO no.	Order quantity	Change-over	Run time (op hrs × 10^{-3})	Total (op hrs × 10^{-3})	End day	Start day
MO1	10 000	20 000	4 × 10 000 = 40 000	60 000	190	186
MO2	5 000	20 000	5 × 5 000 = 25 000	45 000	187	185
MO3	4 000	20 000	6 × 4 000 = 24 000	44 000	185	183

Total in period 10 (days 181–200) = 149 000 op hrs × 10^{-3}
= 149 operator hours

BR02 Blending room 2

MO no.	Order quantity	Change-over	Run time (op hrs × 10^{-3})	Total	End day	Start day
MO1	10 000	0	0.5 × 10 000 = 5 000	5 000	170	169
MO2	5 000	0	1.25 × 5 000 = 6 250	6 250	167	166
MO3	4 000	0	2.5 × 4 000 = 10 000	10 000	165	164

Total in period 9 (days 161–180) = 21 250 hours × 10^{-3}
= 21.25 hours

Note that the actual capacity calculation is very straightforward. Setting up the representative routings can be more complicated. For blending it is necessary to determine how long it takes to produce biscuits equivalent to one finished pack. In this example it proved simplest to incorporate the blending room change-over time into the biscuit making run time assuming an average order size. The times on the routings are based on a campaign of 3 million biscuits taking 15 hours in total to change-over and run three batches of 1 million biscuits each.

This example illustrates how RCCP can be used to assess the load on a resource which is not used by the MPS order concerned. The real routings for packing products P20, P21 and P22 do not involve a blending room, which is likely to be a resource on a real routing for bulk biscuits not a pack.

9.5 Minimal change-over time will be required between Powder A1 and Powder A, if the dilute precedes the more concentrated. Powder B has the earliest planned start-dates so in the absence of any reason to the contrary should follow D which is already in process. The preferred schedule is therefore:

Day	99	100	101	102	103	104	105	106	107
Product	D	C/O	B	B	C/O	A1	A1	A	A

9.6

Advantages

- Planning boards give a simple, easy to understand display of the sequences of jobs and the likely start and finish dates.
- The length of the line of tickets gives a visual indication of the total load on any piece of equipment.

Disadvantages

- Preparing tickets of the correct length is time consuming.
- There is no indication if jobs are scheduled before earliest start or after latest finish.
- Taking account of labour and machine requirements is cumbersome.
- The boards are only visible from one location (e.g. planning office or plant).
- If tickets are accidentally misplaced, information is lost. (The fact that the cleaners may reschedule the factory whilst dusting the boards may be an advantage or disadvantage depending on the effectiveness of official scheduling procedures.)

9.7
(a)

(a) CRITICAL RATIO

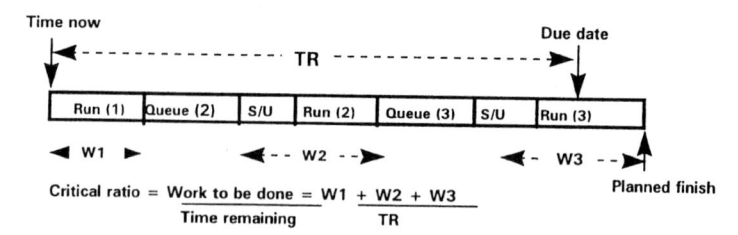

Time now → | Run (1) | Queue (2) | S/U | Run (2) | Queue (3) | S/U | Run (3) | ← Due date

TR spans from time now to due date. W1, W2, W3 indicate work segments. Planned finish at end.

$$\text{Critical ratio} = \frac{\text{Work to be done}}{\text{Time remaining}} = \frac{W1 + W2 + W3}{TR}$$

(b) MAXIMUM EXPECTED LATENESS

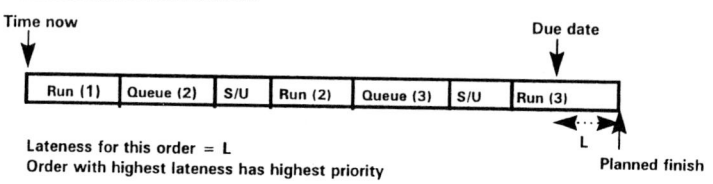

Time now → | Run (1) | Queue (2) | S/U | Run (2) | Queue (3) | S/U | Run (3) | ← Due date, L, Planned finish

Lateness for this order = L
Order with highest lateness has highest priority

(c) LEAST SLACK PER REMAINING OPERATION

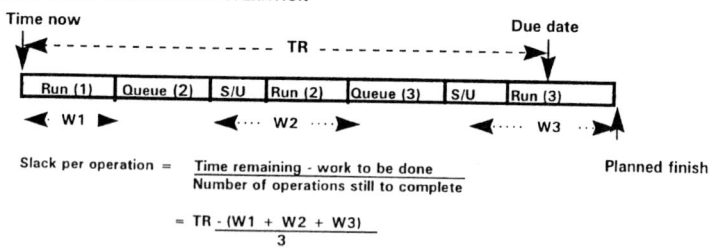

Time now → | Run (1) | Queue (2) | S/U | Run (2) | Queue (3) | S/U | Run (3) | ← Due date

TR spans; W1, W2, W3 segments; Planned finish.

$$\text{Slack per operation} = \frac{\text{Time remaining - work to be done}}{\text{Number of operations still to complete}}$$

$$= \frac{TR - (W1 + W2 + W3)}{3}$$

(b) Critical ratio

Job A

Work remaining	= 3 days of set-up
	+ 2 days run at blending
	+ 3 days run at milling
	+ 2 days run at packing
Total	= 10
Time available	= Due-date − time now
	= 21 − 0
	= 21

$$\text{Critical ratio} = \frac{\text{Work to be done}}{\text{Time remaining}} = \frac{10}{21} = 0.476$$

Job B

Work remaining	= 2 days of set-up
	+ 3 days run at blending
	+ 5 days run at milling
Total	= 10
Time available	= 18 − 0
	= 18
Critical ratio	= $\dfrac{\text{Work to be done}}{\text{Time remaining}} = \dfrac{10}{18} = 0.555$

On this rule Job B has highest priority.

Maximum expected lateness

Expected lateness Job A	= 23 − 21
	= 2 days
Expected lateness Job B	= 19 − 18
	= 1 day

On this rule Job A has highest priority.

Least slack per remaining operation

Slack = time available − work to be done (calculated as in critical ratio)

Job A

Slack	= 21 − 10 = 11
Operations to complete	= 3
Slack per remaining operation	= 3.66 days

Job B

Slack	= 18 − 10 = 8
Operations to complete	= 2
Slack per remaining operation	= 4 days

On this rule Job A has highest priority.

Note that different rules give different answers. No one rule can be said to be best in all situations. Simulation models can be used to choose the best rule for a particular situation, but in practice the differences between them are probably not very important.

9.8 The lists should include the points itemised below.

Queues are beneficial because:

- They enable peaks and troughs in the work load to be smoothed out.
- They protect equipment from running out of work and losing time.
- They give flexibility to the order in which jobs are tackled, permitting a supervisor to minimise change-over times, or make the best use of operator skills.
- They provide in-process stocks to aid recovery from batch rejections, or to meet unexpected demands.

Queues are disadvantageous because:

- They increase work in progress and tie up capital unnecessarily.
- Material in queues takes up space.
- Shelf life is consumed whilst materials queue.
- Material in queues is susceptible to loss or damage.
- Long queues mean long lead times which means slow response to changes in market requirements.
- Long queues increase the difficulty of controlling the introduction of changes in specification.

9.9 Buying a second line will not only provide capacity for future growth but will reduce occupation of the lines by half. That is back to the levels seen when product volumes were half and the average queue was only two batches. Since the lines are interchangeable they can be treated as a single work centre, with a common queue. Stocks awaiting packing should fall from ten batches to two on average, a reduction in value of $8 \times £50\,000$ or £400 000. Notionally at least this sum can be invested at 20% per annum, yielding £80 000 per annum.

To buy the new line for £100 000 costs £20 000 per year in interest and £20 000 in additional running costs, giving a total cost of £40 000. In this case the benefit from stock reduction of £80 000 more than covers the additional costs, and gives a net benefit of £40 000 per annum. The investment is well justified in this case but the case would not be so strong if the in-process materials were less expensive.

Hidden costs and benefits

There will also be service improvements because of the reduced lead times. It should be possible to reduce safety stocks of finished products because with shorter lead times sales forecasts should be more accurate. There may also be other benefits from reduced stock levels such as space savings, less auditing and less risk of obsolescence, etc.

In principle there should be no need to recruit additional operators, because the number of packs to be made remains the same but care is required to ensure that the operators do not become the heavily occupied resource which is causing the long queue.

Also, because of a statistical effect which has not been considered in the text, the queue in front of two lines operating as a single work centre will be less than the average queue in front of a similarly occupied single line. (This effect can be seen in some post offices and banks when a single queue serves several counter positions. The customer at the head of the queue has to wait only until one position becomes free, not until a specific position is free.)

Chapter 10

10.1 Running time is $24 \times 5 = 120$ hours per week per machine

Maximum output per week is:

- *Cold forging*
  Each batch of 10 000 takes 4 hours
  Output per week = $120 \times 0.25 \times 10\,000 = 300\,000$
- *Milling*
  Output per miller = 120×600 per week
  Output from 6 millers = $6 \times 120 \times 600 = 432\,000$ per week
- *Polishing*
  Each batch of 4000 takes 2 hours
  Output per week = $120 \times 0.5 \times 4000 = 240\,000$

Note that the rates given are practical averages, i.e. they allow for the expected amount of disruption and mechanical breakdown.

The facility is not quite able to meet a sales demand of 250 000 fasteners per week by working for five days. The polishing stage is the bottleneck with a capacity of 240 000 per week. Some weekend working, sub-contracting or new equipment will be necessary if sales demands are to be met.

10.2 Stock is brought in at 1.5 tonnes per day, but leaves at only 1.0 tonne per day. The in-process stock increases by the equivalent of 0.5 tonnes per day. After 10 days, if there is no intervention, the stock will have increased by $10 \times 0.5 = 5$ tonnes to 10 tonnes. With the information available it is not possible to say at which stage the stock would be, but if operations continued in this way, in-process stocks would only be prevented from reaching infinity by the bankruptcy of the company.

10.3 Amongst your list should be the following:

- Perfectly balanced plants with equal capacities at all stages are not optimum.
- Ideally capacity should increase at each downstream stage.
- Overall production is limited by the bottleneck.
- Time lost on the bottleneck is lost for good.
- Protect the bottleneck with:
  — buffer stocks;
  — maintenance priority;
  — inspection before the bottleneck.
- If the bottleneck is not at the input stage, gate the input to the bottleneck rate.
- For non-bottleneck stages being idle is not necessarily wrong.
- A realistic achievable MPS combined with disciplined MRP gates the input as required.

10.4 Your list should include the following:

- OPT identifies the bottleneck equipment and, by finite scheduling this stage only, simplifies the scheduling task. Overloads which cannot be resolved are dealt with by pushing excess work out into the future.
  In MRPII, capacity planning identifies the bottleneck and other overloads but leaves the solution of the problems to the planner.
- OPT extends final order completion dates past the requirement date if necessary to achieve a workable schedule. With MRPII this can only be done by manual intervention.
- OPT assumes that bottlenecks do not move as the product mix changes. MRPII assisted by the planner copes easily with wandering bottlenecks.
- OPT, if appropriate, will split or combine orders. With MRPII this must be done manually.
- OPT ensures that plans are feasible with respect to capacity. MRPII will continue to plan with unrealistic loads if the planner does not intervene.

Chapter 11

11.1 Your list will of course depend on the type of business you are considering, but is likely to include the following:

- Unreliable equipment.
- Poor quality – batch rejections.
- Unreliable suppliers.
- Overloaded equipment
- Long lead times making accurate prediction of completion dates difficult.
- Large orders occupy equipment and delay other products.
- Inspection delays.
- Items lost in warehouse.
- Delays in moving materials – shortage of fork lift trucks.
- Long and variable change-over times.
- Incorrect paper work.
- Operator shortages.
- Operator errors.
- Product proliferation.

11.2 Your rocks and actions will be specific to your company. Retain your list until you have worked through Chapter 11 and then review it to see if you can improve it.

11.3 Your list of objections and solutions will be highly personal. It will no doubt include references to cleaning time, the time required to undo all the bolts and to adjust and tune, etc.

Put your list on one side and return to it when you have worked through Section 11.3. See how many amendments you make.

11.4

1. A likely time is 5–15 minutes depending on circumstances.
2. The time for assistance to arrive and complete the job may be as long as two hours. The preparation would have had no cost other than the time involved, perhaps 15–30 minutes.
3. The specialist centre might take two minutes, assuming that all the tyre fitters were not busy. The trolley jack and pneumatic wheel brace used would cost only a few hundred pounds.
4. The team of mechanics would change all four wheels in less than ten seconds, and they will have achieved this speed by carefully analysing the task and practising constantly. However, the cost of the special equipment on the car and the cost of flying the team around the world for a few minutes' action per race will be very high, probably tens of thousands of pounds.

250   PLANNING AND CONTROL OF MANUFACTURING OPERATIONS

Discussion
If the wheel change is regarded as representing a change-over, the exercise demonstrates that the time can be reduced from two hours to ten minutes (a 12-fold reduction) by nothing more demanding than preparation and planning. Investing a few hundred pounds in special equipment by the tyre centre gives a further reduction of 80%. A further 12-fold reduction is possible but at considerable cost. The law of diminishing returns is starting to apply and this final reduction may or may not be cost effective depending on circumstances.

The reduction from two hours to two minutes, a 98.3% reduction, required very little expenditure.

The change from 2 hours to 10 seconds represents a 99.86% reduction. Even if the final 1.5% is deemed not to be cost effective, some of the apparently extravagant original claims from Japan should have been believed after all.

11.5 Change-over reduction permits order sizes to be reduced. Smaller orders mean:

- less work in progress;
- shorter lead times because of shorter run times and, more importantly, less queuing time at each operation;
- less sales stock for the same level of service;
- improved flow and faster response to unexpected customer orders.

In a situation in which capacity is short, change-over reduction can be used to release more time for production. That is, the same number of change-overs is carried out but each one is shorter. However, the major benefits arise if the opportunity to reduce order sizes is taken. Thus there will be more but shorter change-overs. The reduction in order size is probably the single most important contribution to a JIT programme for most companies.

Change-over reduction is relatively easy to initiate because all the resources required usually come from the same area, and high level discussions are unnecessary. Commitment to the project is usually easy to obtain.

The major steps are:

1 Agree an objective and set a realistic target for reduction.
2 Appoint a suitable team and leader. This is likely to consist of:
   - one or more operators;
   - a fitter;

- a first line supervisor (probable leader);
- a mechanical and/or an electrical engineer (may be needed in a consultancy role at times).

3 Make a video or otherwise record an existing change-over.
4 Identify any wasteful activities.
5 Identify activities which can be carried out off-line before the previous job finishes.
6 Identify opportunities for using duplicate equipment.
7 Identify opportunities for simple electrical or mechanical changes to make cleaning or fitting new parts easier.
8 Seek approval for technical changes from engineering management. Carry out the changes.
9 Document new procedures and train staff as necessary.
10 Rehearse and time new procedures.
11 Management recognise achievement.
12 Repeat for next piece of equipment.

11.6 Manufacturing cells have the following advantages over a conventional factory layout and organisation:

1 Control of production between stages is simplified because Kanban methods can frequently be used.
2 Lead times can be dramatically reduced.
3 There is no need to report progress between operations to a central control system.
4 Operators work as a team and morale improves. People with high morale are easy to manage. By introducing a small factory within a factory, large companies can enjoy some of the advantages of a small organisation.
5 Operators work in close contact with each other and are prepared to learn multiple skills and move easily to a point of need.
6 Dedication of a cell to a family of products may reduce the need for change-overs.
7 Accountability for delivering finished products on time is clearly defined.

Disadvantages of cells are as follows:

1 They do not make optimum use of production resources since spare capacity in one cell cannot easily be used to alleviate a temporary overload in another. Flexibility, service and reductions in WIP investment are brought about at the expense of additional capital

investment.
2. Cells can be best applied in a repetitive environment in which families of products using the same equipment in the same sequence can be identified.
3. Cells can be difficult to set up in existing buildings.

An attempt to introduce manufacturing cells is likely to meet the following objections:

1. Our products are not suitable.
2. The unions will not accept it.
3. We cannot knock walls down and move equipment whilst maintaining production.
4. It will cost too much.
5. It is not the way we work.

All or any of these objections may be valid depending on circumstances. To overcome 1, 2 and 5 requires discussion, education and if possible a visit to see a cell operating. The cost must be justified in terms of reduced work in progress and improved service.

Objection 3 is probably most valid for food or pharmaceutical production. The opportunity to introduce cells must be taken when buildings are being designed or extensively upgraded.

11.7 Advantages of Kanban:

1. Simple to operate.
2. Easy to install.
3. Easy to train operators to use.
4. Controls WIP effectively.
5. Reduces lead times.

Disadvantages of Kanban:

1. Requires a repetitive environment.
2. Does not work well with multiple or very different products sharing the same equipment.
3. Does not work well with frequent changes of specification.
4. Is not suitable for big, expensive, low volume products.

A traditional multi-product manufacturing plant is likely to have many different products sharing the same facilities. Some products may be only manufactured infrequently for tenders or special orders, whilst others experience almost constant demand. If manufacturing cells can be established for the high volume repetitive products, Kanban can be used within the cells. The remaining products are then planned and produced conventionally.

11.8 Some reasons for introducing a new product are:

- It will be profitable even after it has paid its fair share of overheads.
- Even if not profitable in its own right, it completes the range and attracts customers who prefer to buy from a single supplier, thus increasing sales of profitable products as well as the new 'loss leader' minor product.
- To spearhead a new range. The first product may be sold at a loss in order to gain market share and publicise the range.
- Although not profitable when carrying fair share of overheads, the product will be manufactured using resources which would otherwise be idle, and will actually increase cash flow and profit. (The danger of this marginal costing approach is that as business grows, the resource will become fully occupied and a case will be made for buying additional capacity. Any new capacity must be justified in terms of the least profitable product made on the resource. It may be more profitable to release capacity by withdrawing the marginal product.)

Some reasons for withdrawing a product are:

- It is no longer sufficiently profitable and uses equipment which can be more profitably used for other products.
- It represents a health hazard to operators or end-users.
- Modifications to the manufacturing plant or process required to meet environmental legislation cannot be justified by the profitability of the products made.
- The product has been found to be dangerous either inherently or when abused by the customer.

For product B, 10% reduction in manufacturing costs saves 1000 × £6 = £6000 per year. A 3% loss of sales because the redesigned product has less user appeal reduces revenue by 30 × £100 = £3000 per year as for product A, but 30 × £60 = £1800 would be saved by not having to manufacture the lost sales. Total savings are £6000 + £1800 = £7800. Subtracting the lost revenue of £3000 leaves a net benefit of £4800.

Because manufacturing costs are a greater proportion of the total for product B than for product A, the value of a 10% saving is greater and the loss of profit from the lost sales is lower, so the design change is beneficial.

It is often difficult to agree on an estimation of any potential loss or gain of sales resulting from a manufacturing led design change, which means that high technology companies and in particular pharmaceutical companies are often reluctant to modify product design in order to achieve JIT benefits. Pharmaceutical and medical companies may also need to modify the registration details of the product subject to the change. This can be an extremely expensive activity which eliminates completely the possibility of benefits from a change to a product specification intended to reduce the cost of manufacture.

11.9 Possible JIT improvements are:

1. Reduce order sizes to reduce WIP, reduce lead times and to increase work flow and flexibility.
2. May require a reduction of change-over times.
3. Reduce queuing allowances to reduce lead times.
4. Reduce transport times by improving layout of equipment if possible.
5. Set up manufacturing cells dedicated to a product family.
6. Introduce Kanban controls where appropriate.
7. Rationalise and simplify products and packaging.
8. Simplify processes where possible.
9. Reduce the number of suppliers.
10. Develop trust with your suppliers. Co-operation not conflict. Use blanket orders with call-off of small delivery quantities.
11. Set up, validate and then accept certificates of analysis. Minimise duplicate testing.
12. Share information on forward work load with suppliers. Book machine capacity in advance. Specify items to be produced only a few days before they are required.

Potential difficulties with JIT:

1. If in defence, medical or pharmaceutical industries, changes to products or processes would result in a need for re-registration, the benefits may not justify the expense.
2. Code of conduct requirements and cleaning problems may set a practical minimum to change-over times in some industries.
3. Batch sizes may be constrained by the equipment available, e.g. the batch must cover the stirrer.
4. In industries which have a legal requirement that each batch, order or delivery must be analysed or tested, too many small orders may swamp the testing facilities.
5. The process of educating suppliers and establishing trust may be costly and time consuming.

6 Giving all of the business for a product or family of products to one supplier makes supply vulnerable to disruption by strikes, fire insolvency or breakdown.

As in many aspects of Operations Management, the risks must be assessed against the benefits before deciding how far to proceed down the JIT road.

11.10 Your list should include the following items:
- Change-over times (or set-up, make ready times, etc).
- Order quantities for fixed quantity order policies.
- Number of days for fixed period order policies.
- Safety stocks.
- Item lead times.
- Queue times.
- Move times.
- Production rates.
- Productivity factors.
- Bills of materials (to reflect changes to products).
- Routings (to reflect changes to processes).

You may be able to suggest additional items.

11.11 Your definitions and service parameters will depend on your particular job. Do you think that your internal customers will agree with your suggestions? Why not ask them? They will probably prefer to be asked for their views rather than be presented with yours.

Chapter 12

12.1 This company's performance for completing orders on time is abysmal. There should be much scope for improvement. An effective improvement exercise, be it based on MRPII or JIT, should yield financial benefits in some or all of the following areas, but the percentage improvements can only be rough estimates at this stage:

1 Increasing sales by improving customer service.
    The Sales Director has claimed that poor customer service is losing sales worth £3 million per year. Only 70% of customer orders are supplied on time. Improving on-time delivery to 90% and avoiding lost sales of £1 million per year (10% of total) is a conservative first target.

	£(000)
Additional income	1 000
Additional costs	
10% of labour	200
10% of materials	300
Net benefit	500

2 Improved purchasing effectiveness
   Assume a 2% saving on £3 million spend
   Net benefit   60
3 Improved labour productivity
   Assume a 3% saving on £2 million wages per annum
   Net benefit   60
4 Stock reduction
   Assume a 30% reduction on a total WIP and sales stock of
   £5.5 million. Assume stockholding costs of 20% per annum
   Stock reduction = £5.5 million × 30% = £1.65 million
   Net benefit = £1.65 million × 20%   330
5 Delaying expenditure
   If better planning and the application of the OPT principles
   to bottleneck management permit the purchase of the
   new machine to be delayed for 1 year, the company avoids
   paying interest to the bank on £1 million at, say, 10% per
   annum
   Net benefit = £1 million × 10%   100

   Total potential benefit   £1 050 000

Assuming that this is an MRPII project, rough estimates of costs will include:

	£(000)
Software, say	200
Hardware, say	200
Education	250
Time of project team. Assume real costs are equivalent to 4 people, full time for 2 years at £30 000 each per annum	240
Consultancy and miscellaneous costs	100
Total cost	£990 000

The figures obviously depend on the assumptions made and those above were chosen for illustration only. The logic behind the calculations is more important than the actual numbers. A significant point is that most of the savings are repeated each year, whilst most of the costs occur only once.

In the example, the general overhead at 60% of direct costs is moderate. Companies with heavy investment in research and/or marketing will usually find that the benefit from increasing sales dominates the calculation, since the fixed costs used to determine selling prices include the high costs of R & D and marketing which do not increase as sales volume increases. The truly variable costs such as materials are a minor element of selling price

In almost all businesses, competitive pressures are increasing. Even for currently profitable companies, to do nothing is to risk a loss of sales to competitors. Avoiding a loss by increasing effectiveness and reducing costs so that selling prices can be kept competitive is just as real a benefit as achieving a gain.

12.2 If a project lasts too long members of the team or supportive managers may change jobs and be lost to the project, the rest of the company becomes tired of waiting and early education lessons are forgotten. Although there is clearly no sudden cut-off point, experience shows that the above problems tend to become significant if the project takes more than two years.

12.3 One objective of the project is to change the way people behave, to introduce a new culture into the organisation. Effective education so that people understand what is being done and why it is necessary is an essential part of this.

The cascade method of education ensures that managers have to understand the subject themselves before they can teach it. A message delivered by one's own manager, and carefully tailored to the environment has more credibility than a message delivered by a relative stranger.

A potential danger is that the message can be distorted as it is passed from layer to layer in the organisation. A quality control procedure is required to minimise this risk.

12.4 The disadvantages are:

- MRPII software is complex. Amendments almost invariably take longer than anticipated and may introduce other errors.
- The supplier may refuse to support modified software or may find difficulty in doing so, even if willing to try.
- Modification will have to be re-applied each time a new release of the

software is available. This can become prohibitively difficult and expensive, thus preventing the acceptance of new releases and access to the associated enhancements.

12.5 The most significant single measure is achievement of manufacturing order due-dates since if these are achieved consistently the plans will be achieved. If the plans were correct in the first place, all other relevant targets will be met.

Index

abnormal order, 52, 55
accuracy of forecasts, 114, 117
Agile Manufacturing, 167
allocated stock, 69, 70, 72
American Production and Inventory Control Society (APICS), 4, 70, 71
Anticipated Delay Report (ADR), 138
APICS Dictionary, 71
Assemble to Order (ATO), 14, 58, 105, 118, 123
Available to Promise (ATP), 52, 53, 57

batch production
bill of materials, 27, 97, 98
bottleneck, 160
BS 5750, 204
business planning, 36, 37

capacity planning, 35, 37
Capacity Requirements Planning (CRP), 127, 128, 130, 132, 134, 141, 142
cells, 165, 175
change-over, 15, 153, 169
commodities, 8
communications with suppliers, 181
Conference Room Pilot, 205
Continuous Improvement (CI), 166, 167, 178, 183
continuous process, 9
control of change, 59
cost–benefit case, 193, 209
Critical Path Analysis, 198

critical ratio, 131
customer service, 6, 10, 12
customer's order, sales order, 28, 52

data, 205
demand, 117
demonstrated capacity, 49
dependent demand, 30, 31
direct extrapolation (forecasting by), 111
Dispatch Meeting, 138
Distribution Requirements Planning (DRP), 120, 122

Economic Order Quantity (EOQ), 77, 79, 80
education, 198, 208
efficiency, 129, 130
electronic planning boards (*Leitstand*), 145, 146
elimination of waste, 167, 183
exception messages, 44, 46, 51, 52, 54, 56, 207
explosion factor, 33

factory layout, 176
family bill of materials, 100, 105
family level forecasts, 118
feedback, 35
finite capacity systems, finite systems, finite planning/scheduling, 141–3, 146, 148, 150

firm planned fence, 44, 45, 65
firm planned order, 45, 67, 70
fixed period order policy, 74–6, 80
fixed quantity order policy, 74, 76
flexibility, 11, 132
Ford, Henry, 1, 5
forecast consumption, 52
free stock, 69, 70
Full Shop Floor Control, 137, 140, 141, 143
functional layout, 176

gateing the input stage, 162
Goldratt, Eli, 148, 160

inadequacies of MRP, 34
independent demand, 30
indirect extrapolation (forecasting by), 111
Infinite Capacity Scheduling/Planning, 132, 141
inspection time, 169
integrated planning and scheduling, 148
internal customers, 186
invitation to tender, 202
invoiced sales, 117
ISO 9000, 204

JIT and MRPII, 184, 208
JIT Spiral, 183, 184
Just in Time (JIT), 118, 166, 180, 183

Kanban, 5, 163, 177

lead time, 19, 84, 86–8, 127, 153, 168
lead time reduction, 118
lean manufacturing, 167
least slack per remaining operation, 140
Leitstand, 146
long term forecasts, 112
lot for lot order policy (L4L), 76
lot traceability, 203

make or buy?, 10
Make to Order (MTO), 12, 14, 47, 208
Make to Stock (MTS), 14, 43, 46, 89, 124, 208
management information, 3
manual planning boards, 145
manufacturing cell, 165
manufacturing orders, 65
Manufacturing Resource Planning (MRPII), 4, 5, 35–7, 148, 150
manufacturing strategy, 9, 10, 12, 14
mass production, 1
Master Production Scheduling, 35, 37, 43, 46, 51, 57–9, 71
material codes, 27
Material Requirements Planning (MRP), 4, 6, 34–6, 57, 70, 143, 146, 148, 150, 153, 163
maximum expected lateness, 140
move time, 169
multipurpose planning grid, 31

network planning, 198
nomenclature, 68, 104
normal order, 53, 56
NRN order policy, 80

on-line systems, 4
open order, 71
operating MRPII, 206
Operations Research, 2, 208
Optimised Production Technology (OPT), 148, 160, 163, 166
optimising algorithm (for scheduling), 147
Option Planning, 48, 101
Order Point, 2, 5, 19, 20, 36
order policies, 74, 79
order quantity, 74, 77, 80
order size, 168
overheads, 11

Pareto principle, 120
Partial Shop Floor Control, 139–43

INDEX

parts list, 27
performance measures, 206
Periodic Review, 21
phantom bill of materials, 99, 104–6
phantom parts, 99, 104
physical stock, 69, 70
planned order, 45, 67, 70
planning bill of materials, 99, 100, 102, 104, 105
planning compromise, 5, 8
potency, 203
priority index, 139, 140
process complexity, 175
product complexity, 178
Production Activity Control, 35, 37
Production Planning, 37
productivity, 6
productivity factor, 129, 130
Project Manager, 195, 200
project organisation, 195
project plan, 195, 197, 199
project publicity, 201
Project Team Pilot, 204
project timetable, 195, 197
projected available balance, 72
projected on-hand, 72
pseudo-bill of materials, 105, 106
pseudo-item, 102, 104
purchasing, 180, 182

quality, 10, 180
Quality Circles, 187
quality control, 185, 186
quantity per, 27, 29
quarantine, 203
queue/queuing time, 84, 85, 132, 150–4, 169

random variations in output, 161
ready for release, 65, 71
ready for release fence, 71
receipts, 68
reducing change-over times, 170, 171
release date, 65

released order, 71
representative routing, 134, 135
River of Inventory, 167
Rough Cut Capacity Planning, 48, 58, 127, 134, 135, 137
routing, 99, 131
routing file, 128
rule based system (for scheduling), 147
run time, 169

safety stock, 20, 43, 44, 83, 89, 90, 93, 94, 117, 122
safety stock, setting, 90
Sales and Operations Planning, 36, 37
sales forecasts/forecasting, 24, 25, 28, 34, 52, 109, 120, 121, 123
scheduled operations, 130
scheduled operations file, 131, 137, 139
scheduled receipt, 70, 72
set-up, 15
short term forecasts, 112
short term scheduling, 137
shrinkage, 96, 97
silence means approval, 138, 206
software, choice of, 202, 203
software, special features, 202
Standard Operating Procedures, 204
Steering Committee, 195, 200
stock holding costs, 6, 15
Stock Projection, 21, 24, 26
suggested works order, 45
suppliers, 180

Task Force, 197
The Goal, 160
Time Phased Order Point, 23
Total Quality Control (TQC), 186
Total Quality Management (TQM)/ Total Quality (TQ), 185, 186
total requirements, 74
two bin system, 21

uncertainty of forecasts, 117, 123

unique selling points, 9
utilisation, 129, 130

work centre, 132
Work Centre File, 128
Work Improvement Group (WIG), 183, 187, 201
work in progress, 168, 169
Work-To List/Dispatch List, 132
works order, 45

yield, 94, 97